My cousin Annie

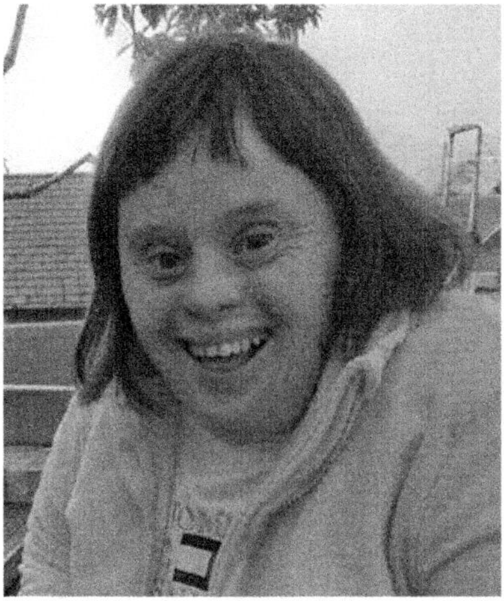

This is my cousin Annie. I have many first cousins and we all agree that Annie is the best of us. She is hugely popular and is great craic. I was in Dublin for an international rugby match in early 2024, and over breakfast I was talking with relatives about a new novel of mine that was just out, The Con Club. Annie spoke up and advised me that I needed to write about her in one of my books. So, here she is.

This is dedicated to all those who try to make the world a better place. Well done and thank you.

INTRODUCTION

If you are yet to figure out the meaning of life, please try the following on for size and see how it fits you. My personal view is that life is about doing good. It's as simple as that, and therefore we should all be trying to do as much good as we can. Simple.

There are many things wrong with the world today. Horrible acts are taking place in some countries, and other countries are behaving in ways that are inhumane and anti-humanity – notably war and conflicts, but also where governments don't give their people a voice. There are things going wrong in families, in personal relationships and in communities. And of course, some institutions, organisations and companies are completely misbehaving, in ways that see them only working in the best interests of a few (often the owners or those in charge) while they make minimal or negative contributions to employees, the environment and humans in general. There are many, many examples, way too many: the oil companies, in the context of knowing about the connections between burning fossil and climate change, but suppressing and denying these facts for many years, to the cigarette companies in the

50s to the 70s who actively hid information that showed smoking was dangerous, to the banks that created the financial crash of 2007/8, to Enron – and more local to the UK, the Grenfell Tower fire and the Post Office scandal, also known as the Horizon IT scandal. Go online; you will find many examples.

A common denominator across all of the above is people. It's people who are doing the bad things, and in that regard, the solutions are with people too.

Selfishness, power and greed appear to be at the heart of these issues which cause so much damage. Badness is real, and its different levels of badness that create these issues, up to the furthest end of the spectrum, which takes us into the zone of evil.

But why is there so much badness?

Most people don't set out to do bad or haven't got 'doing bad' as their objective or goal, but that's what is being achieved.

It's okay for us to have self-interest. In fact, according to the Dalai Lama, it's essential to our survival as individuals (Dalai Lama & Hougaard, 2019). But there's obviously a line that gets crossed, where self-interest becomes selfishness, and then greed kicks in, and by then we are well down that road and into the territory of badness.

Many cross this line because they don't realise that it actually exists, but even if you do know, the fact that it's an invisible line doesn't help.

We need people to understand that self-interest is okay and is required and isn't an issue or something to be ashamed of, but that there are limits to self-interest and we all need to be wary of selfishness.

Many people do bad things out of ignorance or blindness, because they haven't set their own personal compass. This lack of a specified positive goal or objective means they stray into the domain of doing bad, and then this becomes their norm. They never know otherwise; or they become too ashamed to admit who they have become; or they think they now have too much to lose; or they are unable to change, because change, as we all know, can be very difficult to achieve.

So how do we deal with this, how do we improve this? For starters, we need people to set themselves a goal of doing good. This will get them actively thinking in a positive way about what is good and about how to do good. People aren't stupid, and for many this simple act will help to steer them down the right road and then keep on this road.

Unfortunately, there are a small number of people who set out with badness as a goal, and sometimes these people are the ones running companies or countries, and obviously they have influence, power and money, which is a worry and a problem. I'm not going to focus on them now; instead, I want to think about working with the majority.

So, how can people understand what it is to do good? There are loads of ways to help here:

Understanding and drawing on utilitarianism, which is about delivering actions that bring the greatest good for the greatest number of people. With utilitarianism, you focus on creating happiness and wellbeing, and you try to prevent harm and pain.

Considering what Elkington (1999) calls the Triple Bottom Line of profit, people and planet – aimed at companies but good for individuals too. We can't just look at money and finances in isolation or as the only objective anymore; we have to consider people and the planet too. This means minding the environment and doing things that help it, while also focusing on people – and a good way to think about people might be through the prism of wellbeing, not just financial but also physical, emotional and social, which I will come to soon.

Building self-awareness, as this enables us to think about others differently and to be more accepting of them, which creates better teamwork and harmony.

One of the ways I hope to do good is through sharing some of my own ideas, concepts such as Mind the Gap, Grow Great Teams and the RISE UP model.

The other way is to help people to become better leaders in their personal and professional lives – to *Just Do Good*. I hope to do so through this book, helping readers to think about the concept of leadership in terms of personal leadership, leadership within communities, and leadership in the more traditional sense, in companies and countries.

There are lots of journal articles and books about leadership, many of which I have read and enjoyed. Often, though, these texts use examples of politicians and companies etc., and as a result many people struggle to engage with them, because they disagree with the political standpoint of the texts, or they might be supporters or critics of some of these brands and politicians. As people, we can at times all be quite biased and tribal.

But with films, engagement is simpler. Generally, we align with the protagonist, the lead character, and understand them and their actions, even if that person commits negative acts. Therefore, I think films are an excellent medium for exploring leadership: because we're engaged and aligned with the film, we're more open to taking on any leadership lessons that it might contain. Much of this book looks at lessons learnt from the films that I call my Significant Sixty, and we will come to these later. First, I want to introduce you to some key concepts used in this book, starting with a leadership/engagement model I developed a few years ago.

PART 1: THE FOUNDATIONS

CHAPTER 1:
RISE UP

I was studying business and leadership as part of an MBA (there are other types of masters' degrees too, and I'm of the view that if you want to do one, you should, but equally if you don't want to do one, that's fine) and I learned that Pink (2009) had interesting ideas around motivation, and I already knew that Storey and Holti (2013) had written one of the best healthcare leadership models I've encountered. I began thinking about a range of other concepts and theories, and I realised I had a number of my own ideas on the subject, and then it came to me, the bare bones of RISE UP. But I sat on it and I did nothing. In truth, I was busy with other aspects of life and work, and also during this time I unexpectedly wrote a couple of novels.

But then in my work, RISE UP began to... rise up in my thoughts. As part of my job, I was travelling around England and Wales, meeting lots of staff and informally interviewing them. I needed to ascertain what was good and not so good in the company, to help triangulate facts and get a clearer picture of how things were, so we could then work to fix the things that weren't functioning, the things that were negatively impacting on culture and quality. While having an informal chat with people, I would ask a range of questions, and there were three questions that I always asked everyone:

1. What is good about work these days?

2. Is there anything that frustrates or worries you?

3. If I could get the CEO to fix one thing that would make your working life or the lives of your colleagues better, what would it be?

Then I started to theme the answers, and after a thousand interviews, I could see that I had a model, as every matter raised by staff fitted into RISE UP. Once I had the model in place, I checked it with the next 1,300 people I interviewed, and that demonstrated the same: RISE UP had legs.

Red sky in the morning

Insights from the Office for National Statistics, the Bank of England, McKinsey, Deloitte, Gallup and NHS Digital suggest that there have never been as many vacancies across multiple industries as there are today, which is putting pressure on staff retention. This was the case before and during the Covid-19 lockdowns, and it continues to be a problem.

These staff shortages make it even more vital that organisations are able to hold on to the people that they have in the first place. Not being able to do so will have serious consequences. To start with, it will make the workplace a more difficult place for those staff who remain, and over time this increased pressure is likely to encourage them to move on too. Of course, this will impact on quality standards, with a negative effect on consumer satisfaction and perhaps safety. These are genuine threats to organisational brands, their market position and their long-term survival. And while you may be able to get new staff, they will not necessarily be the type you need.

It's impossible to swim out of a downward spiral, so it's imperative to ensure that we don't find ourselves in such a position in the first place. We need to heed the shepherd's warning.

Happy staff stay: RISE UP

Much has been written about employees and how to keep them happy and satisfied. My goal is to add to the existing body of work by offering a model that not only makes sense but is easy to remember and apply, so that practitioner impact is maximised – which means organisations can hold on to their people and do whatever it is they do as organisations brilliantly. I hope RISE UP achieves this.

As organisations we can't not get involved. We can't just let people walk out the door; we have to RISE UP and we have to RISE UP now.

With my model, I slightly sidestep the work of Maslow (see Chapter 3) and centre RISE UP more in the domains of intrinsic and extrinsic motivation. I don't discuss money at all; I take it as accepted that money is always part of the equation, in the same way that you need bread to make a sandwich. I zone in on the hidden bits, the filling between the two slices, the factors that are given less attention but that are in reality truly vital. It's worth noting that many of these factors won't cost an organisation much or anything at all to address, and importantly *all* of them are within the organisation's power to address and resolve – that is, if they have the desire and courage to do what at times might feel uncomfortable, which is RISE UP.

Generally speaking, happy staff stay. We need to keep them happy. But how? It's as easy and as hard as this: help them to RISE UP.

Raison d'être
Independence
Stimulation
Expertise
Unite
Process-fixing

Here's how the model works:

Raison d'être

Raison d'être is about having a direction. What is it all about? Who am I? Why do I exist? How do I contribute? What do I contribute? What do I contribute to? Sometimes life and career intersect, but not always.

What's clear is that people need to know their raison d'être in the workplace. As people, we are passionate. But if we don't know what our raison d'être is, we're like flat tyres. We exist, we can move, but it isn't pretty, it isn't right, the motivation isn't really there.

At recruitment level, if you can hire people with a raison d'être that's aligned with your industry or sector, you're immediately onto a winner. Recruiting these types of individuals will do much for your retention as they will stay forever.

For employees who are already in place, helping them to recognise and understand their raison d'être will have a positive impact too. For some it turns on a light bulb, taking them out of the darkness, and they start to understand how they're making a difference. For others, the passion was already there, and this just joins the dots for them in terms of self-awareness. For some, even if they didn't and still don't quite have a passion for the work, it helps them to appreciate that they're making a contribution. Finally, for a small few it will help them to recognise that this line of work isn't for them and they can move on to something they're more suited to. This isn't a bad thing: given that emotion is contagious, a negative employee can be very damaging, a catalyst that pushes good employees into the arms of other organisations.

Some managers feel embarrassed about doing raison-d'être type activities, and this can be one of the obstacles to enlightening staff.

Independence

Independence is about having a say, having influence, feeling listened to, feeling valued. It's the opposite of feeling that things are being done to you. This is huge when it comes to feeling like a person, like a human, as opposed to being a number or just another cog in the machine. It appeals to a person's sense of self, their sense of self-worth. If you believe you don't have a say, that your contribution isn't valued, then why would you stay? Some do stay despite this; they have their reasons for doing so and probably never reach their potential in the workplace. But many leave.

Imagine how differently people would contribute if you managed to 'switch them on'. When you're able to create an environment where staff believe they are listened to and have influence, straight away they start to feel important, they feel liked, they feel respected.

Managers who fear change or enjoy hierarchy can be an obstacle to this. It's about a sense of democracy.

Stimulation

Stimulation is about all the Human Resources stuff. How do we do recognition? How do we do rewards? How do we do acknowledgement? How do we do thanks? It's about doing things like meaningful supervision. It's about doing appraisals, properly and positively. It's about having systems in place to publicly acknowledge people who are doing a good job or making an invaluable contribution. This can be annual award ceremonies. It can be 'employee of the week' nominations.

Complacency as a manager – believing that you have all of this sorted – can be an obstacle here. You have to keep doing it. Just like your staff have to keep turning up and doing what they do every day, so do you. It's not a one-off task.

Expertise

Expertise is about our need to be good at something. Chefs have their signature dish. For a dancer it might be a specific move. Sports teams have individuals who are a specialists and so should all business and organisational teams. Being an expert helps us to feel good about ourselves; to know, 'I'm that person. I have that skill or that ability. I'm the main person for this. I'm the specialist.'

Expertise is strongly connected to identity. It's so important for people to be able to feel good about themselves, especially when you consider that most of us are awake for at least 112 hours every week. A lot of people struggle with low confidence and think they aren't good enough. It's amazing the amount of successful people who feel like this. Some of these people have imposter syndrome. However, for others, the root cause is simply not understanding what success actually is, or how it looks for them.

But there is something great that people can believe in: they can believe in themselves. That starts with being good at something, anything. Being an expert in something: dandelions, a rugby spin pass, coffee, zebras, anything. In the workplace it might be spreadsheets, keeping the peace, organising things, the medication round. For some, it might be about doing degrees and diplomas at various levels, being coached, or being pushed for promotion opportunities and other kinds of learning. Or it might be as simple as being the best that you can be. Expertise doesn't look the same for everyone.

Creating a workplace where people can feel like a winner is great for their self-esteem. Managers who fear being less knowledgeable than their juniors can be an obstacle here.

Unite

Unite the people. We have to operate in teams. Organisations are teams within teams within teams. Silos are generally the enemy. Also, we live and work in families and communities. This has been the way since the beginning of time. It's for safety reasons. We need friends. We need others. There needs to be connectivity. Connectivity is like electricity.

All of this means we need to learn how to deal with conflict. We need to know how to build teams. We should be using tools like the Myers–Briggs Type Indicator, the Predictive Index and DISC. We should be helping people to understand their own strengths and the strengths of others. You need more than flour to make a cake. You need all of the individual strengths in place for a team to be brilliant. Help people understand their work objectives, what needs to be achieved and why. Involve them in change. Link it all up for them. Get everyone into the boat and rowing in the same direction.

Staff with personality problems, powerful groups with vested interests and managers who can't create authentic followership can be obstacles here.

Process-fixing

Process-fixing is about sorting out what doesn't work. It's a bit of a catch-all too, as all the other bits of RISE UP can also turn up here. There are always things that don't work in the workplace. Sometimes these are physical things, but sometimes they're invisible things that can be classified as the unwritten rules. Not addressing what's broken is very frustrating for staff and creates huge dissonance and dissatisfaction. In the end, people just give up and go, 'I'm banging my head against a brick wall. The IT doesn't work. The change was done poorly. The food in the canteen is rubbish. There's no parking. My manager doesn't listen. I don't know how promotion happens around here. Nothing works. Nothing ever changes.'

Sometimes there are things that can't be fixed, but many things can. Listening is important here too. Find out what isn't working, acknowledge that you know. Fix what you can and communicate with everyone about the changes. Also point out what can't be fixed and explain why. If you don't communicate all of this, negativity will fill the void and create its own narrative. Be seen to listen. Be seen to care.

Disorganisation and poor communication can be your biggest obstacles here. Process-fixing should be a never-ending cycle.

As I mentioned previously, every other part of RISE UP can also show up here. However, if you're a winning organisation, an organisation that learns, then none of the other five factors should show up here regularly, as those matters should have already been addressed.

Red sky at night

RISE UP can create the 'red sky at night' effect for organisations. It's a model that you can use to analyse your teams and organisations and take appropriate action wherever you have deficits. RISE UP is about genuinely achieving wellbeing for people and organisations. This is the key. Achieve this and staff will stay. The meek may indeed inherit the earth, but in the meantime, only organisations that RISE UP will thrive and survive.

RISE UP is for us as individuals too

RISE UP can also work for us as individuals, in our personal lives. And assist us with understanding our needs and how to help ourselves. Let me demonstrate:

- **Raison d'être:** Have I got a raison d'être? Well, if you haven't, you need to start thinking about how to get one and then follow it.
- **Independence:** Am I really listening to myself? Like, really listening, and doing the things I really want to do?
- **Stimulate:** Am I being kind to myself? Am I having a supportive internal dialogue with myself? Am I telling myself about the good things about me?

- **Expertise:** Am I thinking about my strengths? Am I developing my strengths? Am I playing to my strengths?
- **Unite:** Am I engaging with those around me in a positive way? Am I being kind to others? Am I playing a part in making those relationships honest and meaningful and supportive?
- **Process-fixing:** Are there things in my life I'm not happy about? Am I identifying these? Am I trying to understand them? Am I trying to find solutions? The goal here isn't to actually fix everything that's wrong in your life; it's to be compassionate with yourself, to listen to yourself, to acknowledge the issues, to try to find solutions, and where they can't be found, to accept you've tried your best and accept the situation.

CHAPTER 2: OTHER CONCEPTS FROM ME

In this chapter and the next, I share other concepts that I will use in this book to help explore and demonstrate leadership. The following are my own ideas:

The Sistine Chapel

There are many cities that should be on your 'to visit' list, but in my opinion, one that's definitely worth a visit is Rome. Now, if you ever go to Rome there are many places there that you must see, such as the Colosseum and St Peter's Basilica, but top of the list for me has to be the Sistine Chapel. Words can't adequately describe it. You stand there and look up at the ceilings and are struck not only by the fact that the beautiful artwork is about 500 years old, but that someone had the idea and then the actual ability and audacity to create such a marvel. It's awe-inspiring, breathtaking and thought-provoking.

But what you never hear people talking about when it comes to the Sistine Chapel is the front door. Not a word. Not a thought. Nothing. Yet here's the thing: if it weren't for the front door and the doorway, there wouldn't be a way in, and no one would ever get to see the beauty within the building. The door and doorway are hugely important.

Something similar happens with leadership. There are millions of articles about leadership. Many love it and are hugely interested in it, but very few people acknowledge or are interested in the doorway into leadership, and that doorway is self-awareness. Without self-awareness, it's really difficult to be a decent leader. It's probably the single most important thing when it comes to developing your leadership ability, because once you start to become self-aware, you also start to think about others in terms of their strengths and limitations, and this is the beginning of understanding how to build great teams.

And how can we develop our self-awareness? There are many different ways, from reflection and 360-degree feedback, to listing our strengths and weaknesses, or doing some tests like the Myers–Briggs Type Indicator, the DISC personality test and the Hogan Personality Inventory.

Grow Great Teams

This concept is connected to self-awareness. But the greatest example of Grow Great Teams is when we turn on the TV and watch professional sports teams. You can use any great sports side as an example, but I will take the Argentina football team that won the World Cup in 2022. A really good team.

Good teams know the strengths and weaknesses of every player, and then, as much as they can, they play to people's strengths and try to limit the damage that can be caused by their individual limitations. This is obvious with sports, but we don't give it enough attention in the workplace.

Back to Argentina. The world champions. Now hugely confident. Let's go back to that tournament and make two changes. We still play with eleven players, but we swap two: Lionel Messi, one of the greatest players ever, maybe the greatest ever, who plays in a striker position, and Emiliano Martinez, their goalie, who is one of the best in the world at this moment. Let's put Martinez up front and Messi in goal.

Martinez might be capable of breaking the ball down or holding it up for others and might score the odd header, but he won't cause anywhere near as much damage as Messi would up front, so straight away, Argentina will score a lot less often. Then, Messi in goal: I'd fancy my own chances against him, so prolific strikers, I imagine, would expect to have a field day. Messi just wouldn't have the stature to do a good job there. With this formation, Argentina would lose every game against decent opposition, yet they'd be playing the same eleven players, only swapping two. The impact, very quickly: heads would dip, and eventually they would lose their confidence, and this would affect their self-esteem, and this champion side would start to feel like it was a rubbish team full of losers.

So why don't we apply this learning in the workplace?

Why aren't we letting people play to their strengths more?

Football teams never pick 11 strikers or 11 goalkeepers, for obvious reasons: they would lose. Badly. They pick for differences. They pick for different strengths. It's the same with rugby. You wouldn't pick 15 scrum halves or 15 flankers for your team, because you would lose. And if you played your best player, who is frequently your out half, as a prop, you would lose; and again, if you moved your prop to the out half position, you would lose.

Let's be smart and Grow Great Teams. Growing Great Teams is about building positivity and motivation, by allowing people to play to their strengths, as much as you can.

Mind the Gap

You might think I'm referring to the routine announcement at many of the London Underground Tube stations advising people not to make a misstep into the space between the train and the platform, but I'm not. Or if, like me, you grew up in rural Ireland, you may be calling to mind a time a farmer asked for your support to stop cattle escaping through a hole in the hedgerow while he mended it with some fencing, but it's not that either.

If you ever watch eight-year-olds, boys or girls, playing soccer, you'll notice one thing in particular. You can say to them, 'keep your structure, keep space between you and pass to each other,' but once you throw in the ball, immediately they converge together. All of them. They all try to get a boot on the ball, and eventually one does, and the ball goes flying over to a different part of the park. Then they all swarm over there together and, again, they converge. They try to get a boot on the ball, and eventually one does, and the ball flies over to another part of the park. Again, they all swarm over to the ball, they converge, and this goes on and on and on and on. This is what the game becomes.

What's fascinating is that when you're dealing with 12-year-olds, boys or girls, playing soccer and you ask them to keep their structure, keep space between them and pass to each other, they do it. They don't converge. That's right, they don't converge. This is significant. Why don't they converge? Because you asked them not to, and they have awareness, so they don't. Awareness.

Convergence happens in organisations a lot. It happens in management and leadership teams a lot. You end up getting a convergence of strengths. It's common. It just happens. Why? Well, like is attracted to like. Dominant strengths dominate. Junior staff mimic the behaviours of senior people. There's a tendency to engage in groupthink. You see, convergence is normal, and the fact it happens isn't a problem. But not recognising that it's happening is a huge problem. If you have a convergence of strengths, then because we all have weaknesses, that means you're also getting a convergence of those same weaknesses. And this causes problems. This is the gap.

When you have leadership groups that have these

homogenous strengths, these are communicated out in an invisible way, like the way in which radio stations work. Staff on the same frequency as the leaders generally pick up the communication, and this switches them on, and then they raise their heads and are able to see the people with the same strengths as them, and they understand that these strengths are valued, and they feel like they're connected.

The weaknesses of the leaders are really missing strengths. And these missing strengths don't get transmitted out, meaning staff with these particular strengths are never switched on, and they start to believe that their strengths aren't valued. As a result, they don't feel like they're connected. And, disappointingly, they believe they don't belong. And then they leave, or they stay and feel unmotivated and unvalued.

How do you address this? It's easy. Just like with the 12-year-olds who don't converge, you start with developing awareness of the issue. You can take it a step further and shine a light on it, like with the Hawthorne Effect, which is an experiment from the 1920s, that maintained that people modify their behaviours in response to believing they are being observed. And you can take it a step further still and actively address it. How? Well, you start by measuring individual strengths and weaknesses. Take care here, as you don't want people to feel 'got at' and persecuted. Once you have clarity on the missing strengths (i.e. weaknesses), you go and find people with these actual strengths, and then you put them in visible positions of influence. Now, you might be unsure what these types of people actually look like and where to find them, but this is easy too. Analyse the types of people who've left the organisation; it will be them.

One degree of longitude on a map is sixty-nine miles

People do lots of good things for others. Lovely acts of kindness and goodness. Things that make a difference. But frequently we don't realise the impact because we don't always get to see the results. I've worked with people who do lots of small things for colleagues that will have helped those people in their relationships with their partners and children. But at work they don't get to see or know this. Healthcare staff have a huge impact on their patients and the patients' families, which then changes how they think and behave towards those surrounding them in their personal and professional lives. These acts have a significant reach, and this is all doing good.

Take the five million people in Ireland. If they do one decent act every day, that's five million acts of kindness each day and 1.825 billion acts a year. That's a huge amount of goodness. The population of India in 2025 is approximately 1.5 billion. If every person in India does one act of kindness a day, that equates to 547 billion acts a year. Just one act a day very quickly becomes a huge amount of goodness.

We don't always realise the value of doing small acts of kindness. We think they're small and don't matter, but they all add up. I do a lot of hiking and sometimes I use maps. And on the map, one degree of longitude looks like it's tiny and meaningless, but in reality, it's huge, especially if you try to walk that one degree, because in reality it's sixty-nine miles.

The Panama Canal

The rationale for building the canal made a huge amount of sense. Ships that needed to reach the Pacific from the Atlantic Ocean and vice versa had to travel around Cape Horn, using the Drake Passage and the southern seas. These seas are rough, stormy and dangerous. And in addition, this journey uses up a huge amount of fuel. So, they built the canal, to save fuel and ensure a safer journey.

And while they were building it, ships had to continue with the arduous journey around the Cape. Even when there was only 50 metres of the canal left to build, they still had to travel via the Cape; they couldn't just ditch that route and start using the canal. Why? Because the canal wasn't ready, and any ship that tried to travel that way would have ended up grounded, and every ship behind it would have crashed into the ship in front of it. It would have been carnage and chaos.

In industry – take health, for instance – there is always talk about making transformations, about switching to a different way of working, changing systems etc. But what always happens is that before the new system is fully built, we start using part of it, and it isn't set up for this, so it fails, and the older system doesn't get switched off either. As a result, we end up having backlogs, confusion, frustration and chaos in the now-stretched older system and the new system that isn't fully ready yet. There are, of course, reasons why this happens, but nothing can improve until we fully create the new system before starting to use it. Think Panama Canal.

CHAPTER 3:

IDEAS DEVISED BY OTHERS

Brian O'Driscoll's new way of thinking

Between his biography (2014) and a particular YouTube video (2017), Irish rugby great Brian O'Driscoll talks about a time when he was no longer happy playing rugby. He wasn't enjoying it. He went to see a sports psychologist, Enda McNulty, who played for the Armagh All-Ireland-winning Gaelic football team. Enda asked Brian to recall a time when he was madly in love with his rugby. Brian spoke about the 2001 Lions tour to Australia. He said he was buzzing then as he was doing things he loved, like using his speed and skill to beat players and make exciting plays and score tries. The psychologist was able to work out that at some stage since then Brian had stopped thinking about and working on his strengths and become ultra-focused on his weaknesses and trying to improve them. The psychologist pointed out that this was sapping his energy and was turning the game he loved into something negative and a chore.

Enda's advice to Brian was to stop working on his weaknesses and instead put the time into making his strengths even better strengths, because it was these strengths that set him apart from others and made him the brilliant player that he once was – the player who was making the big breaks happen and loving the satisfaction that was coming from being brilliant.

So, Brian stopped working on his weaknesses and focused his attention on improving his strengths. He found the joy in rugby again, and in the 2009 Six Nations, he played a pivotal role in Ireland winning their first grand slam since 1948. He ended up being nominated for World Rugby Player of the Year, and there's a strong case to be made that maybe that year he deserved to win it, but one can't argue with the fact that it went to the great New Zealander Richie McCaw.

Newton's Third Law of Motion

Isaac Newton gave the world many things. For the purposes of this book, I'm most interested in his third law of motion: *for every action there is an equal but opposite reaction.*

Maslow's Hierarchy of Needs

Maslow's ideas are well known and widely written about. He theorised that human needs can be separated out and categorised and then placed into a hierarchy. He put the needs into a pyramid to demonstrate that they come in building blocks: to reach the top of the pyramid, you must have your needs met in each subsequent tier. He builds upwards from physiological needs, to safety needs, to feeling-loved needs, to esteem needs, before you hit the top of the pyramid and you self-actualise.

Maslow (1943) explains our needs as follows:

1. Physiological needs, such as air, clothing, food, heat, housing, sex and sleep.

2. Safety and security needs, such as being financially, physically and psychologically safe.

3. Needs to belong and feel loved, such as affiliation, being part of a group and meaningful friendships.

4. Esteem needs, such as acceptance, accomplishment, achievement, recognition and status.

5. Self-actualisation needs, which are about achieving your full potential as a person, being the best you can be, the best version of yourself.

Schein on Culture

Edgar Schein is the expert/guru in organisational culture. He defines culture as follows:

> The Culture of a group can now be defined as a pattern of basic shared assumptions learned by a group, as it solved its problems of external adaption and internal integration, that is seen to have worked and as a result is valid and taught to

> new people as the correct way to perceive, think, and feel in relation to these problems. (Schein, 2010, p. 18)

Another useful thing Schein (2010) says about culture is that it can be broken down into three things:

1. **Artefacts:** These are visible, like signs and posters, uniforms, cleanliness and order.

2. **Espoused values and beliefs:** These are what it says on the tin: the values and beliefs that people say they have.

3. **Basic underlying assumptions:** These are invisible. They definitely won't be written down. They are what people really think but keep quiet about unless you are one of them. They are real, powerful and the culture is built on them.

Let's see how we can apply these three factors to understand culture. Imagine you're visiting a factory to explore the culture there.

First, you zone in on equality, diversity and inclusion (EDI). There are signs and posters up on the walls (*artefacts*) showing that the business takes EDI very seriously.

The factory is in a country where people are predominantly Caucasian, but it's in an area that's 50 per cent Caucasian people and 50 per cent people of other races. What shows up in the *espoused values* is interesting. The factory management and staff are saying that they're anti-racist, and respect all races, and believe in equal opportunities. These are great things to say.

Now, you've come to the factory as an outsider, and so the people there are unlikely to tell you the truth about the *basic underlying assumptions*, because you're not one of them and they don't trust you. But you can find out what the basic underlying assumptions are, because these will show up, if you know where to look. For example, I said the area is 50 per cent Caucasian, and yet you find out that 80 per cent of the workforce are Caucasian, and 100 per cent of the people in management positions are Caucasian. And when you explore disciplinary matters, you find that even though only 20 per cent of the workforce are non-Caucasian, it's 75 per cent of the non-Caucasians who find themselves in disciplinary hearings.

This suggests that there is a culture problem, as the business is *saying* it's a particular kind of organisation, but it's actually clearly the opposite. On this occasion, you can deduce that the basic underlying assumptions contain bias and prejudice against non-Caucasian people. The artefacts, espoused values and basic underlying assumptions don't align. Therefore, the organisation needs to do some alignment work, but also some very important work on bias and prejudice.

Wellbeing

There are many expert opinions on what wellbeing is, and they all usually agree that it refers to how a person feels about themselves, how they might describe their level of happiness, how they feel about their physical and mental health. And how things like their finances and how well they eat and sleep, impact this. Wellbeing is also shaped by having meaningful ways to pass your time and the support that you receive from being in a friendship group.

Its widely reported that there are four, five or even six wellbeing pillars. The four I promote in this book are emotional, financial, physical and social.

Definitions of leadership

There are many definitions of leadership, and in this book, I'm drawing on two. The first is from Edgar Schein:

> When we are influential in shaping the behaviour and values of others, we think of that as leadership. (Schein, 2010, p. 3)
>
> And the other is from McKinsey:
>
> Leadership is a set of mindsets and behaviours that aligns people in a collective direction, enables them to work together and accomplish shared goals, and helps them adjust to changing environments. (McKinsey & Company, 2024)

However, as you read, feel free to use your own subjective interpretation of leadership.

PART 2: THE SIGNIFICANT SIXTY

And now, finally, we move on to the films – or movies if you prefer. The 'Significant Sixty' are the films that I'm using to help broaden our understanding of leadership. I started with over 100 films compiled from a variety of '100 best movies ever' type lists. I wrote up about 80 of these and then decided that this was too many for what I wanted to achieve and distilled it down to these 60.

Each chapter that follows focuses on a different theme that I believe relates to leadership. I've subjectively categorised each film under one theme, but in fact most of these films have a number of themes within them and could just as easily have been placed in a different chapter. Before getting into the themes, I begin with the three films which I believe teach us the most, my 'on the podium' movies.

CHAPTER 4:

MY THREE ON THE PODIUM

From a leadership learning perspective, these films are my podium three, but I won't go so far as to allocate their medals a colour. I start with a film that many view as one of the best films ever.

1: *The Godfather* (1972)

The storyline

Maybe the best film case study of people, life and organisations that exists. The film was directed by Francis Ford Coppola and based on Mario Puzo's novel. It stars many big names, with Marlon Brando playing the Godfather, Vito Corleone, and Al Pacino his youngest son, Michael. It centres on organised crime and the mafia families. Michael is a medal-winning marine who loves his family but has no interest in being part of the crime cartel. His father, Vito, respects and supports this.

In *The Godfather*, a drug baron invites Vito Corelone to do business with him, in order to benefit from his connections. Vito politely declines, however, as he's involved with a number of politicians, to their mutual benefit, and he believes that by getting involved in the drug trade, he would alienate the politicians. Vito is the leading mafia don, and his unwillingness to get involved with drugs makes it difficult for some of the other mafia families. The drug baron is connected to another mafia family, the Tattaglias, who attempt to kill Vito, shooting and severely injuring him. While Vito is incapacitated, the drug baron puts pressure on his eldest son, Sonny, played by James Caan, to accept the drugs deal.

Meanwhile, Michael visits his dad in hospital, and foils another hit on him. This proves to Michael that the NYPD captain is on the payroll of the drug baron. Michael recognises that because he isn't involved in crime and is viewed by the mafia bosses as a lightweight, he's the only one who can get close to both the drug baron and the police captain, and he agrees to a meeting with them both, to resolve the current disputes. At this meeting, he assassinates them both.

This leads to a big fallout amongst the five leading mafia families, and for his safety, Michael has to seek refuge in Sicily. He survives a number of attempts on his life there, but his older brother Sonny is murdered back in America. All of this leads to Vito calling a meeting with all the mafia heads to try to broker a peace deal. A deal is agreed and Michael returns home, a bona fide criminal.

Vito is old now and knows his time is limited and that Michael will have to take over from him. Vito makes

Michael aware of how this will be received by the other mafia families and who will strike at him, how and why. Vito dies, and what he told Michael is what plays out, but because his father had warned him and Michael took what he said seriously, he's ready and waiting. Michael shows his ruthlessness and strategic aptitude by having all the dons of the leading families assassinated at the same time, and his brother-in-law, too, for his betrayal of the Corleone family. This immediately announces Michael as the most powerful and dangerous mafia don.

Leadership lessons

There are many lessons here:

> Vito is a great coach to his son, Michael, which shows the value of coaching.

There can be benefits to having someone like Sonny, who can cause fear through being a hot head, but the real lesson here is that this also presents others with the opportunity to exploit you. Hot heads in companies can get things done, but ultimately, they will compromise themselves. They lack emotional intelligence and emotional regulation.

The film is an example of how the best leaders are sometimes the people who don't want the leadership responsibility. Sonny wants it and has it and isn't good at it, whereas Michael doesn't want it at all, but has to take it on and is excellent.

The film shows the transformation of Michael from being a war hero who's in love with Kay Adams (played by Diane Keaton) – a person who's honest and straight, who sits outside the family's criminal businesses and has zero interest in them – to becoming the ultimate criminal, feared and respected by all, and now someone who no longer views Kay as his equal and worthy of the truth, but as someone to be lied to. This shows us how circumstances can create change.

If Vito had recognised, he was no longer capable in the job, he could have managed the succession planning, thus preventing the other families from trying to assassinate him. This probably would have prevented the whole mess. Instead, the combination of the emotion from the failed assassination, the love Michael has for his now-vulnerable father (who the other families are still trying to kill) and the genuine weakness of his other brother, Fredo, mean that it's only Michael who can save his father's life, by getting access to and killing the other mafia leader and the dodgy cop. The consequence is that Michael has to flee to Sicily and is now a marked man, and in addition, there's now a bigger war amongst the mafia families, which leads to Sonny being murdered and Michael's new Sicilian wife too. A lesson here is that once you go down the wrong road, there's no going back, as the system and the people within the system make it hard to do so, and this is Michael's life in the film. But one thing that Michael displays is good judgement: time after time, he makes good decisions.

Culture and Edgar Schein

Culture is huge in the film in terms of what is accepted and expected in these families of organised crime. They have their own set of rules and values, their own structures and systems, and their own way of dealing with grievances and disciplinary matters.

Remember Schein's definition of culture:

> The Culture of a group can now be defined as a pattern of basic shared assumptions learned by a group, as it solved its problems of external adaption and internal integration, which has worked well enough to be considered valid and, therefore, to be taught to new members as the correct way to perceive, think, and feel in relation to these problems. (Schein, 2010, p. 18)

Remember, too, that Schein (2010) says culture can be broken down into three things: artefacts, espoused values and beliefs, and basic underlying assumptions.

We can look at the mafia families in *The Godfather* in two ways:

- **From the outside:** To people outside of the mafia, the families' artefacts and espoused values are ones of order and being law-abiding, and they won't share their basic underlying assumptions. But the authorities are looking at what they do, and they see lots of crimes. So outsiders can see a cultural misalignment. This is deliberate, however: as the mafia families are setting out to deceive and stay out of trouble, they have to set out their artefacts and espoused values in this way.

- **From the inside:** Through the eyes of an insider, we see the families' artefacts are ones of honour and respect and looking presentable. The espoused values are ones of working within the families, being respectful, abiding by the mafia rules and working together, but also accepting that if a dispute breaks out, murder is allowed. What's great about films for this exercise is that we can see the basic underlying assumptions of the film characters, because we have access to what they think. We can see that the basic underlying assumptions agree with violence being allowed and necessary under certain circumstances, and we can see this in the action too, as there are murders. Therefore, within the mafia there's alignment from an analysis perspective, and what you can say about the culture is that it can be brutal.

Why is the culture like this? That's easy. It goes back to Schein's definition earlier in the book, that culture is a pattern of basic shared assumptions learned by a group, to solve problems of external adaptation and internal integration. That is seen to have worked, and as a result is valid and taught to new people as the correct way to perceive, think and feel in relation to those problems.

The reason the culture is like this, is that the mafia families evolved into this way of being, because it made sense to them, and it gave them the solutions that they needed to survive and function.

Key takeaways:

- Having the right coach adds value.
- Emotional intelligence is essential, as if you're prone to losing your temper, you will fail.
- Understand culture.

2: *Saving Private Ryan* (1998)

The storyline

This is a brilliant war movie, written by Robert Rodat and directed by Steven Spielberg. It's set in Normandy, France, in 1944, during World War II. The opening scene takes place on 6 June, D-Day, and the US army is trying to land on Omaha Beach as part of the Normandy Landings. The beach has been fortified by the Nazis and the American soldiers are being decimated by enemy machine guns. Captain John H. Miller (Tom Hanks) rallies a bunch of men taking refuge but is under heavy fire on the beach and then leads them to destroy a machine-gun nest before getting off the beach to reach the previously planned rendezvous point.

Unbeknown to Miller and his men, three out of the four brothers of the Ryan family have been killed in action. A general at the Department of War decides that this is a huge loss to the mother of the Ryan family, and orders that the fourth Ryan brother, James Francis of the 101st Airborne Division, played by Matt Damon, needs to be located and returned home to his mother. Unfortunately, Ryan is missing. When Miller gets to the army camp, he is tasked with finding Ryan and bringing him back safely so he can be transported home. He uses some of his current men, but also recruits some others to help him with this mission.

The team starts tracking Ryan, and the first place they head to is the town of Neuville-au-Plain. It's here that Private Caparzo, played by Vin Diesel, disobeys an order and does what he believes is the right thing to do, by saving a young French girl. His death is a huge disappointment to the team, and is personally felt by Miller, but he doesn't show this to the others.

A short while later, Miller and his men believe they have found Ryan and that the mission is concluded, but in fact it's a different James Ryan, a James Frederick Ryan. They then head to the planned meeting place of the 101st Airborne Division, and he isn't there either, but they encounter a soldier who advises that Ryan got new orders to go and defend a bridge in a town called Ramelle.

On the way there on foot, the team aren't detected by a hidden Nazi machine-gun nest, but Miller believes that he and the men are obligated to attack and take out the nest. The men don't want to, as they see it as an unnecessary risk and not part of their current set of orders. Miller leads the attack, and they manage to destroy the nest and kill a number of Nazis, while taking one Nazi prisoner. Sadly, their medic, Wade, dies in what is a very emotional scene. This has a huge impact on the men, and some of them want to execute the Nazi prisoner, though one man argues that to do so would be an illegal act. Miller, it appears, is unsure what to do, but agrees to release the desperate prisoner, ordering him to turn himself in to the next Allied patrol he comes across.

This decision leads to more conflict, with Reiben a soldier played by Edward Burns, looking to step down from the unit because he disagrees with their releasing the prisoner and thinks the mission is rubbish, as Ryan isn't worth the lives of his two dead colleagues. This puts Burns into direct conflict with Sergeant Horvath, played by Tom Sizemore, who pulls out his pistol and threatens to shoot Reiben for desertion.

Miller skilfully intervenes to de-escalate the situation. He knows the men have a series of bets in place to try to guess what he does for a living back home, and when he declares he's an English teacher, all the soldiers are immediately distracted. He then explains that losing men is very upsetting to him, and that his mission is really to follow his orders, whatever they are, and hope that these help the Allies to win the war, so that he can go home to his wife and kids. If finding Ryan helps to make that happen, then he will do it, he says, and if Reiben wants to resign from Miller's company and go to another one, he will make it happen, without a consequence for Reiben. Then he heads off, back in the direction they were heading, to try to find Ryan. Miller's men have been positively impacted by him and they follow his lead.

They encounter Ryan – Matt Damon – in Ramelle, and he is very upset that his brothers are dead, but out of integrity, he won't abandon his fellow soldiers. This frustrates Reiben and others; as they see it, they have had two friends killed because of Ryan. But Ryan respectfully enquires about their dead colleagues and displays good emotional intelligence. After a short while, Miller comes to terms with Ryan's decision to stay and sees the goodness in it.

Some of Miller's team think they should stay to defend the bridge with Ryan. Miller, as the only officer present, takes command of everyone there and decides to do the prep work to try to defend the bridge from the Nazi tanks that will be coming. This displays innovation, strategic thinking, teamwork and leadership.

The team display great courage, but take on heavy losses, and are about to blow up the bridge as planned, to prevent the Nazis from getting control of it. However, air support arrives, destroying the tanks and forcing the Nazis to surrender. Millers is fatally wounded, and just before he dies, he tells Ryan to make sure that in his life he earns the sacrifices that Miller and his men made for him.

The film closes with the elderly Ryan and his family at the grave of Miller in a Normandy cemetery. Tearfully, Ryan confesses to him that he has never forgotten him, and that he hopes he earned the sacrifice that Miller made for him back then.

Leadership lessons

In *Saving Private Ryan*, Miller displays great leadership throughout. Miller is driven by his *raison d'être*, which is to win the war, by following orders, even if he dislikes them, and in doing so, be part of the wider effort to bring an end to the tyranny of the Nazis and the evil of Hitler. In his darkest and most difficult moments, he leans into *raison d'être*, to make sense of the craziness around him, and aligns this with getting home to his wife and children, an overarching *raison d'être*.

What he radiates as a person more than anyone else is also his biggest strength: he creates followership. His men follow him. It's about more than Miller having the authority; they really believe in him. They see he's authentic, they see he's fair and compassionate, and they see he tries to do good.

Miller also has a great understanding of how to build and manage a team. He knows how to use the bolshy and pushy Tom Sizemore (Sergeant Horvath), who uses different tactics in the team to the ones Miller uses, and he recognises the skill sets of others, such as Barry Pepper (Private Jackson), a brilliant sniper. As much as possible, Miller has everyone playing to their strengths.

He's a good listener, as demonstrated when he clearly explains to his team why they have to take on the risk of storming the machine-gun nest, even though they all believe that this isn't their task and they should stick to finding Ryan. And Miller's men listen to him. One of the most poignant things in the film is how all of this inspires Ryan to spend the rest of his life trying to do good. This is driven by Miller's final words to him before he dies, regarding the sacrifice that Miller and others have made for Ryan. The words are 'earn it'. Miller achieves much, and a lot of that is done by engaging his men, which is attributable to his ability to listen.

In highlighting a war film, it's important to acknowledge that killing people is fundamentally a bad thing. However, history dictates that war is sometimes unavoidable, and even though Miller is involved in the killing of others, his actions and everything that he's trying to make happen come from a position of decency: he's definitely trying to do good.

Another point about Miller is that he makes good decisions, which shows he has good judgement.

And finally, in this role Miller certainly Minds the Gap; he recruits quite a heterogeneous bunch. He also applies Grow Great Teams and the Brian O'Driscoll approach.

Eisenhower

Bear with me. Yes, this is tangential, but it is connected to the film and leadership. The planning and delivery of the actual D-Day Landings was overseen by General Eisenhower. It's fair to say that the operation was a success, but it did come at a great cost in terms of the lives of Allied soldiers. A number of years later, Eisenhower was a two-term president of the United States. On his departure, as all presidents do, he gave a farewell address. His was about ten minutes long and was given in January 1961, just before he was succeeded by JFK. Here's a quotation from his speech:

> A vital element in keeping the peace is our military establishment. Our arms must be mighty, ready for instant action, so that no potential aggressor may be tempted to risk his own destruction.
>
> Our military organization today bears little relation to that known by any of my predecessors in peace time, or indeed by the fighting men of World War II or Korea.
>
> Until the latest of our world conflicts, the United States had no armaments industry. American makers of plowshares could, with time and as required, make swords as well. But now we can no longer risk emergency improvisation of national defense; we have been compelled to create a permanent armaments industry of vast proportions. Added to this, three and a half million men and women are directly engaged in the defense establishment. We annually spend on military security more than the net income of all United State corporations.
>
> This conjunction of an immense military establishment and a large arms industry is new in the American experience. The total influence – economic, political, even spiritual – is felt in every city, every state house, every office of the Federal government. We recognize the imperative need for this development. Yet we must not fail

> to comprehend its grave implications. Our toil, resources and livelihood are all involved; so is the very structure of our society.
>
> In the councils of government, we must guard against the acquisition of unwarranted influence, whether sought or unsought, by the military-industrial complex. The potential for the disastrous rise of misplaced power exists and will persist.
>
> We must never let the weight of this combination endanger our liberties or democratic processes. We should take nothing for granted. Only an alert and knowledgeable citizenry can compel the proper meshing of the huge industrial and military machinery of defense with our peaceful methods and goals, so that security and liberty may prosper together. (Eisenhower, 1961)

What is fascinating about this is that this is a successful ex-army general who achieved much in World War II giving this warning, some 15 or 16 years later, as a departing president, and this was way back in 1961. It leads me to questions about how countries, the world and the leadership of the world have evolved. Where are we today? Has Eisenhower's warning been heeded in any way? Has the military-industrial complex become more or less powerful since then?

As leaders, we need to be aware that our actions and inactions have an impact. It's a bit like Newton's third law of motion: *for every action there is an equal and opposite reaction*. It might be that the reaction isn't always exactly opposite or exactly equal, but there will be something.

So, the American need for weapons in World War II created the military-industrial complex, and that has evolved into what it is today, with far-reaching political and global decisions around power and finance. And of course, it was the Nazis' behaviours in Europe that gave birth to these American needs (I am ignoring Japan here). And what gave rise to the Nazis and Hitler was a combination of things, including a global financial downturn that was felt very severely in Germany, and what were objectively believed to be extreme and unfair financial penalties imposed upon Germany by France and the UK in the Treaty of Versailles, as punishment for their role in World War I. But WWI was caused by the aristocrats who ran all the European empires trying to undermine, manipulate, overthrow and control each other, a macro form of *Game of Thrones*.

Actions create more actions, and we evolve and evolve, not always in positive ways. There will always be a reaction. Therefore, we should always be conscious of this and make the best decisions, with an eye on always doing what is good.

Key takeaways:

- Listening to others is important.
- Followership is strongly connected to real leadership.
- Humility helps to build trust.
- Teams make things happen.

3: *Erin Brockovich* (2000)

The storyline

This movie is based on the true story of Erin Brockovich, and she's played by Julia Roberts. It's directed by Steven Soderbergh and also stars Albert Finney.

Erin is an unemployed single mother of three children. She has been injured in a road traffic accident by a doctor and is suing him. Her lawyer, Ed Masry, is played by Finney. He expects to win the case, but Erin misbehaves in court when being cross-examined and loses the case. Erin blames Masry. A determined person who's at her wits' end, she's frustrated with Masry for not returning her calls, and she turns up at his office and makes a bit of a scene. She convinces Masry to feel some sympathy for her hardship, and he reluctantly gives her a job, at her request.

Erin is given files about a woman called Donna Jensen of Hinkley, California. The Pacific Gas and Electric Company (PG&E) are buying her house, and Erin needs to help Donna with this process. Because there are medical records in the file, Erin goes to visit her. Erin's inquisitive mind and her willingness to go the extra mile help her put two and two together. Donna and her husband are suffering from different forms of cancer, and PG&E have been paying for a doctor to help treat them. Through doing some detective work, Julia discovers that PG&E have been heavily contaminating the water supplies in the Hinkley region with a carcinogenic agent called hexavalent chromium and lying to the residents about this.

When Erin returns to the office having been away for over a week, Masry sacks her for not coming to work. But then he rehires her when he understands that she's been working away from the office, and that his not knowing this was a miscommunication issue.

Erin travels to Hinkley on several occasions and meets most of the residents, whom she starts to develop a rapport with. They start to trust her. Most of them are ill with cancer, and all are being helped by the PG&E doctors. These residents have been duped by PG&E into believing that their conditions have nothing to do with PG&E and the chromium.

Representing all the residents, Erin builds a class action lawsuit against PG&E. But a difficulty of the case is that it's limited, against the local plant only and not the wider company or the board, as they're saying that they never knew, that the information was withheld from them, and that therefore they're not liable.

Masry knows that PG&E will use every trick in the book to block and delay the case, maybe even until every cancer sufferer is dead. He explains to Erin that the only legal option open to them to bring this to a head reasonably quickly is to use a process called disposition by binding arbitration. However, that will require nearly all the residents agreeing to this. Erin meets all 634 of the residents who are impacted and gets all of them to sign up.

While she's there, an ex-employee of PG&E approaches her. He's upset that his cousin, who also worked at PG&E, recently died from cancer. He says that he can help Erin, but she's unsure how he can. Luckily for her and all the residents, he was given the task by PG&E of destroying lots of documents, but he didn't do it; in fact, he kept them. He presents them to Julia, and it turns out that some of them highlight that as far back as 1966, the board of PG&E knew all about the poisoning of the groundwater in Hinkley, and ordered the local site to ignore this, to keep it secret and to continue as they were.

The judge finds on the side of the residents, and orders PG&E to pay them damages of $333 million. Masry surprises Erin by giving her a much bigger bonus than what she asked for; he gives her $2 million, which leaves her speechless.

Leadership lessons

Erin Brockovich demonstrates the most dreadful aspects of corporations, where regardless of the consequences to people outside of the company, their only focus is on making money, and they spend the rest of their time denying they're doing anything wrong and putting as much energy and resources as they possibly can into lies, fraud and corruption. Absolutely awful.

The film shows the bias and lack of opportunity afforded to people who haven't got professional qualifications, who lack money and whose personal lives are a little chaotic, represented by Erin, despite the fact she has a huge desire to work and also has a great work ethic. It shows how socially siloed the workplace can be, and in my opinion what's at the heart of all this bias is the inability to see, hear and understand the lives of others, because all we really know is what we know, which is how we all subjectively live and see the world. Masry shows us how being exposed to others can allow us to understand them, and then as a result be more compassionate and create the conditions needed to empower them, by making things fairer. He does this for Erin.

There is also a lack of listening from the law firm in general, in that they've failed to recognise the trends and the scale of the misbehaviour of PG&E until Erin arrives.

This film also connects with *Saving Private Ryan*. In war, soldiers do terrible things, and to justify these they say they were 'just following orders'. In companies, sometimes the employees and leaders too, do dreadful things, but won't necessarily view it as doing bad, they will excuse their actions as just following orders, and keep their head down and get on with it. Sometimes those that do raise their head above the parapet are othered and excluded. You will be aware of many well documented cases where whistleblowers have been very badly treated.

Erin's leadership skills are huge; in fact, they're as good as it gets. She's good at detail, interested and inquisitive. She's highly motivated, intelligent and cunning. She's fearless, fair and warm-hearted. She's resilient, with a 'never give up' attitude. But most importantly, she knows right from wrong and is prepared to put it all on the line in order to do good. She's in my top ten leaders featured in this book, which we will come to later (see Chapter 26).

Key takeaways:

- Greed is a driver of harm to people and the environment.
- Psychopathic behaviour exists.
- Lies are a way of life for some.
- Determination can overcome greed and other negative forces.
- Bias exists and we need to be aware of it and the damage it causes.
- Effort is essential to achieving results.
- Decency is a great value to build connections and good things.
- Accountability is essential in tackling corporate greed and criminality.
- Overcoming the odds is possible.
- Fairness is what we should be aiming for.
- Great leaders achieve for others, especially the vulnerable.

CHAPTER 5:

AUTHENTICITY

4: *The Truman Show* (1998)

The storyline

The Truman Show is a movie directed by Peter Weir and starring Jim Carrey as Truman Burbank. Truman doesn't know that his whole life is just one big TV show, with everyone else a paid actor and him the main star: he's completely in the dark. At birth, Truman was adopted by the TV company, and he lives in a fake town that's actually a huge set on a studio lot. There are thousands of secret cameras hidden from him.

The script for the show has Truman falling in love with Meryl, played by Laura Linney, but love being love, it doesn't happen like that for Truman, and instead he falls in love with Sylvia, played by Natasha McElhone, an extra, so the show sacks her. This doesn't stop Truman from having feelings for Sylvia or dreaming about her, even though he ends up marrying Meryl.

Truman is about to turn 30, and he starts to develop an awareness of things not being what they seem, and he becomes quite suspicious of several small things, which leads him to believe that there's something inauthentic about his life. This leads to him trying to leave town, but several things happen, some big, to stop him at this time. To try to calm Truman down and get him to stay in the town, so he can continue to make money for the big studio, the show's producer reintroduces the actor who played his father, who died. It appears that Truman has bought the elaborate storyline regarding his dad, and everything goes back to normal, it seems.

But Truman has managed to sneak onto a sailing boat and is heading for what he hopes is freedom. The producer, who has access to wave machines that can control the sea, dials up a storm, but even though Truman nearly drowns, this doesn't deter him, and he manages to keep sailing, until he safely crashes the boat into the wall of the set. From there he finds an exit door to the real world, where he is met by Sylvia, who has been following the show and knows that Truman reciprocates the love she has for him. The show ends, and all the viewers find something else to watch.

Leadership lessons

The Truman Show highlights the importance of trusting your gut instinct. Truman senses that things around him aren't right, and that people aren't being straight with him. It also gives us the opportunity to think about ourselves as individuals within a system or organisation or team that isn't behaving in the right way, and the role we're playing by being compliant. The exception to this in the film is Woman B, who is authentic and has the right morals, but she finds herself in the minority and powerless, and is removed by the TV executives.

Truman displays great bravery, in that he takes action to uncover the truth, he challenges the powers that be, and as he makes his escape, he stands firm and achieves his goal despite all they do to try to stop him.

The film also gets us thinking about really understanding who we are as people and leaders. The film challenges us by asking us to be the kind of person who'll do the right thing, even when no one is looking. This tells you what your true character is. This idea is generated by the fact that we see Truman all the time, even when he believes no one is looking, whereas all the other people on the show are actors, and behave one way when the cameras are rolling but a different way when off the set.

The film takes us into the areas of authenticity and integrity. In the real world we might ask, why do the leaders of the UK water companies pay their board members huge incomes while failing to deliver any meaningful infrastructure or strategic work, and damaging the environment by having sewage regularly flowing into rivers, lakes and the sea?

Truman appears to have financial wellbeing, and most of his biological needs are met, and he feels safe and secure. But he doesn't fully believe that he belongs in the town, and even though his self-esteem is strong (which enables him to be brave), he knows he doesn't have true love, in terms of a genuine romantic relationship and proper friends. We see how all this impacts his emotional wellbeing. What's great is that Truman takes control of his life and does something about it.

Key takeaways:

- Trust your gut.
- Be brave.
- Be authentic.

5: *Legally Blonde* (2001)

The storyline

This is a comedy of sorts, starring Reese Witherspoon. Reese is Elle Woods, a fashion branding student at California University Los Angeles. Her boyfriend Warner takes her to lunch, and she's expecting him to propose to her. Instead, he dumps her, and his reason is that he wants to be a big-time politician and Reese is too flaky and will make it more difficult for him, as he'll be taken less seriously because of her.

Determined to win Warner back and prove she's a serious person who can achieve big things, she studies hard and wins a place at Harvard Law School.

While at law school, she quickly realises that she's quite different to the others there. She puts it down to a California versus East Coast thing, but it's really a class thing, as the other students are grandiose, privileged and snooty.

Warner, who's also at HLS, gets engaged to a fellow student and ex-girlfriend of his, Vivian. Elle is annoyed with Warner for dismissing her as not living in reality and not being bright enough to win one of the professor's internships, and she shows grit and determination. She ends up being one of three people chosen as interns to help the professor with a high-profile case of a wife who's accused of murdering her husband. The other two interns are Warner and Vivian. The woman, called Brooke Windham, is someone Elle greatly admires. They strike up a good relationship. Vivian becomes impressed with Elle and confides in her that Warner only got the internship because of his father's connections.

Emmet, a junior partner working at the same firm as the professor, is very impressed with Reese. One night, the professor makes a sexual advance towards Reese, and she resigns from the internship, disappointed and frustrated. When she finds out, Brooke sacks the professor from the case and appoints Elle as her leading lawyer, under the supervision of Emmet, which is all allowed legally.

When cross-examining Brooke's stepdaughter, Chutney, Elle – drawing on her knowledge of fashion and beauty – notices that a number of things don't add up in her story. It's to do with hair perms and washing them and what happens if you do. It means that Chutney couldn't have been taking a shower when her father was shot, which she claimed was why she didn't hear the gunshot. This leads to Chutney admitting that she was the one who killed her father.

Brooke is cleared and Elle is championed by the media. Warner asks Elle to take him back, but she declines, and she becomes good friends with Vivian, who has dumped him. Two years later Elle graduates, and Emmett intends to ask her to marry him, now that he has his own law firm.

Leadership lessons

In *Legally Blonde*, Elle has to deal with a huge setback, and she uses it as an opportunity to prove to herself and others that she is capable of a great deal. She displays huge courage in putting herself out there, taking on the risk of failure and just going for it.

In the film, Warner shows us the pressures that society can put on people to conform to a way of thinking that allows societal strata to thrive, as he removes himself from Elle's life because of what she is not, as opposed to championing her for what she is. This is a societal, organisational and individual failure in the real world, where an individual's actual value is frequently not recognised. The plus column for everyone, our strengths, is what really matters. Yes, we should be self-aware and aware of our limitations and other people's, but these should just be declared to highlight self-awareness and humility, and then parked, as they're not important or relevant. Warner clearly demonstrates narrow thinking and bias.

Elle shows what can be achieved with hard work and drive, firstly by getting into Harvard and then by winning the internship and graduating.

There's a theme of white male privilege too, which is huge in many societies, and again this is demonstrated by Warner, who is getting ahead due to his father's connections rather than his own abilities and merit. This is also represented by the sexual advance from the professor.

Elle shows us the power of authenticity. She's a great example to us of having the confidence to be who we are. She is herself throughout the film, and benefits from it: Vivian starts to admire her for it, Brooke is drawn to her, and of course, so is Emmet.

There's so much pressure sometimes on people to pretend that they're something they're not, and it's damaging to them. They're telling themselves that they're not good enough as they are, but it isn't true. Being who you are is a gift to yourself and everyone else. In truth, the people who are prepared to be themselves are the great creators, because they actually enable genuine connections to form, and they weaken the need and case for negative conformity, which is really only driven by a dangerous and damaged minority.

This film is femininity at its best, and this is the main Equality, Diversity and Inclusion angle of the piece, but it's about much, much more besides. It's about being brave enough to be yourself, accepting yourself as you are, and it's also a story about the weakest in society challenging the prevailing establishment and power structures.

The film demonstrates a toxic culture and how to challenge it by being authentic and values driven. There is plenty of *raison d'être* with Reese, *independence* in that she listens to herself, *expertise* in that she plays to her strengths constantly, and *unite*, which she does by creating followership with the people around her that's very much about their connecting to her authenticity and values. She is a great leader.

Key takeaways:

- Societal silos exist, and they exclude others, creating disadvantage.
- Toxic cultures damage people.
- Authenticity is a key builder of trust.
- Integrity is a leadership trait worth having.
- Effort can help to move mountains.
- Skills are worth developing as they add value.
- Kindness is a wonderful human trait.
- Great leadership overcomes adversity.

6: *Some Like It Hot* (1959)

The storyline

This is a comedy film, written, produced and directed by Billy Wilder, and starring Marilyn Monroe, Jack Lemmon and Tony Curtis.

The film, set during the prohibition era in Chicago, is about two musicians Joe, (played by Curtis) and Jerry, (played by Lemmon) who witness a mafia boss and his men committing some murders. They know they have to get out of town. Through a musical booking agent, they learn that there's work for a saxophonist and a cellist in a group who are heading down to sunny Florida, but it's a female group. They disguise themselves as women (Josephine and Daphne) and take the train with the group to Florida. On the way down they become friendly with the lead singer of the band, Sugar Kane, played by Marilyn. The two guys really like Sugar and compete for her time and affection, but Jerry's intentions are unclear, whereas Joe is madly in love with her.

To try to win Marilyn's affections, Joe adopts a second disguise, as the millionaire heir to Shell Oil. Meanwhile, Jerry, as Daphne, is being pursued by a real elderly millionaire man who owns, amongst other things, a boat. Joe convinces Daphne to set it up so that Joe can use this boat to seduce Marilyn.

Another tactic used by Joe (posing as a millionaire) is to pretend that he's no longer interested in women, and isn't interested in Sugar. This spurs her on to have some interest in him. Then he taps into Sugar's competitive nature by stating that if he ever met a woman who could get his libido flowing again, then he would marry her. Sugar sees this as a challenge, with the added benefit of acquiring someone rich.

This is all happening while the trio are the entertainment act in a well-to-do hotel. It just so happens that this hotel is chosen by US mafia leaders for what could be described as a mafia AGM, and attending are some of the men that Jerry and Joe have run from. These gangsters realise that the two female musicians are really the two male musicians from Chicago who witnessed the murders. Of course, then they pursue them.

The duo has to leave very quickly. Joe, in love with Sugar, has to come clean to her if he wants to keep her, and he explains that he's not a female musician, nor a millionaire Shell Oil heir. She concludes that she loves him anyway. Jerry, in his role as a woman, is now somehow engaged to the elderly millionaire with the boat, and Jerry/Daphne convinces him to help all three of them to escape.

On the yacht, Jerry, still dressed as Daphne, explains to the elderly man that they can't get married because he's really a man. The millionaire seems unperturbed by this and happy to marry him anyway, which appears to totally confuse Jerry, and then the film ends.

Leadership lessons

As much as I like the characters and the film, Joe and Jerry are liars and fraudsters. Of course, they take on the identities of women to save themselves from death, which raises the question: what would it take for any of us to pretend to be something or someone that we're not? I imagine the stakes would have to be high.

The film raises the issues of authenticity and trust. Are the duo trustworthy? Many people in organisations and society are inauthentic. They aren't doing it to hoodwink anyone; they do it out of fear. They don't feel psychologically safe to be themselves, because they might be dismissed or targeted in some way, or given the harder tasks to do, or get paid less, or miss out on the supervisor roles, which pay more and lead to other opportunities.

Joe's deception pays great dividends for him, as he manages to escape the mafia and he wins the woman of his dreams. But this is only because Sugar can see past the two disguises he was wearing, and she believes that the person at the core of those two disguises is the real him, and this is what she's really connected to. Most people don't like to be deceived and may not be as forgiving and understanding as Sugar.

Jerry, on the other hand, has yet to figure out how he'll get out of the situation that his deception has landed him in.

Maybe if I'm forgiving of Joe and Jerry, the lesson is that sometimes we can find ourselves in a difficult or dangerous situation, in way over our heads, and just to survive, we have to adapt and be ruthless and different to how we usually are. Maybe sometimes you have to be inauthentic.

Key takeaways:

- Some people are inauthentic out of fear.
- Psychological safety is what many people need to thrive.
- Deception has many layers to it.

7: *Grease* (1978)

The storyline

Grease is a musical movie set in 1958, at Rydell High School. Student Danny Zuko, played by John Travolta, has a summer romance with Sandy Olsson, Olivia Newton John, who's on holiday from Australia, after they meet on the beach. At the end of the summer, Danny has to head back to school, and Sandy, to Australia.

However, Sandy's parents decide to remain in the US, and she enrols at Rydell High, where Danny is the leader of the T-Birds greaser gang. At this point neither is aware of the other being present in the school. Sandy has been befriended by a group of girls called the Pink Ladies. Both Danny and Sandy recount their summer encounter, but differently: Sandy describes a very romantic liaison, and Danny tells a more macho story that makes him maintain his cool, tough-guy image with his gang.

Rizzo of the Pink Ladies has an issue of some kind with Danny, and when she realises that Sandy is describing him as her summer romance, she organises for her gang to bump into Danny's gang, with the intention of causing Danny some tension and embarrassment. And that's what happens. Both Danny and Sandy are delighted to see each other, but very quickly, Danny feels vulnerable, and understands that he needs to be cool and dismissive of her, to maintain his status within his group, and this hurts the genuine and authentic Sandy.

The Pink Ladies have a sleepover, and Rizzo mocks

Sandy's good, clean-cut image. Rizzo leaves and has a date with Kenickie of the T-Birds, and they end up having sex in his car. Their get-together is interrupted by a rival gang member, Leo, of the Scorpions, who's in his car with his girlfriend, Cha-Cha.

The next day, Danny meets Sandy and says sorry for his poor behaviour the night before, and they agree to go on a date. Their date becomes a whole-gang affair as all their pals turn up, and a row between Rizzo and Kenickie sees them break up.

There's a school dance, with a dance competition that's broadcast live on TV and hosted by DJ Vince Fontaine. Danny and Sandy do well, and as many of the other competitors are tapped on the shoulder and out of the contest, it starts to look like they might be in with a chance of winning. To manipulate and annoy each other, Kenickie and Rizzo have brought Leo and Cha-Cha as dates. Kenickie and Leo start fighting, and an emotional Rizzo runs away.

Without meaning any harm, one of Danny's drunk friends pulls Sandy away from Danny and the dance floor, and before Danny realises and can do something to pull her back, Cha-Cha seizes the moment and drags Danny back to the centre, to finish the dance off with her. A devastated Sandy runs from the hall, and the prize that Danny and Sandy should have won is now given to Danny and Cha-Cha.

Then Rizzo starts to think she might be pregnant, and when Kenickie finds out and tries to support her, she insults him and pushes him away.

The big race day between Leo and Kenickie, in his car Greased Lightning. The winner gets to keep both cars. Kenickie is knocked unconscious just before the race, so Danny stands in for him. He wins, and Sandy, who is watching from afar, is delighted, and accepts that she still loves him. She enlists her friend Frenchie, a trainee beautician, to help her change her image to the type that she thinks Danny will prefer.

On the last day of school, Rizzo realises she isn't pregnant, and she and Kenickie get back together. When Danny and Sandy meet, they see that each has completely changed their image and style to fit in with the other. Sandy is now dressed like a greaser and Danny as a more conservative, traditional schoolboy. They drive off in the Greased Lightning car.

Leadership lessons

In *Grease*, there is gentle inauthenticity at play with both leading characters. Danny and Sandy are their genuine selves at the beginning of the film when they have their beach summer romance. However when we next see Danny, he is behaving and dressing differently, in order to be the alpha male of the T Bird gang at the school. It's an identity that enables him to survive and thrive there socially. When Sandy then turns up as a new student at the school, she is still her genuine self. There is confusion and conflict between them due to Danny's inauthenticity, and she is offended by his macho behaviour which she doesn't understand or recognise. To win her back, Danny tries on other softer identities but with little impact. By the end Sandy wants to become what she thinks Danny wants her to be, so that she will be wanted by him, and this is at the exact moment when he forgoes his fake gang identity and reverts to being the genuine Danny from the summer romance at the beginning. The Sandy at the end is really just a dressed-up, made-up, unnatural Sandy, but clothes aside, she's still the same Sandy underneath: sweet, honest and nice. A few hours later, she'll probably revert to her usual clothes, but of course we'll never see that, as the film ends where it ends.

Danny has a lot of *unite* ability, and unites his pals, the T-Birds, quite easily. Even when he changes at the end, it's likely that they too will soften their image to remain connected to him, as they seem to believe they belong with him, hence his ability to have their followership. Danny makes mistakes, but eventually he realises he needs to be true to himself or he won't achieve his most important goal, which is being an item with Sandy.

In terms of group dynamics, there's a lot of kindness in the female friends, with only Rizzo driving a level of unkindness and toxicity at times, which she occasionally applies to keep the other girls in check. She applies this a lot more with Sandy: she belittles her and makes her feel uncomfortable, to keep her in her place, which in her opinion should be at the bottom of the hierarchy, and not really part of the group. Rizzo is very threatened by Sandy. Some of you may have had this done to you in life and work, and you'll certainly have seen it happen to others. Sandy is obviously upset by Rizzo, as the toxic behaviour is unwarranted, and all of this tells us a lot about the psychology of Rizzo. We need to have the self-awareness to recognise when we're feeling threatened without good reason, so we can curb our instincts to behave like Rizzo. However, Sandy has a lesson for us all, as she always maintains her dignity and her integrity. She is a great servant to doing good.

Key takeaways:

- Self-awareness helps us to be authentic.
- Fickleness won't create genuine happiness for you.
- Authenticity enables us to make genuine connections with others.
- Dignity is something we sometimes sacrifice to fit in, but we shouldn't.

> Authenticity is at the heart of transparency. It allows others to see exactly who you are . This helps them to make a judgement call on your character and whether you are their type of person or not. The opposite of authenticity might be that a person is fake or a fraud, so you can see that being authentic is important. Authenticity is key when it comes to having others trust you. And this plays a role in creating ***true*** followership (as opposed to just followership, as some people follow others who aren't authentic, but that says a lot about them too).
>
> First you need to find out who you are. Then you must practise telling the truth. Practise aligning your words with your actions.

CHAPTER 6:
SELF-AWARENESS

8: *Rocky* (1976)

The storyline

The heavyweight boxing champion of the world, Apollo Creed, played by Carl Weathers, is organising a title defence to coincide with the American Bicentennial. His opponent pulls out five weeks before the fight with an injury and getting a credible replacement isn't possible. He decides to give a local contender an opportunity to fight him, and likes the sound of the Italian Stallion, which is the name Rocky goes by.

Rocky (played by Stallone) is by his own admission 'a bum', an average boxer who's never made use of the abilities he has, which are that he can take a beating and make great body shots. His life now is boxing in local, low-level bouts while he's making a living as a debt collector. But then this opportunity presents itself.

Rocky hires elderly ex-boxer and local gym owner Mickey, played by Burgess Meredith, to train him. They do unusual things, like wood chopping, practising body shots on beef carcasses, and speed work that involves catching a live chicken.

Rocky also begins a relationship with the shy Adrian, the sister of his friend Paulie. Rocky trains hard while Apollo doesn't, as he thinks he only needs to turn up to win, and instead focuses on the promotion of the fight.

The fight takes place on New Year's Day. In the first round, Rocky secures a knock-down, which is the first time Apollo has ever tasted the canvas. Apollo immediately stops fooling about and imposes himself. It looks like Apollo wins the majority of the rounds, and it goes the full 15, with both of them suffering bad injuries.

The fight ends with both men on their feet, and Apollo is declared the victor, after a split decision.

Leadership lessons

Sylvester Stallone not only played the lead role but he wrote the film. On a personal level, Stallone had excellent self-awareness, in that he knew that he was a good fit for the part – he had the *expertise* in some regards – but also that he would never be a traditional leading man. Therefore, this was a rare opportunity for him to get a lead role that was a very good fit for him. The studios didn't want him, just the script, but he persevered, and eventually they agreed a deal: they would make the movie and he would play Rocky. For their $1 million investment, they made $225 million at the box office.

Rocky changes in the movie, and towards the end

humility, raison d'être, confidence and self-awareness combine. In terms of listening, Rocky becomes brilliant at listening to himself and figuring out his values, and he changes his behaviour and starts to be a better person. In contrast, Creed has lost touch with himself, some of his values are negative and he isn't listening to anyone.

This is a love story too, one where two people who are imperfect as individuals combine to be a great couple. This is brilliantly described by Rocky in a conversation with Adrian's brother Paulie:

> Paulie: You like her?
> Rocky: Sure I do.
> Paulie: What's the attraction?
> Rocky: I dunno. She fills gaps.
> Paulie: What's 'gaps'?
> Rocky: I dunno. She's got gaps, I got gaps, together we fill gaps.

This is at the heart of all teams. There are no perfect humans and there are no perfect staff members, and accepting and understanding this allows you to build a good team. You bring together a mix of people, allowing them to play to their strengths, and if you do it correctly, you can combine the different types of strengths, meaning the weaknesses of each individual are covered by the strengths of another.

What Rocky brings as a leader is humility, self-awareness and confidence, but also an ability to live in the moment, a huge work ethic and a willingness to make the very most of every bit of his ability. All of these are significant.

Apollo is outstanding as a boxer and fighter and is leagues ahead of Rocky. He's very confident and rightly so, but he lacks humility; there is none. He's become arrogant and a little narcissistic, but he definitely isn't grandiose, as he really is a brilliant boxer. Rocky needs to get fit, make improvements and find a game plan that suits his strengths: to soak up the punches, and when he can get close, unleash his powerful body shots.

Rocky is also on an emotional journey of self-acceptance and he's supported by only a handful of people who love and care for him, his girlfriend Adrian (played by the excellent Talia Shire, sister of Francis Ford Coppola) being one. The night before the fight, Rocky has the humility to admit to himself and then to Adrian that there's no way he can win the fight, that Apollo is too good. But the power of *raison d'être* presents itself to him, and he resets his life goal. As he says, he's a bum and a loser who's achieved nothing in life, but now he has the opportunity to differentiate himself, to refine his identity, and to prove that he's a somebody, not by beating Apollo, but by managing to go the distance with him, and in doing so, be the first person not to be knocked out by the brilliant Apollo.

What follows is something I call the psychology of sport, the psychology of winning, the psychology of expectation. Rocky is humble and confident and prepared. Apollo is underprepared and overconfident, and he can't reset his thinking fast enough in the cauldron of the occasion. You see this every now and again in sport. A good example from rugby is the Leinster v. Munster European Cup semi-final in 2009. Munster turned up thinking that was all they needed to do, but Leinster were really up for it, and the rest is history. In the film, Rocky nearly wins; in the process he takes an almighty beating, but he dishes one out too. He goes the distance, and in doing so, achieves his goal.

Key takeaways:

- Self-awareness helps us to be authentic.
- Effort helps us to move mountains.
- Humility helps to build trust.
- Acceptance gives us the freedom to create happiness.

9: *A Simple Plan* (1998)

The storyline

This is a movie that stars Billy Bob Thornton and Bill Paxton as brothers Jacob and Hank Mitchell and Bridget Fonda as Hank's wife, Sarah. Hank and Sarah live in rural Minnesota. Hank has a management job at the local cattle feed mill, which is a good job. Sarah works as a librarian and is pregnant. Jacob is an ordinary, not very bright layabout.

Jacob, Hank and a friend of theirs, Lou, are out hunting in the snowy wilderness when they come across a downed aeroplane. The pilot is dead, but there's over

$4 million there too. Hank wants to hand the money in to the authorities, but the other two convince him not to. Hank compromises and they all agree that he should take the money for safe-keeping, and that when the spring comes and the plane is found, if no one comes forward to claim the money, they'll split it three ways and all leave the area.

The sheriff comes along, and a jittery Jacob says something about a plane crash, but then he and the others backtrack from this, coming up with some rubbish story about hearing a plane. The sheriff buys it and leaves.

The trio make a pact not to tell anyone, but shortly after this, Hank tells his wife, Sarah. She advises Hank to put some of the money back in the plane, so that when the plane is found, no one will suspect anything. Hank brings Jacob with him, but as they're doing this, an elderly farmer, Dwight, comes on the scene on his snowmobile. Jacob panics and hits him with a log. However, the farmer isn't dead, and as he starts to regain consciousness, Hank weighs up the situation and suffocates him. They crash the farmer and his snowmobile off a bridge, to make it look like the farmer died accidentally.

Sarah does some detective work, and learns that the money is a ransom for a rich woman.

Lou, who is down on his luck and broke, gets drunk and demands that Hank give him his share now. Hank refuses, but starts to worry when Lou tells him he will go to the police and inform them that Hank killed the farmer. Jacob told him. Sarah plants a seed in Hank, telling him that he needs to set Lou up for the murder and she comes up with a cunning plan.

Hank, Jacob and Lou are drinking late at night, but Hank remains sober. Playing a bizarre acting-out game, he gets Lou to say that he killed the farmer and to give a little explanation about how he did it. Hank records this false confession. Lou is hugely disappointed and then angry about being tricked. He pulls out a gun and threatens to shoot Hank. A worried Jacob, who wasn't happy about Hank tricking his friend Lou, shoots Lou dead in order to save his brother. Lou's wife comes upon the scene, and in obvious distress she shoots at Hank. Hank uses Lou's gun to kill her. Hank and Jacob convince the sheriff that the couple killed each other in a drunken domestic dispute.

The FBI come and meet the sheriff, as they're looking for a missing plane that they fear may have crashed in the area. The sheriff recalls Jacob saying something about a plane, so he asks Hank and Jacob to help the special agent, Baxter. They agree to help. Sarah is suspicious and does some digging and finds out that Baxter isn't from the FBI at all but is one of the kidnappers. She warns her husband.

When Baxter, the sheriff and the brothers head out together to the area where they said they heard an aeroplane engine, Hank brings a revolver for safety. The four of them split up to look for the plane. The sheriff comes across it, but before Hank can warn him that Baxter is a kidnapper, Baxter shoots the sheriff dead. Baxter orders Hank into the plane to get the money, thinking Hank is an unarmed hick, but when his concentration is momentarily broken, Hank uses this opportunity to shoot Baxter dead in self-defence.

Jacob arrives and Hank explains the false story that they'll have to tell to keep their cover intact. Jacob – soft, not so bright and now depressed – has been struggling with guilt over all the deaths that they've been responsible for. He wants to use this situation to end his own life as he can no longer go on. He pleads with his brother to kill him, but to make it look like Baxter did it. This horrendous position is hard on Hank, but he yields and does what his brother asks, killing him using Baxter's gun.

The real FBI come to town and they believe Hank's story. He isn't under suspicion. As an aside, they make Hank aware that a lot of the ransom money is missing, but they aren't worried, as the serial numbers of the notes have been recorded, so when whoever has it spends it, the FBI will become aware and catch the thief and recoup the money.

Hank and Sarah realise that everything has been for nothing, and they aren't going to be rich and will have to stay where they are, living a life that Sarah says she now hates.

Leadership lessons

Who are we really, what makes us tick? What is happiness, what does it look like? Are we chasing the right goals, and if we achieve them, will we actually be happier? And finally, is happiness to be found in the simpler things in life? All the characters in *A Simple Plan* appear to be happy to a degree. Hank and Sarah are, and Jacob is with his pal Lou. But in the end, Jacob and Lou are dead, and Hank and Sarah are stuck in the depths of unhappiness that they'll never rise from again.

The film explores trust, and there are levels of trust between them all, some very strong bonds indeed, but none of them can withstand the pull of the millions, greed, which tears them apart. Booze and an inability to manage emotion fires a number of the characters into paranoia and betrayal. The film shows the importance of trust, and chilling out, in terms of not being impulsive but instead waiting, processing the situation, regrouping and reaching an agreement. Emotional intelligence and emotional regulation are missing with many of the characters. All the characters display poor judgement, as many of their decisions are poor.

Key takeaways:

- True happiness is sometimes found by recognising the good things already in your life.
- Self-awareness helps us to be authentic.
- Acceptance gives us the freedom to create happiness.
- Greed corrupts.

Self-awareness is key to building strong relationships. It stops you from accidentally offending other people. It helps you to understand them. It's a key to personal happiness, as you'll be able to get more from your relationship with yourself and with others. It's important when it comes to preventing and minimising conflict, and when you have to collaborate, compromise and negotiate. It's essential when trying to build teams.

There are different ways to build self-awareness. It might be through reflection, 360-degree feedback, listing your strengths and weaknesses, or doing some tests like the Myers–Briggs Type Indicator or the DISC personality test.

CHAPTER 7:

SKILL SET

10: *Pulp Fiction* (1994)

The storyline

This movie announced Quentin Tarantino to the world; he wrote and directed the film. It's set in the criminal underworld. What's unique about this movie is how Tarantino cuts up the leading stories and knits them back together in a way that doesn't follow the usual chronological order of most movies. For that reason, it's not easy to explain the plot etc., but I'll give it a try.

Jules (Samuel L. Jackson) and Vincent (John Travolta) are hitmen who work for crime boss Marcellus Wallace (Ving Rhames). They do a job together where both of them should have ended up dead. This is life-changing for Jules, who sees this as some sort of divine intervention, and he decides to quit killing and crime, once they return a briefcase to Wallace, which is the job they agreed to do. Jules proves he has changed in his ways, as he doesn't kill the small-time criminals who try to rob him in a diner, instead giving them his money and buying them their lives.

This storyline intersects with other storylines, one of which follows Vincent as he takes Wallace's wife, Mia (Uma Thurman), to an event at Wallace's request. They get on well, but afterwards, while Vincent is in the toilet, she finds his stash of heroin, mistakes it for cocaine, and takes a massive overdose and nearly dies.

Another storyline has boxer Butch (Bruce Willis) agree to throw a fight for Wallace. He double-crosses him, and Wallace issues a hit on Butch and sends Vincent after him. Butch ends up killing Vincent, but shortly after, becomes entangled in a shoot-out and chase with Wallace. They end up tied up in the basement of some rapists, and while Wallace is being raped, Butch manages to untie himself and escape, before returning to rescue Wallace, meaning they're no longer in conflict with each other, as long as Butch tells no one and leaves town immediately.

There's another storyline involving Jules and Vincent, where Vincent accidentally shoots a lesser criminal while they're travelling with this guy in the back seat of their car, making an almighty mess. It necessitates them having to hide out in the suburbs, as if they continue driving, they'll get arrested, so they head to a house owned by Jimmie, played by Tarantino himself, an acquaintance of Jules's. Wallace calls in a favour from another acquaintance, Winston Wolfe (Harvey Keitel), who specialises in clean-ups and body disposal, and all of this needs to be done before Tarantino's wife returns home.

Leadership lessons

In *Pulp Fiction*, trust raises its head. Butch, the professional boxer who never quite made it, double-crosses master crime boss Wallace. The rules of the underworld, according to this film, appear to be different to the corporate world and other industries. There wasn't a legally binding document/contract between the men; it was a verbal agreement, which Butch broke, causing a lot of problems for Wallace and the others who were betting on Butch to go down in a particular round. To save face, the rules are (culture) that Wallace now has to kill Butch, and he sends his best man, Vincent, out for this task. However, circumstances arise that bring Butch and Wallace into a physical confrontation, and both end up unaware of their surroundings and they're captured by a couple of rapists. Butch manages to free himself to escape, but instead of fleeing alone, he rescues Wallace, meaning they bring their feud to an end by negotiating another deal. Wallace won't kill Butch now, and will call off his hitmen, but Butch needs to leave town immediately, never return and never mention anything about Wallace being raped to anyone. It's a great example of how different organisations have different rules in place, rules that you can't necessarily see or understand, but they're there, so be aware.

Vincent and Jules are a good example of two strangers who are very different but come together to form an excellent team. They don't panic when they find themselves in high-pressure situations, such as when they could easily end up in prison or dead. They stay calm. In addition, when they find themselves in over their heads in the blood-splattered car, they have the good sense and insight to hide at Jimmie's home while they phone Wallace, to whom they're accountable, to get his help with a solution. He sends in Winston Wolfe to oversee the tidy-up. This is a good example of knowing the limits of your abilities and reporting up the line to the person who's accountable to get support, and then allowing a specialist to do a specialist job.

Key takeaways:

- Experts are useful.
- Know the rules/culture of the ecosystem you're part of, and abide by these or face the consequences.

11: Jaws (1975)

The storyline

Jaws is another film directed by Steven Spielberg. It stars Roy Scheider as Martin Brody, the police chief of a seaside town and Richard Dreyfuss as a marine biologist, Matt Hooper, who come together to hunt down and kill a huge, man-eating great white shark.

The film starts with a woman going for a late-night swim. She gets pulled underwater and her dead body is found washed up on the beach the next day. The coroner says it's death by shark and Brody, worried for the public, closes the beaches. This puts him into conflict with the mayor, who needs the beaches to be open, especially in the summer months, for the town to generate its income. Under pressure, the coroner changes his mind and says the death was the result of a boating accident.

All is fine until a boy is killed by the shark, and Hooper arrives and examines the body of the woman and advises that it was a very large shark that killed her. The death of the boy gets a lot of media attention, and a bounty for the shark attracts hunters and wannabe hunters from far and wide. A tiger shark is killed and the mayor opens the beaches again, but Hooper and Brody aren't convinced. Hooper opens up the shark and doesn't find any human remains. The mayor, Hooper and Brody argue, but the mayor refuses to accept that the killer shark is a very large great white.

On a hot Fourth of July weekend, people jam up the beaches. The shark enters a nearby lagoon, killing one person and attempting to kill Brody's son. This is enough to convince the mayor to hire a very experienced shark hunter, Quint. Quint, Brody and Hooper head out to catch and kill the shark. They manage to harpoon it, but the shark doesn't appear to be badly injured at all and disappears.

The shark returns during the night and rams the boat, knocking out its power, meaning the boat is drifting and helpless and taking on water. They fix the engine, and with the power back, Hooper tries to call the coastguard, but the drunk and arguably now grandiose Quint wants the acclaim for himself and breaks the radio. The men manage to harpoon the shark again, but this time with a line on the harpoon that's connected to the boat. The huge shark drags the boat backwards, and it takes on more water. The power fails again and the trio are stranded.

They implement another plan, which fails, and ends with Quint being eaten alive and Hooper going missing underwater. As the boat sinks, Brody tries one last idea. He shoves a scuba tank into the shark's mouth, and then when the opportunity presents itself, fires a shot at the tank, causing it to explode and kill the great white, saving himself and Hooper, who resurfaces.

Leadership lessons

In *Jaws*, Brody represents doing good and the greater good, whereas the mayor is thinking less about people's safety and is more focused on economics instead. Whether this is due to a vested interest of some kind, we never know, so we must assume that he's just worried about the local economy and the impact the shark attacks will have on his popularity and being voted back into office at the next election. This is something that we see with political leaders quite a bit, in terms of why they're making short-term decisions and why they're so focused on economics. But why is there never a proper focus on longer-term issues, even existential ones like climate change? Economics is always a leading election issue, generally the most important, especially for the short election cycles of four to five years that are in place in most democracies.

Brody represents the leader who always wants to do the right thing morally, and he's genuinely interested in safety and wellbeing. Both he and Hooper represent innovation and pragmatism. They appear to have all the Maslow ideas in balance, and their wellbeing is balanced too, which might explain why they achieve success. Take note: they also have a strong *raison d'être*. I believe they have *independence* to a degree, and clearly they have *expertise*.

The shark hunter, Quint, is poor at risk analysis, is overconfident and thinks he's more knowledgeable than he is. These character flaws cost him his life and nearly do the same for the others. These traits present themselves in teams and on boards quite a lot, where people have expertise and they grow in confidence from this, but if they aren't self-aware, they can develop a false sense of their abilities and start to think they can also make good decisions about things they know very little about. In organisations, this presents as senior staff who fail to listen to others and fail to recognise the value of the expertise of others, especially those who are more junior than them. Think the financial crash of 2008, the lack of care for the economy and society that the bankers had, their lack of diligence, their inability to look beyond the end of their noses. Think about the leadership of the NRA, and the lobbyists who enable American citizens to carry military weapons and the impact this has on the corporate world (dollars), but then also the impact on society in terms of deaths on the streets and in the schools of America every week.

Key takeaway:

- Recognise the expertise of all those around you, and harness it to do good.

We all have a skill set, but the difference that comes from knowing you have one and not knowing can be the difference between having good self-esteem and poor self-esteem. There is a connection between skill set and self-awareness, in that if you're self-aware, you're likely to know what you're good at and what you're not good at. Knowing your skill set can enable you to play to your strengths. This can keep you from playing to your weaknesses, so that you're perceived as competent and proficient rather than incompetent. And then there are the successes, failures and consequential feelings and emotions that come with knowing and not knowing your strengths. Figure out your strengths. Figure out your weaknesses. Then decide if you want to strengthen your strengths or lessen your weaknesses. Build from there. Specialise or generalise, that's up to you – just know, and then decide.

CHAPTER 8:
EMOTIONAL INTELLIGENCE

12: *Goodfellas* (1990)

The storyline

Goodfellas is a mafia movie set in America and directed by Martin Scorsese. The lead character is Henry Hill, who's played by Ray Liotta, and other leading characters are played by Robert De Niro (Jimmy) and Joe Pesci (Tommy).

The film tells the story of Henry Hill, who's impressed by the sway, respect and control the mafia have in his Italian community in New York. He starts hanging out with them via their businesses, which are a front for their crimes, and ends up working for them, serving an apprenticeship. Then, on graduation as a young man, he works for Jimmy and Tommy. Henry ends up marrying the feisty Karen.

A 'made man' is mafia slang for someone who has a certain serious status within a mafia family. Billy is one such man, with a different mafia family to the one that our three leads are aligned to. Billy insults Tommy, and the short-fused Tommy kills him, with assistance from Jimmy. They quickly bury him upstate, hoping to avoid the consequences of killing Billy. In mafia circles, you cannot kill a made man without the permission of a mafia leader, a don.

Jimmy and Henry have to collect money owed to their don from a gambler. They do, but the FBI have been monitoring this situation and arrest both of them, and they end up in prison. To provide for his family, Henry has his wife bring him drugs in prison, which he sells to other inmates. By the time he gets out, he has a successful drugs business with Jimmy and Tommy, and they run this against the express order of their don, Paulie.

Jimmy organises a raid on a multimillion-dollar haul of jewellery and cash at JFK Airport, and his team start living it large – which Jimmy ordered them not to do, as he didn't want to draw any police/FBI attention to them. He has them all murdered, apart from Henry and Tommy, to control the situation and prevent the authorities from being able to apply pressure on some of the team to rat out others.

Tommy is invited to a mafia event, where he thinks he's about to become a made man. However, mafia leaders have become frustrated with his behaviour and deem him untrustworthy and out of control. So instead they kill him, for something he thought he'd got away with the killing of the made man, Billy, years earlier.

All of these things, in addition to the impact of Henry's cocaine addiction, make him quite paranoid. However, despite his paranoia, he continues to take risks and is arrested by the cops. His wife, Karen, destroys as much evidence as she can, to support Henry, but this means they now have no money. Paulie realises that Henry has been lying to him and has been dealing drugs against his orders, so he ends their working relationship.

Then Jimmy approaches Henry about doing a hit (murder) together. Henry thinks it's a ruse, to isolate him so that Jimmy can actually kill him. Paranoid and annoyed with Paulie and Jimmy, feeling betrayed by these men whom he'd previously viewed as family, he feels scared, cornered and without options. So he goes to the FBI and cuts a deal to inform on others, for the guarantee of a place in the witness protection programme. He gives evidence in court that leads to Paulie and Jimmy going to prison, and then he and his family, now in the programme, move to a suburb somewhere and live a boring life.

Leadership lessons

With *Goodfellas* there are similarities to *The Godfather*, which is to be expected given that it's also about organised crime and the mafia. There are also differences. Paulie is the don for all the main characters mentioned above, but he isn't as strategic or as brilliant a don as Brando and Pacino's Corleone. This demonstrates the impact of great individual leaders in terms of their thinking, their strategic ability, their attitude to risk, their ability to predict others' behaviours, and their resilience.

In this film, the value of coaching and mentoring from someone brilliant is highlighted by its absence: Pacino's character had his father and this benefitted him greatly, whereas in this movie, Henry, Jimmy and Tommy just have Paulie, and he isn't up to the task. I must also highlight here that even though Vito Corleone is great, he couldn't guide his other two sons, Fredo and Sonny, to success, which reminds us that every great coach needs good players too, to be able to make a serious impact.

Tommy, like Sonny Corleone, demonstrates that hotheads can create fear, which is useful, but they're also impulsive and can be easily provoked and therefore manipulated into their own downfall. Michael Corleone creates fear too, but it's a different type of fear, one you can't manipulate or create; it's very real.

Stress and the inability to manage it leads to Henry abusing cocaine, and as a result, he loses his ability to keep a clear head and make smart decisions. He also loses his self-awareness. He becomes reckless, and this gives the authorities the opportunity to catch him out. He grasses everyone up, which demonstrates that when some leaders get caught doing wrong, they'll give everyone else up, to save themselves. We see this with Bud Fox in *Wall Street* too, and the lesson here, like with *Macbeth*, is that once you go down these dark roads, there's no turning back.

The film also demonstrates the importance of supporting your people. Henry was in the gang, yet when he went to prison, his mafia family didn't help out his wife, leaving her to fend for herself. This frustrated Henry, making him feel that they didn't really care for him, or that he didn't really belong, which created resentment, and made it easier for him to be disloyal to them all when he was trapped by the feds.

Goodfellas steps into the area of integrity too. Yes, you can argue that integrity doesn't really fit with the underworld and criminals etc., which is a fair point, but within their culture there are unwritten rules about honour and the importance of family, and these were missing from Paulie and others when Henry needed them. There is, as expected, lots of psychopathy on show, arguably with most of the characters, but especially with Tommy. If leadership is about alignment and keeping others on side, Paulie fails, as do Jimmy and Henry, but the person who fails the most here is Tommy, and it effectively kills him. He loses his ability to influence.

Everyone here is striving for Maslow's security and safety. They appear to have it at times, when they're part of the group and obeying all the rules. However, other than Paulie, they don't really have safety, as they have to constantly earn money for their superiors and there are consequences if they don't: at the very least, changes to the pecking order and humiliation; other times, something worse. There is zero psychological safety. The characters' biological needs are met, and their financial wellbeing is generally okay. What they're all really aiming for is *independence*, as they already have *expertise*. Independence for them will be achieved by having more power and money. They all have *raison d'être*, but sadly, it's to do wrong. This negatively impacts on everyone's emotional wellbeing, especially that of Henry and Karen, and everyone else is either killed or in prison, so they lose everything.

Key takeaways:

- A good coach makes a serious impact.
- Losing your temper and not having control of your emotions will cost you dearly.
- Manage your stress in the right way.
- Create and support alignment with others.

13: *Heat* (1995)

The storyline

Heat is a movie written and directed by Michael Mann, starring Al Pacino as leading LAPD detective Vincent Hanna, and Robert De Niro as master criminal Neil McCauley.

McCauley and his crew rob an armoured truck, netting themselves $1.6 million. But for no reason, their new recruit Waingro shoots one of the guards dead. This is against the ethos of the gang and wasn't part of the plan. It means that should McCauley's gang be caught, the charges against them would be murder as well as armed robbery. As such, they can't take any chances with leaving any witnesses to this crime, so they kill the other guards. It's a ruthless decision, but one based on need and survival.

Of course, murder gets more attention – or heat, for want of a better word – and rightly so, and Hanna is given the case to solve. McCauley, seriously aggrieved with Waingro, sets the scene to execute him, but Waingro manages to escape.

An informant tips Hanna off that one of McCauley's men was involved in the robbery. Hanna has him followed, and this leads him to McCauley and the whole crew. Hanna knows what their next job is going to be, and he intends to catch them all in the act. However, a single noise from one of the cops on Hanna's team is enough to spook McCauley, who, smartly, cancels the robbery.

McCauley senses that the heat on him is very high. He has a new girlfriend, whom he's serious about, and he feels ready to step away from his life of crime and make a real go of things with her. McCauley is aware of another job, a big one, for $12 million, and is tempted into taking the risk.

A tip-off from McCauley's enemy, Van Zant, a criminal with no morals (or different values to McCauley), makes Hanna aware of the big heist that McCauley is in the process of pulling off. The cops arrive at the bank just as McCauley and his crew are leaving, and there's a huge shootout, with casualties on both sides. McCauley manages to escape, and he learns that it was Van Zant and Waingro who leaked his plan to the cops. McCauley knows where Van Zant is, so he locates and kills him; it's overdue revenge. He doesn't know where Waingro is, so he sticks to the plan he made with his girlfriend, and they get ready to leave the country.

Hanna knows that McCauley won't be caught now, but then he realises that there's bad blood between De Nero and Waingro, and he knows the hotel where Waingro is hiding out. He leaks this information, to lure McCauley to that hotel. McCauley takes the bait, and kills Waingro, but as he's departing, Hanna spots him and gives chase, which leads to a shootout between the pair and, eventually, the death of McCauley.

Leadership lessons

In *Heat*, McCauley appears to have his life under control, and all aspects of his wellbeing seem good. He demonstrates *raison d'être, independence, expertise* and *unite* quite well. But emotionally, he feels like he's missing something: love. He links having complete financial independence with creating the platform for freedom that means he can leave criminality and have a life of leisure and love.

Hanna also scores well for *raison d'être, independence, expertise* and *unite*, but his emotional wellbeing is a mess. His *raison d'être* is positive though, whereas all the other leads are bad guys and so their *raisons d'être* are bad.

With the bad characters, we encounter violence and hate, and a belief that they can steal and kill, and they very clearly demonstrate the downsides of being bad-tempered, untrustworthy and double-crossing in nature. This mostly applies to Waingro and Van Zant, to be fair.

Both McCauley and Hanna are great team leaders and are strategic and intelligent. In the end, it's McCauley's need for revenge that leads to his death. If he'd had the ability to walk away at this stage, he would have achieved all the goals he had set for himself, but he didn't. Maybe this was a lack of humility, or the trappings of narcissism. Be aware of your flaws and weaknesses; don't let them derail you.

Key takeaways:

- Humility is important.
- Success sometimes breeds arrogance.
- Manage your emotions.

14: *Mrs Doubtfire* (1993)

The storyline

Mrs Doubtfire is a comedy that stars Robin Williams, Sally Field and Pierce Brosnan.

Robins is an actor, Daniel Hillard, and has three children with his wife Miranda (Field), who's a career-orientated interior designer. They haven't been getting on, and following a heated argument about their son, Miranda tells Daniel that she's sick of him, that he should move out immediately and that she wants a divorce. Daniel tries to talk her out of this, but to no avail.

The judge gives Miranda sole custody of the kids, as

Daniel has no fixed abode and no job, but advises that if he gets those things sorted in the next few months, then custody can be shared. Daniel gets an admin job working for a TV studio, which means he can now get an apartment, but he isn't seeing enough of the kids, so is unhappy. He finds out that Miranda is looking to hire a nanny for the kids, and disguises himself as an elderly Scottish woman, Mrs Doubtfire, applies for the job and gets it.

After a while, the kids warm to Mrs Doubtfire, and thrive with her, and Miranda starts to rely on her and builds a meaningful friendship with her. This all happens while she continues to view Daniel, her husband, as a frustrating loser. The kids twig that Mrs Doubtfire is their dad, and agree to keep the secret, so that they can all spend time together.

Daniel gets an interview for a TV show, and this interview is actually a sit-down dinner. But it's happening at the same time, in the same restaurant, as a family dinner that he has to attend as Mrs Doubtfire, and also present is Miranda's new boyfriend, Stu, played by Brosnan. Humour and chaos ensue as Daniel moves back and forth between the two tables. The TV producers love the idea of Daniel hosting the TV show as Mrs Doubtfire, but as he applies the Heimlich manoeuvre to save the choking Stu, his mask falls off and Miranda can see that it's him. She's understandably furious about the lies he's been telling.

In court, Daniel loses any opportunity for joint custody, as the judge is annoyed by his behaviour, and he will have to make do with supervised visits. The TV show becomes a hit, and all parties begin to realise that they could have behaved differently towards each other during the course of the film. Miranda thaws towards Daniel, recognising that he's good for the kids – and, indirectly, her – and she presents him with the opportunity to share custody, which he gratefully accepts.

Leadership lessons

In *Mrs Doubtfire*, Miranda and Daniel brilliantly demonstrate how emotion, miscommunication and poor management of other people's expectations can turn two balanced people who love each other into a warring couple, which has a negative impact on all involved, but especially the children. Daniel is destroyed by not being able to see his kids and not having a place to live or a regular income puts him at a disadvantage when it comes to having access to the children. Miranda's lawyers fight hard for her, which is easy under the circumstances, and initially she just does what they say she should.

To get access to the kids, Daniel finds a huge *raison d'être* and has the inspired idea to disguise himself in order to win the new position as the children's nanny, just to be with them. It's a massive act of love and shows what you can achieve when you have a clear goal and a huge desire to make something happen. It's inspirational, creative and entrepreneurial in nature. Obviously, in the funniest of ways he gets found out, but Miranda eventually sees the levels he's willing to go to for his children and softens towards him, and they make informal arrangements around access to benefit the children. In addition, the disguise that Daniel wears is so brilliant that he ends up catching the attention of some TV producers and gets his own children's show.

Collaboration and the ability to compromise are hugely important in leaders. For much of this film, both parties are poor at this. They both fail to listen.

Key takeaways:

- Collaborate and listen.
- Emotion is powerful.

> There are terrible pitfalls and consequences to not having emotional intelligence, as demonstrated in the films in this chapter. Emotion is a very powerful thing, and it needs to be controlled.
>
> You need to understand what triggers you and also what triggers others, so you're not triggering them. It's important to recognise changes in others, to be able to read them. What is their body language telling you? What language are they using; is it different? Get into the habit of pausing before you react to something, the old 'count to ten' advice. It's also good to develop your listening skills, and one way to get insights into other people is to ask them how they're feeling.

CHAPTER 9:

GREED

15: *Wall Street* (1987)

The storyline

This film was written and directed by Oliver Stone. Charlie Sheen is a young small-time stockbroker, Bud Fox, who idolises renowned Wall Street heavyweight Gordon Gekko, played by Michael Douglas; he wants to impress him and do deals with and for him. Fox pursues Gekko in an obsessive way, and eventually Gekko grants him some of his time. Out of sheer desperation to get validation from Gekko, Fox shares insider information with him that he innocuously learned from his dad, a union worker with Bluestar Airlines.

Gekko buys a load of Bluestar shares and makes huge profits from them. He decides to give Fox a large amount of money to invest on his behalf, meaning Gekko is now a client of Fox's. None of the investments make any money, and some lose money. Gekko is about to end the relationship, but instead he convinces Fox to spy on a well-known English investor. They figure out that the English guy is going to try to buy a particular steel company, so Gekko buys a big chunk of shares in the company, meaning the English guy has to pay Gekko above the odds to get ownership of the steel company.

Fox starts to earn big himself now and is enjoying the trappings of this wealth. He's becoming a name and makes money for himself and Gekko with lots of illegal insider-trading deals. Without realising it, he's caught the attention of the authorities, the Securities and Exchange Commission (SEC).

Fox convinces Gekko to buy Bluestar Airlines, by highlighting why it's such a lucrative business, and thinks that Gekko will make him the new CEO of it. However, he soon realises that Gekko is planning to break it up, sell it off in pieces and legally empty the pension fund, meaning Fox's father and work colleagues would lose everything. Even though this deal would make him mega rich, Fox is now angry with what he sees as Gekko's lies, and out of concern for his father, who has just had a heart attack, Fox comes up with a plan to double-cross Gekko and save the airline.

Fox and the president of the airline union do a deal with the English investor for whom Fox had previously caused problems, selling him a controlling share at a discount after he agrees to save the airline. Fox then makes a number of plays that mean Gekko has to offload a lot of his shares in the airline at a loss, and once Gekko understands that the English guy is the new majority shareholder of the airline, he knows that he's been double-crossed by Fox.

Any delight Fox feels about saving the airline is short lived, as he's arrested for all his illegal activities by the SEC. Fox then does a deal with the SEC for a shorter sentence, which involves him wearing recording equipment and tricking Gekko into admitting his involvement in all of the illegal trades, thus handing his one-time idol Gekko over to the authorities for a certain prison sentence.

Leadership lessons

In *Wall Street*, Michael Douglas and Charlie Sheen play compelling characters. They love and want money, money, money, and all its trappings. That is what drives them. Fox idolises Gekko and wants to be him. They both display ruthlessness and single-mindedness, which are attributes that can benefit organisations, but you rarely see these listed as values anywhere, and you rarely see them in job descriptions.

The film gives us an insight into some of the types of people at the heart of the financial crash of 2008. Would Fox and Gekko score highly on the ICD-11 medical diagnostics for psychopathic and narcissistic personality disorder? Probably. Are they chasing financial wellbeing? Perhaps they are, but by achieving it in the way they do, they create financial wellbeing problems for others and badly damage the emotional and physical wellbeing of others too. Their whole concept of wellbeing is massively out of balance. In many ways, what they are is psychopathic, though in the end, maybe Fox is less so. But even though he saves others, is he really just saving himself? And don't forget, in doing so, he sells out his idol and mentor, Gekko.

This film is a great example of the wrong kind of values. You can't trust anyone here, and many organisational gurus and relationship experts explain that trust is the main building block of all things good, and without it, you don't have anything real or tangible. This is a good lesson in greed and psychopathy, and it may offer insight and an explanation as to why the worst things going on in the world right now and in the past actually happen. No one is listening to anyone else; there's no uniting of people.

Going back to Edgar Schein, you should by now be able to analyse and understand the culture here. Remember:

> [Culture is] a pattern of basic shared assumptions learned by a group, as it solved its problems of external adaption and internal integration, that is seen to have worked and as a result is valid and taught to new people as the correct way to perceive, think, and feel in relation to these problems. (Schein, 2010, p. 18)

And, Schein tells us, culture can be broken down into artefacts, espoused values and basic underlying assumptions.

What do you think the culture is in *Wall Street*? Greed and dishonesty.

Key takeaways:

- Greed causes so much damage and needless pain.

- Psychopathy plus greed = danger.
- Toxic cultures are created, but so are positive ones.

16: *Trading Places* (1983)

The storyline

Trading Places is a comedy. It stars Dan Aykroyd as aristocratic snob and commodities broker, Louis Winthorpe III, and Eddie Murphy as a street hustler con artist, Billy Ray Valentine.

A pair of elderly brothers, the Dukes, witness a confrontation between the director of their brokerage company, Winthorpe, and petty criminal Valentine. They decide to create a social experiment, betting each other that if they swap Valentine's and Winthorpe's lives and professional circumstances, this will change how they both behave, with Winthorpe falling to pieces and becoming a wreck and a criminal, and Valentine becoming respectable, well behaved and a success.

The Dukes organise for a shady, borderline-criminal person on their payroll, Beeks, to frame Winthorpe. Beeks hires a prostitute, Ophelia, played by Jamie Lee Curtis, to frame Winthorpe as a thief and a drug dealer. The Dukes have him sacked from his job, freeze his credit cards and bank account, and kick him out of his sumptuous home, which belongs to the company. His friends disown him. While this is happening, the Dukes bail Valentine out of his police cell, and give him the house and job that were previously Winthorpe's.

Valentine, who is smart, quickly becomes a success. Meanwhile, Winthorpe bumps into Ophelia and recognises her as the person who accused him of doing some of the things that got him sacked. She recognises that he's an aristocrat, and that his luck will change again, so she takes him in and agrees to help and support him, as a business deal.

Winthorpe becomes aware that Valentine has his job and home and is convinced that Valentine somehow had him set up. He decides to take revenge on Valentine and set him up in turn. At the Dukes brothers' Christmas party, a drunk and dishevelled Winthorpe plants drugs in Valentine's desk. This doesn't go according to plan, and to escape the situation and the event, Winthorpe pulls a gun on everyone and flees.

The Dukes believe that this concludes their experiment, and they exchange a dollar as part of the bet. But Valentine overhears this, along with their intention to sack him, and to forget about the loser Winthorpe, whose life they have wrecked.

Winthorpe attempts suicide, but is saved by Ophelia and Valentine, who explains to them both everything that has happened and why. Winthorpe and Valentine learn that Beeks, who is on the Duke brothers' payroll, works for the government, and he has an agriculture report on orange crop forecasts that hasn't been publicly published yet. Winthorpe remembers the Dukes making large payments to Beeks off the books, and both he and Valentine realise it must be so that they get to see the report before it's released, and with this insider information, they can safely bet on the orange crop markets and make huge profits.

Valentine and Winthorpe intercept Beeks, tie him up and lock him in a cage with a gorilla on a train. They change the report so that it says the opposite of what's actually going to happen to oranges, and make sure the Dukes get this false report.

Valentine, Winthorpe, Ophelia and the butler for the house where Winthorpe, and now Valentine, live pool every cent they have, and using the insider knowledge, they make the right investments in oranges. The misinformed Dukes, meanwhile, invest heavily in oranges in the opposite way and lose everything. The now rich foursome move to a paradise island, with all four now friends, and Ophelia and Winthorpe a romantic couple.

Leadership lessons

In *Trading Places*, the Dukes represent privilege. They have power and are insulated from the problems of ordinary people. Despite this, they have to cheat and stack the deck of cards in their favour illegally. They aren't able to use intellect and skill to increase their wealth; instead, they're bribing an official to make a killing on the stock exchange. In the real world, those with extreme wealth frequently bend and break the rules to assist themselves, believing the rules that apply to ordinary people don't apply to them. The 0.01 percenters, the billionaire class etc. There's a large EDI issue here, as the lack of equality in this film is vast and striking. The Dukes could use their position and power to do good, but they don't.

The film proves something that we already know, which is that money and privilege create an unfair advantage, and those without it have a harder life, and it's more difficult for them to get ahead.

Another thing the film demonstrates is the importance of true friends. After he's sacked, Winthorpe is blanked by all his buddies, and he learns that they were never really his friends at all and never had his back. It turns out that people he has nothing in common with but who have integrity and a belief in fairness support him when he's down, Valentine and Ophelia.

The film superbly makes points about wellbeing for us, and shows how the financial shapes the physical, emotional and social, to the point of destruction with suicidality. *Unite* is very powerful here, as is *expertise* amongst the good guys, once they start working together as a team.

This film also demonstrates the importance of the bottom tier of Maslow's pyramid in terms of biological needs like food and shelter, which are basic needs and arguably human rights, though many people across the world haven't got them. When these needs aren't met, it creates insecurity and a lack of belonging, and it completely removes the chances of people actualising or achieving anything in life, as they're barely surviving. People with the ability to build other people up and improve their lives really should just do it.

Key takeaways:

- Friendship is essential for happiness in life.
- Honesty is a brilliant behaviour to possess and role model.
- Authenticity helps to build trust.
- Privilege stunts the personal growth and self-awareness of some people.

17: *The Last of the Mohicans* (1992)

The storyline

This movie is based on the novel by James Fenimore Cooper from 1826 and is set during the French and Indian War of 1754–63. It's directed by Michael Mann and stars Daniel Day-Lewis.

Major Heyward is a British officer who arrives in Albany and is tasked with bringing the adult daughters of Colonel Munro to his base, Fort William Henry. His guide is Magua, a Huron who's falsely presenting himself as Mohawk. He leads Heyward and about 50 of his soldiers into an ambush by Magua's war party. All of the soldiers are killed by the Hurons, but Heyward and the Munro daughters are saved by an adopted Mohican called Hawkeye (played by Day-Lewis), and his Mohican father and brother, Chingachgook and Uncas. They kill all the Hurons, apart from Magua, who escapes. The three Mohicans agree to help Heyward and the women get to Fort William Henry.

It becomes clear that Hawkeye and the elder Munro

daughter, Cora, are attracted to each other, which is difficult for Heyward, as Cora declined his proposal of marriage.

The fort is under siege by the French, so Hawkeye and his relatives have to sneak Heyward and the women into the fort using their knowledge of the area. Colonel Munro is disappointed to see his daughters, as the fort isn't safe, and he had written to them advising them not to come, but they tell him they didn't receive the letters.

Once Munro finds out that General Webb is near, about 20 miles away at Fort Edward, he becomes more positive, as he knows that the soldiers stationed there under the general could help him win his current battle. He dispatches someone to get the reinforcements.

Day-Lewis has a number of friends in the militia who are supporting Munro and fighting on his side. Hawkeye tells them the truth about Huron war parties going up and down the river and targeting the settler farms belonging to the militia men. This obviously concerns them, so they tell Munro that they have to leave to protect their land and families. Munro had earlier agreed that they could do so, but now he goes back on his word. The militia men sneak away in the night, supported by Hawkeye, who provides sharpshooter protection against the French. Hawkeye doesn't leave, as he wants to remain close to Cora, to protect her. Munro charges Hawkeye with sedition, and he's arrested and sentenced to death.

The French general makes Munro aware that he's now in position to take Fort William Henry, and that he intercepted the letter intended for General Webb at Fort Edward, so no reinforcements are coming. Therefore, Munro can either let everyone die or negotiate a surrender. Munro agrees to surrender, and he and his men are allowed to march to Albany.

This goes against an agreement Magua thought he had with the French general, and enrages him. He hates Munro, because he killed Magua's family, and Magua wants to get revenge by killing Munro and his daughters.

When Munro and his soldiers are passing through a narrow piece of land with woodland on either side, Magua and his tribe attack them, killing Munro and many others. Hawkeye, Chingachgook and Uncas save Cora and her sister Alice, and flee the battle with Heyward. Magua and his men pursue them, and Hawkeye and his family know they can't stop them being captured, so they slip away, after Hawkeye reassures Cora that he will find her.

Magua takes the three Britons to the chief of the Huron tribe. Hawkeye interrupts Magua while he's talking with the chief, and he pleads for the lives of the Britons. The chief decides that Heyward should be returned to the British, Alice should be given to Magua and Cora should be burned alive. Both Heyward and Hawkeye plead for Cora's life, offering to die in her place. The chief accepts Heyward's offer, allowing Cora and Hawkeye to leave.

Hawkeye, Chingachgook and Uncas pursue Magua to free Alice. Uncas is ahead of his family by some distance and kills many of the Hurons in pursuit of Alice, with whom he seems to have a bond. He reaches Magua, but isn't a match for him, and is killed, his body thrown off a cliff. This has an unforeseen impact on Alice, who chooses to end her life by leaping off the cliff.

Hawkeye and Chingachgook catch up with the rest of the Hurons and Magua. They kill many of them, and Chingachgook challenges Magua to a fight. Chingachgook is wily and skilful and kills Magua. Afterwards he prays to the gods and declares himself 'the last of the Mohicans'.

Leadership lessons

Remember Newton's third law of motion: *for every action there is an equal but opposite reaction*.

In *The Last of the Mohicans*, Magua is single-minded in his hatred for Munro, and his *raison d'être* and everything he does is about causing the colonel as much pain as possible and then killing him. This comes from the trauma Magua experienced years earlier when Munro's soldiers killed Magua's wife and children.

This film incorporates the theme of wickedness in terms of colonialism and all the hateful acts associated with it, all in the pursuit of power and wealth, at a cost to the indigenous tribes, who are militarily weaker and peaceful, until provoked. There's no good with colonialism; it's totally wrong. These acts of evil are acts against humanity, and of course, sadly, it's still happening today.

All Munro's acts are in pursuit of power and wealth for England, and this provides him with a strong *raison d'être*, which also enables him to commit acts against humanity and be very willing to lie and break promises and do the opposite of what he should know to be right. He lacks integrity. Uncas, Chingachgook and Hawkeye prove that you can do good and have a good *raison d'être*, and they're driven by this throughout. To some degree, so is Munro's oldest daughter, Cora. Hawkeye has extra *raison d'être*, as he has a laser-precision insight that Cora is his special love in life, and his every act is to keep her safe and in the end to rescue her.

Expertise is evident throughout this film, as everyone has clear strengths, otherwise they wouldn't survive in this wild, lawless world. But *independence* is weak here, which is something that's common with dictatorships, autocracies and countries that have been imperialised or colonised. No one has a say.

The film brilliantly captures culture. Artefacts, espoused values and basic underlying assumptions are very clearly aligned. The hidden assumptions aren't actually hidden, but are clearly on show. It's a toxic and deadly culture.

From a wellbeing perspective, there's no balance; it's all about financial wellbeing, which destroys all the other pillars for everyone else, but also the British. Throughout, Day-Lewis's character displays good judgement, as most of his decisions turn out to be good ones.

Key takeaways:

- Greed causes so much needless pain.

- Lies can be harmless but also deadly.
- Dishonesty dilutes and eventually drowns our integrity.
- Imperialism is the opposite of humanity.
- Evil exists and frequently it is accompanied by power and greed.
- Teamwork makes you realise and appreciate the importance of others.
- Integrity is a leadership trait worth having.
- Honour yourself by honouring others.

18: The Untouchables (1987)

The storyline

This film tells the story of how Eliot Ness builds a team to take down the Chicago mob boss Al Capone during the Prohibition era. It's directed by Brian De Palma and stars Kevin Costner as Ness, with Sean Connery and Andy Garcia also on his team. Capone is played by Robert De Niro.

Capone is in a commanding position and controls the illegal alcohol trade across the whole of Chicago. Ness, an agent of the Bureau of Prohibition, has been given the task of bringing Capone down. He has no success, mainly because Capone has paid spies in the police force, meaning Ness is either foiled by them or Capone is tipped off.

Ness comes across James Malone, (Connery), a straight cop, who agrees to help him, and they start hiring unknowns from the police academy, those who haven't been corrupted yet by the dodgy cops or Capone himself. This is where they get George Stone (played by Garcia) from. They also bring in an accountant from Washington DC. They trust no one, and to Capone's frustration, they start to have some success, to the point that the press calls them 'the untouchables'.

Wallace, the accountant, discovers that Capone hasn't filed any income tax documents for a number of years. The team decides to target him for tax evasion, as his crime syndicate is very hard to penetrate with everyone loyal to and scared of Capone. Capone's network tries to bribe Ness, to no effect, and then they target his family, meaning he has to move them out of town.

On the Canadian border, the team intercepts a large shipment, killing a number of gangsters and getting their hands on one of Capone's bookkeepers. They convince the bookkeeper to give evidence against Capone, but they become complacent and underestimate Capone, and he manages to kill the bookkeeper and Ness's accountant.

Malone twigs that the police chief leaked the whereabouts of the accountant and the bookkeeper. Malone roughs up the police chief and finds out the name and location of Capone's chief accountant, Walter Payne.

Capone's number-one hitman, Nitti, goes after Malone and kills him, but Ness and Stone reach him before he dies, and he's able to advise them of the train that Payne will be taking to leave Chicago. This leads to a shootout at Union Station and Ness captures Payne, who agrees to testify.

In court, the hitman Nitti is present and is searched. Ness sees Malone's address written on a matchbook in his possession. Ness now knows that it was Nitti who killed Malone. Realising this, Nitti flees. Ness catches him on a rooftop. Nitti mocks Ness, telling him that he won't be convicted. Ness realises this might be true, and seeking revenge for his dead friends, he kills Nitti by pushing him off the tall building.

A piece of paper in Nitti's coat shows that all the jurors are on Capone's paylist. This leads to the judge deciding to switch his jury with a jury from another courtroom. Capone is convicted and sentenced to 11 years in prison.

Leadership lessons

In *The Untouchables*, Ness and his team never feel they're untouchable; it's a media thing. But Capone thinks he's untouchable, and he is – that is, until he isn't.

In modern society, some corporations believe they're untouchable, and it's easy to understand why they believe this, because there are no consequences for their poor and arguably criminal behaviour. Examples are the water companies in the UK and the oil companies in general. And then there were the shenanigans in the UK with how PPE contracts were handed out during the Covid pandemic, and indeed the £37 billion that was paid out for a track and trace system that didn't work, though other countries had a track and trace system in place that did work, and it only cost them a few million. Where did all that money go, where is it? These people are the modern untouchables. All of this is doing bad, and what we want in our companies and societies is for people to do good. That can require a carrot, but for some people it appears it really needs a stick. These people have to be held to account and dealt with according to the letter of the law, or others will assume that it's okay to behave in this way, and it will keep happening.

What Ness does well here is hire the right types of people. He hires for values, i.e. those who aren't corrupt, and then he hires for a skill set – he knows what he needs. Then, finally, he lets everyone play to their strengths and he doesn't micromanage.

Being adaptable is also modelled here. The team can't get near Capone to make things stick to him: he's too smart, no one will testify against him and he distances himself from the big crimes. So, they get him for tax fraud instead. That's easier to do, and they achieve it.

A word of warning: Ness loses his composure and his faith in the system and steps into the darkness when he kills an unarmed Nitti in cold blood. He crosses the line and is now a tainted good guy, as opposed to being a bona fide good guy. When doing good, we need to know what good is and what it isn't. Ness forgets this at that moment. Emotion gets the better of him.

The film demonstrates to us that autocratic dictator types create cultures of fear where they're the single ruler and rule-maker. Clearly, this is a pursuit of extreme financial wellbeing to the detriment of all other wellbeing pillars, and ultimately this damages everyone. These are toxic cultures. These rulers undermine and sabotage everyone from a Maslow safety and security perspective. By holding others down, they push themselves up.

Key takeaways:

- Toxic cultures are created, but so are positive ones.
- Greed causes so much needless pain.

19: *Raiders of the Lost Ark* (1981)

The storyline

This action movie, directed by Steven Spielberg, is set in the pre-World War II era, with the Nazis on the rise in Europe and elsewhere. Archaeologist Indiana Jones (played by Harrison Ford) is attempting to find the Ark of the Covenant before the Nazis and their archaeologist, Belloq. Jones's fear is that the holy power that the Ark possesses will be used for evil by the Nazis.

Jones is approached by army intelligence personnel, who explain that the Nazis are digging in Egypt to locate the Ark. Jones goes to Nepal, to meet an ex-girlfriend, Marion, as he knows her father is an expert on the Ark. The Gestapo know this too, and arrive there at the same time as Jones, and he saves her from them. Marion has a medallion belonging to her now deceased father, that to the trained eye, has encryptions on it that show where the Ark is hidden in Egypt. They head there together.

Using the medallion, Jones realises that the Nazis and Belloq are digging in the wrong area. Jones assembles a small team, and they find the Ark. But the Nazis, who are nearby, intervene and take possession of the Ark. Jones and Marion escape, and they pursue the Nazis and Belloq across sea and land. They're captured and overwhelmed by the superior forces.

Jones tries to convince Belloq not to hand the Ark over to Hitler, and not to test its power first. But Belloq, obsessed with the power of the Ark, opens it, and releases the spirits within that are universally connected to the Ark. Jones and Marion have closed their eyes, so they don't see what is going on, but they hear everything. Belloq and the Nazis present are destroyed by the spirits, and the Ark is resealed. When Jones and Marion open their eyes, they find everyone else has disappeared, and only they and the Ark remain.

Jones hands the Ark over to the American authorities, who put it in a huge storage building with thousands of other artefacts and boxes.

Leadership lessons

In *Raiders of the Lost Ark*, Jones is the ultimate hero. Academically brilliant and great in the field too. Physically capable, interesting, charismatic and someone with sound morals.

The movie pits good against bad, the bad being the Nazis and those working for them. It also shows the downside of people meddling in things that they don't understand, represented by the Nazis, who have power and think this gives them the authority to do whatever they want. This is an issue in organisations where those with authority but not necessarily ability or expertise make decisions that have an impact on others. In this case, the Nazis think they're entitled to the power of the Ark and incorrectly assume that whatever power it possesses will align with them, but it doesn't. In organisations and society when those with authority but not necessarily ability or expertise make decisions, it's the opposite of real listening.

Jones is the embodiment of RISE UP; he lives it. He generally makes good decisions and has sound judgement. From a wellbeing perspective, his life also appears to be in balance. By contrast, the Nazis and other bad faith characters are striving for money and power, and their behaviour negatively impacts on all the wellbeing pillars. They're actually striving to diminish and destroy everyone else's wellbeing, and their needs according to Maslow's hierarchy. Their *raison d'être* is badness.

Key takeaways:

- Listen, truly listen.
- Power in the wrong hands, a homogenous minority, is dangerous for the heterogeneous majority.

20: *Spartacus* (1960)

The storyline

This is a movie directed by Stanley Kubrick and starring Kirk Douglas, Laurence Olivier, Peter Ustinov, Tony Curtis and Jean Simmons. Douglas also produced it. It's set in the first century BC in the Roman Empire.

Spartacus (played by Douglas) is a slave in an open mine who's disobedient and belligerent, and as a result he's sentenced to be starved to death. He comes to the attention of a visiting Roman businessman, Lentulus Batiatus (played by Ustinov), who buys him, with the intention of training him in his gladiator school.

While at the school, Spartacus develops a strong bond, which becomes a romance, with Varinia (played by Simmons), a female slave who works as a serving woman. Batiatus is visited by a powerful senator, Crassus (played by Olivier) who is aiming to become the next leader of Rome. Crassus buys Varinia, and to the annoyance of Batiatus demands a spectacle, ordering that Spartacus and others fight to the death. Draba, an Ethiopian, gets the better of Spartacus, but defies the Roman visitors and spares him. Instead, he attacks the visitors, but is wounded by the guards, and killed by Crassus.

The atmosphere amongst the gladiators is tense and angry, and to try to get some calm, Batiatus encourages the Romans to depart, and sends Varinia to Crassus's residence in Rome. Marcellus, one of the trainers at the gladiator school, dislikes Spartacus, and uses Varinia leaving to insult and tease him. Spartacus kills him, and this triggers a riot where the gladiators turn on the guards, killing them and taking control of the school. They all leave and hide in the mountains.

The escaped gladiators elect Spartacus as their leader, and he decides to lead them out of Italy, after which they can head to their homelands. As they travel across the country, they steal money from the Roman gentry, which they will use to pay the pirates of Cilicia to ship them out of Italy. More and more slaves join them as word of their mission spreads. The escaped Varinia joins them, as does Antonius (Tony Curtis), who helped her escape. Very quickly, Spartacus has so many slaves with him that what he has assembled is an army. Varinia, meanwhile, becomes pregnant.

The Roman senate is now in a state of worry, as every army they have sent against Spartacus has been defeated. Crassus has been trying to use the situation to get complete control of the Roman armies, but another powerful senator, Gracchus, who despises Crassus, has been blocking this by ensuring his mentee, Julius Caesar, has control over half the armies. However, Caesar views one of Gracchus's actions as being disloyal to Rome. Gracchus has paid the Cilician pirates to take the slave army out of Italy.

Caesar joins Crassus, and they make a deal with the pirates, who don't turn up to transport Spartacus and his slave friends to freedom. Crassus also spreads panic in Rome that Spartacus is coming to kill them all, which means he gets what he wants, which is total control of the armies.

Trapped and surrounded by the armies of Rome, Spartacus tries to rally his followers, saying that even if they die, they have given slaves a voice and hope. On this occasion they lose badly. The Romans win and want Spartacus, yet they can't identify him. They offer to spare anyone who points him out. Spartacus is about to step forward and declare himself, but just before he does so, someone else steps out, saying, 'I'm Spartacus.' Then another does the same, and another and another, practically every man.

Crassus has them all sentenced to death by crucifixion. He recaptures Varinia with her baby and attempts to make her commit to him in the way she did to Spartacus, as some sort of way to deal with the fact that Spartacus's people align with him and love him in a way no one does with Crassus. She rejects him, and out of spite and hatred, he's determined to find Spartacus.

Crassus has an advantage, in that he knows what Spartacus looks like because he was at the gladiator school. He finds him and forces him to fight with Antonius. The winner will be crucified. Out of love for Antonius, Spartacus kills him, meaning he will have to endure the painful crucifixion.

Batiatus locates Varinia and helps her and her baby to escape. As they leave Rome by road, they encounter Spartacus, nailed to his cross and just about alive, and she presents her son to his father, Spartacus.

Leadership lessons

In *Spartacus*, *expertise* and *unite* are huge, with the

slaves and indeed the Romans. You expect this of the Romans given that they're a well-trained army, but it's a testament to the leadership style and ability of Spartacus that he gets such alignment with his people that they become a group that's able to match and defeat the Romans. Spartacus possesses the ability to create real followership, which is extra special when we consider the decency of what he's trying to achieve: freedom and equality for a large section of society, those at the very bottom of it, the enslaved.

What defeats them in the end is the lengths that the moneyed and powerful are prepared to go to, to keep their power and wealth, with Caesar and Crassus paying the pirates not to take Spartacus and his followers away from Italy by sea, which they had promised to do. This means that Spartacus and his followers end up with another battle on their hands, one that they haven't planned for and aren't prepared for. Perhaps they should have foreseen that the pirates weren't to be trusted and should have had a Plan B. But in fairness there couldn't really be a Plan B; this was their only option, apart from staying where they were previously, enslaved. Their achievements and their strategy were good, and the right ones.

The film shows how Maslow's hierarchy of needs is undermined, deliberately, to stop people from thriving, so that they can be held down by others. It also shows how those with wealth see those without wealth, as merely an opportunity for exploitation, to greedily increase their own wealth. The Spartacus character generally makes good decisions and has good judgement.

Key takeaways:

- Loyalty, loyalty, loyalty. Someone has your back.
- Freedom is something all humans deserve.
- Power corrupts.
- Evil exists, and we can subdue it, as long as we admit it exists.

> There's no real value to be had from greed. It's important to understand this. The films in this chapter exemplify evil, corruption, toxic cultures, lies, dishonesty, psychopathy, and imperialism. This is what greed creates. It's okay for us to have self-interest, which is something the Dalai Lama advised is essential to our survival as individuals, but there's obviously a line that gets crossed where self-interest becomes selfishness, and then greed kicks in.

CHAPTER 10:
PSYCHOPATHY

21: *Braveheart* (1995)

The storyline

The movie is different from the history it depicts, but let's stick with the movie. The story follows the trials and tribulations of Scotsman William Wallace (played by Mel Gibson) who sets himself the goal of gaining freedom for his country, which is under the rule of the English king, Edward I.

Early in the movie, as a child, Wallace is orphaned as his father is deceived and killed by the king's men. Wallace is taken to Rome by his uncle, a cultured man who believes in education, and Wallace learns the art of war, but also many other things, including Latin and French. He returns to Scotland and marries and stays out of anti-English politics – that is, until his wife is brutally murdered by a local English lord. Using his knowledge and skills, he leads a group of men against the lord, killing him and his men.

This sets him on a course of wanting to free his

country from English rule, and he leads his ever-growing group of followers to victory in several battles against English lords in Scotland. His honesty and passion shine through in his authentic leadership, and people connect with this and the goal of freedom.

His next battle is the Battle of Stirling, and it brings Wallace into contact and conflict with the Scottish nobles, who want to agree terms with the very strong English army and gain more land. Wallace wants the battle, as this is the only way to remove the English from Scotland. His military acumen comes into play and he executes his plan perfectly, with support from the Scottish noblemen, and they defeat the English army. He quickly understands that the noblemen view themselves as better, more important, than the ordinary men of Scotland, and are less interested in freedom, as they do quite well from a land and money perspective with things as they are.

Wallace leaves Scotland and the noblemen behind and invades England, and following another battle, he takes over York. King Edward has made a few attempts at tricking and assassinating Wallace without success, but he has also been moving pieces on the chessboard while Wallace holds York, namely he sails with an army from England, Ireland and Wales to Scotland to destroy Wallace's people. Wallace returns to Scotland and this leads to another battle, one which Wallace loses, after he's been betrayed by the Scottish noblemen, who align themselves with the English king, for increased titles and money.

However, Wallace escapes, but is later captured by the father of Robert the Bruce, who undermines and betrays Robert the Bruce and Wallace, again for increased land and titles. Then Wallace is executed.

Leadership lessons

In *Braveheart*, Wallace is all about doing good and *raison d'être* is huge for him, and these create strong followership. He's a smart man and trusts people, though some ultimately betray him, which leads to his death. He took a chance trusting the noblemen. In many ways he wasn't aligned with them.

In terms of Mind the Gap, he's a senior leader who could have aligned the common folk of Scotland, but silver, gold and land were more appealing to the Scottish noblemen. What they and the English king were able to do was create a *raison d'être* for their ilk which was all about power and wealth and self-interest.

Wallace is a great listener to the majority, whereas the English king and Scottish noblemen are deaf to the ordinary folk and are listening only to themselves. This can be an issue in companies too, where the board are viewed as being in their ivory towers, ignoring everyone else. Some of us may have worked in companies like these, and there are lots of examples of such companies in history, like the East India Company and, in recent times, Enron. And of course, the English water companies, where the boards of directors loaded these companies with debt, then paid out much of the money taken in loans as dividends, didn't modernise the infrastructure and are responsible for the constant flow of sewage into the rivers, lakes and seas of England. They're clearly failing on the Triple Bottom Line.

Both Wallace and the English king are good at uniting others, by very different means, and in terms of *process-fixing*, the English king learns his lessons quickly and makes improvements, but Wallace fails to do so in terms of managing the Scottish nobles. But as a leader, who would you want to be led by and who would you really want to be, Wallace or King Edward? What's great about the film is that you can answer that question without feeling conflicted in any way. We would all probably want to be led by Wallace and aspire to be a Wallace type, but what about in the real world? That becomes more difficult, because traditional allegiances take hold. This is seen in democratic elections around the world, where some parties who are or have been doing poorly and causing huge grief still have a core following, and sometimes gain as much as 25 per cent in an election with multiple parties in play, but in countries where there are only two main parties, like the USA, they can achieve anything from 47 per cent to 53 percent, depending on whether they win or lose.

Wallace has confidence and humility, which are admirable leadership traits, and in organisations people tend to respond well to leaders with these strengths. The English king and Scottish lords, however, have no humility, yet they still have power and authority.

In reference to Mind the Gap, King Edward and the Scottish noblemen are clearly psychopaths of different levels, and when it comes to selection processes, blood counts for much, and they want to keep things as they are because they're the ones who benefit. This crops up in organisations too: like attracts like, and those hiring feel more comfortable with having the same kind of people as them about. Sometimes they protect themselves by appointing the same types as them, it feels safe. Other times when they appoint people the same as them, it is because they believe they have to, as those who are different to them, are actually inferior, and why would they want them around.

Wallace, on balance, makes some bad decisions, which is down to poor judgement, but he's still very strong for followership and having the right values.

Key takeaways:

- Honour yourself by honouring others.
- Inequality disadvantages and hurts the weak, it's a terrible thing.
- Power corrupts.
- Psychopaths in the corporate world can do good, but you must set them the right objectives.

22: *Training Day* (2001)

The storyline

This movie is set in Los Angeles and stars Denzel Washington as a highly respected and successful narcotics detective (Alonzo Harris), and Ethan Hawke as a more junior police officer (Jake Hoyt).

Hoyt has to spend a training day with Harris as part of an evaluation/appraisal process to get a promotion. They catch some teenagers smoking marijuana and confiscate the stash. Harris puts it in a pipe and pressurises Hoyt to take a puff of it. Hoyt declines, but Harris makes a big deal out of it and chastises and manipulates Hoyt and pulls his gun on him. Hoyt knows Harris isn't going to shoot him, but it's an awkward situation, so to keep the peace while he's trying to adjust to Harris's behaviour, he smokes a little. Then Harris laughs as he tells Hoyt that the cannabis was laced with PCP, a more illegal substance. Hoyt doesn't know if he's being pranked or if Harris is telling the truth, but he knows that Harris is toying with him, and wonders if this is all part of the assessment.

A little later, it becomes clear to Hoyt that Harris is corrupt and dangerous. What should be a routine search for drugs and money at a known criminal's house turns very dark. The police team with Harris are close friends of his, and they uncover $4 million of the criminal's drug money and without resistance the criminal gives it up. Harris's team order Hoyt to shoot the criminal, but he refuses, so they shoot the criminal dead, and then plant evidence and create a story to explain the shooting as self-defence. The local police are about to arrive when Hoyt is told by Harris and his corrupt team that according to the story, Hoyt is the hero and the shooter. Hoyt refuses to go along with this and is told it's this or they will kill him, but then they manipulate and blackmail him by telling him that he smoked their PCP earlier without knowing it, and that it would now show up in a routine blood test, so he therefore needs to comply with them or they will set him up. He recognises that he has no choice and has been entrapped.

Hoyt is pleased that the day is coming to an end and just wants to get the day over and signed off, and then he can get on with his life and career and put this messed up day behind him. Harris advises Hoyt that they have one small thing to do before the day ends, though, which is to visit the residence of a gangster. Harris leaves Hoyt in the kitchen with a few gangsters as he attends to some business in a different room. The gangsters in the room jump Hoyt, and it becomes clear that Harris has left by a different route and has hired these gangsters to murder Hoyt.

They drag him into the bathroom and are about to shoot him when a wallet in Hoyt's possession falls onto the floor. It belongs to a teenage girl whom Hoyt saved earlier in the day from a rapist. That's what he tells the gangster who is about to shoot him, when they question him as to why he has the wallet of the girl, who is the gangster's cousin. He doesn't believe Hoyt, but phones his cousin, and she confirms she was saved by Hoyt. The gangster releases Hoyt, as he now owes him one, and has also realised that Hoyt is a genuinely good cop and nothing to do with the rotten Harris, whom they all despise. Hoyt is also made aware that Harris has until the end of this day to pay the Russian mob $1 million as compensation for killing one of their own following an argument in Las Vegas.

Hoyt goes after Harris, confronts him, fights him and escapes with the drug money that Harris needs to save his skin. The Russians don't get their money and they shoot Harris.

Leadership lessons

With *Training Day*, the 'doing good' thing is big. It's huge with Hoyt, and ultimately saving the teenage girl is what saves him later on. Harris clearly stepped away from doing good long ago and is now immersed in criminality and corruption. Like attracting like is evident here too, and all of Harris's crew are rotten to the core and a team for a reason.

A big lesson for Hoyt is to always follow your values and the right standards. He shouldn't have smoked the pot. He knew it was wrong, in a minor way but nonetheless wrong, and this action was used against him by Harris to entrap him. The lesson for leaders is that some people will try to compromise you so that they have something on you that they can use as leverage at a time that suits them. Also, you'll encounter people in the workplace who are successful, but also very psychopathic, ruthless and self-serving, and you might not be aware of this side of them, as they only show it in certain circumstances. We need to trust others, but we should never step away from doing good and living our values. Sometimes you'll encounter a CEO or a very senior leader who has some people around them who don't appear to add any value. Occasionally, the rumour mill tells yarns about these individuals having worked together for a long time, and the CEO being stuck with Person X, as Person X knows some of the mistakes and perhaps misdemeanours the CEO has committed in the distant past, and the CEO needs the skeletons to stay in the closet!

In this movie *raison d'être* is clearly strong with both leading characters. With Hoyt, it's in the right way, to do good, which is what we should all aspire to. Obviously with Harris it's in the most toxic of ways, to serve his selfish needs.

Harris is a good example of a person who rules by fear and authority but has no genuine followership. Indeed, he's despised by nearly everyone, and they have no loyalty towards him. This is demonstrated by the criminal passersby who congregate to see him and Hoyt fight. Once Hoyt starts winning, no one takes up Harris's bribe to shoot Hoyt and they aren't responding to Harris's threats either. They all want rid of Harris, and Hoyt is the opportunity. In organisations, you can have people with the wrong behaviours, but once they see that a majority, or certain seniors, have the right values, they realise that their time is up and they either change their ways or leave. This is a big culture thing.

Key takeaways:

- Sometimes you get what you deserve.
- Once you choose to do bad, that's your lane, and getting out of it can be extremely hard.
- Live your values.

- Psychopaths in the corporate world can do good, but you must set them the right objectives.

23: *Goldfinger* (1964)

The storyline

Bond, played in this movie by Sean Connery, is in Miami, and he's been asked to keep an eye on Goldfinger, a gold bullion dealer. Bond sees that Goldfinger is cheating in a card game using a female employee, Jill (played by Shirley Eaton) who's monitoring what cards the other players have via binoculars and relaying this via an earpiece to Goldfinger. Bond interrupts Jill, and uses her mic to speak directly to Goldfinger, forcing him to lose the card game.

Bond sleeps with the Jill, but is knocked out by Goldfinger's bodyguard, Oddjob. When Bond regains consciousness, he finds Jill dead beside him, naked and covered in gold paint. He understands immediately that Goldfinger has no sense of humour, demands loyalty from his people and is very dangerous.

MI6 gives Bond the mission of figuring out how Goldfinger smuggles gold internationally. Bond plays golf with Goldfinger at his country club in England and bets him a bar of gold that he can beat him. Bond tricks him and wins. Goldfinger is annoyed and warns Bond to stay away from his business and gets Oddjob to display his strength by squashing a golf ball into dust with his clasped bare hand.

Bond spies on Goldfinger and follows him to his lair in Switzerland. He manages to get into the lair and hears Goldfinger bragging about how he melts and shapes gold into structural parts of his Rolls-Royce, enabling him to transport it without detection. He also overhears him mentioning Operation Grand Slam, which saves his life. Bond is captured and tied to a steel table and is about to be killed using a laser when he blags about Operation Grand Slam, saying that MI6 knows about it. Goldfinger decides to spare him for now, as killing him might alarm MI6, which could put the operation at risk.

Pussy Galore, a female pilot, transports them to a farm in the USA on Goldfinger's private jet. Bond escapes from the cell he's locked in and sees that the mafia are meeting with Goldfinger. He manages to hear what is proposed at the meeting. Goldfinger is going to release a nerve gas that will knock out and incapacitate all the soldiers and guards at Fort Knox, allowing his men to steal the gold there. Goldfinger offers to give the mafia a share, as a thank you for all the items they have already supplied him with to make the project a success. The mafia leaders present all laugh at him, so he locks them in the room and gases them all to death.

Bond is captured again, and in a confrontation with Goldfinger tells him that the plan won't work, as there is too much gold and it would be impossible to move this very heavy metal and then hide it. He then twigs from Goldfinger's behaviour, and from recognising a Chinese government agent, that actually Goldfinger's plan is to explode a Chinese dirty bomb, thus contaminating all the gold, decreasing its value and pushing up the price of the rest of the gold in the world, much of which is owned by Goldfinger and China.

Pussy Galore is central to the plan, and she and her gang of female pilots spray the gas all around Fort Knox from their planes, knocking out all the army and security people. Then Goldfinger's small army brings the dirty bomb into the vaults and switches on the timer, to count down to the explosion of the bomb. But Goldfinger's army unexpectedly comes under attack from the Fort Knox soldiers and security, who were only feigning unconsciousness, following a tip-off from Pussy Galore, who switched the knockout gas for a neutral substance.

Bond is locked in the vault with Oddjob, and manages to kill him, but is unsure how to defuse the bomb. Before Bond makes a mistake by cutting the wrong wire and actually activating the bomb, a bomb expert is able to get access to the vault and switch off the bomb. Goldfinger manages to escape, but he wants revenge on Bond, so pursues him, and Bond kills him.

Leadership lessons

The biggest lesson in *Goldfinger* is how power and extreme wealth totally corrupt. Goldfinger has huge wealth already but just wants more and more and will attain this by doing whatever is necessary. It's a good example of psychopathy too, and it raises the question of what level of regulation is the right amount, and how we should control the flow of big money through tax havens etc., and through tax too perhaps. The 1%

of the 1%, the mega rich again. The film is also a good example of how the obsession with financial wellbeing of a minority can have a huge negative impact on the physical and emotional wellbeing of the many.

Goldfinger also shows us something that we see in the world today and have seen in the past too, which is that there are people without morals who are ready and willing to align with badness. Their reasons for doing this may be connected to how they get their recognition, or to do with needing to feel important, or maybe it's just a form of greed in terms of being well-paid, and the example here is all of Goldfinger's people.

Raison d'être is big with both Goldfinger and Bond. *Expertise* is big with many characters here, notably Goldfinger, Oddjob, Pussy Galore and of course Bond. *Independence* is missing. A psychopathic or power-driven person always impacts those around them in the *independence* domain. They are in charge and they decide and they dictate.

Bond is adaptable, in that he's able to use some knowledge to bluff and lie and create doubt in Goldfinger's mind that maybe Bond does know the truth, and therefore he decides not to kill him at that moment. It was a close call, and Bond could have died. He displays calm under immense pressure.

Another matter excellently demonstrated relates to EDI. Pussy Galore is a strong female character, maybe stronger than how women were portrayed in film and society at that time, but it's completely ridiculous to think that her attraction to Bond would ever be enough for her to sacrifice everything she has and just switch allegiance from the bad guys to the good guys. It's fantastical and certainly of its time and not based in reality then or now.

Goldfinger is a major psychopath, but Bond is psychopath too. Bond tends to make good decisions, which show that from a judgement perspective he's very strong.

Key takeaways:

- The extreme and selfish obsession with financial wellbeing by a tiny minority, can have a huge negative impact on the physical and emotional wellbeing of the many.
- Greed causes so much needless pain.
- Sometimes you have to bluff.

24: *Shane* (1953)

The storyline

Shane is a Western starring Alan Ladd as the eponymous gunslinger. Shane arrives in what appears to be a quiet valley in the middle of nowhere in Wyoming. He's a stranger to the townsfolk. He's a quiet man of very few words and has a vibe of being serious and someone not to be messed with. We know he's a top-class gunfighter.

He's hired by small-time farmer Joe, who's a decent, hardworking man living on the land with his wife, Marian, and young son, Joey. Joe tells Shane how he and a number of other small farmers are being harassed and bullied by a big cattle baron, Rufus Ryker, who's hired numerous dodgy henchman types to force the farmers off their land by leaving or agreeing to sell to Ryker at well below market prices.

Shane heads into town on his own, to buy things for the farm at the general store. There's a saloon next door. Shane heads into the saloon to buy and bring back a soda for the boy, Joey. Ryker's men are drinking there and one of them does a lot to provoke Shane, but Shane retains his composure and ignores the taunts and acts of aggression.

The next time Shane comes to town he's with farmer Joe and some of the other small farmers. Shane and Joe have a brawl with most of Ryker's men and they win. A vexed Ryker warns that the next fight will be with guns. Ryker goes out and hires an obvious bad man who's also an excellent gunfighter, called Jack Wilson (played by the outstanding Jack Palance).

One of the harmlessly ordinary but proud farmers is in town on his own and is taunted and mocked by Palance into drawing his gun. He doesn't stand a chance against the extremely fast Palance and is easily killed.

At the farmer's funeral, most of the other farmers have decided to give in to Ryker and just go somewhere else and start again. However, while they're gathering, their homes are unguarded, and Ryker's men set one farmer's house on fire. This angers them into changing their decision, and now, united, they will stay and put up a fight.

Ryker views Joe as the stubborn and resilient force in the group of farmers. He invites him to a meeting to negotiate a way forward, but his real intention is to kill him. One of Ryker's men has tired of all the wrongdoing, and he makes Shane aware of what Ryker intends to do. Shane tells Joe and tries to convince him not to go, but Joe won't back down. Joe's wife begs Shane to intervene, and he does. They fight, and Shane knocks the farmer unconscious. He says goodbye to Joe's wife, and heads into town to tackle Ryker by himself.

We never learn what drives Shane to commit this act of goodness. Is it that he knows Ryker is evil and Joe and his family are good, and believes he needs to step in to protect them, knowing what will happen if he doesn't? Or is he looking for redemption for the bad acts he may have committed in his life?

He goes to town and kills Wilson in a gunfight, along with Ryker and all of Ryker's men that were present.

Leadership learning

Shane is a great example of the good and the bad, the right and the wrong, the powerful versus the weak and the moneyed versus those without. It shows how money buys power, and how someone can exert their will by any means including darkness just to increase their wealth and power. It's all here.

This is a story that lays out the reality of many societies, in which oligarchs lobby and win over politicians to do their bidding, to the disadvantage of the many. Examples include energy companies, water companies, gun makers and defence companies.

Shane has a past, maybe a bad one, but we're not told about this; we just know that he was once a brilliant gunslinger, and it becomes clear that he still has that dangerous ability. It's interesting to see that Ryker recognises Shane isn't to be messed with, and instead tries to buy him. Some bullies and dictator types have the ability to see the resilience and strength in others, and they try to win them over somehow, to strengthen their position and at the same time leave the vulnerable without protectors. When the Shanes of this world work to do good, they minimise the damage that the autocrats create.

It's also fascinating how the Wilson types do things to mock, trick and manipulate others to compromise themselves, to lose their composure, and they try to tilt the playing field to suit them and their toxic ways. But when they meet a strong and skilful force for good, they lose, to the benefit of the majority and the greater good. In companies and societies, *expertise* types who have a desire to do good can really add value and do a lot of good. It comes down to having a *raison d'être* that's aligned with doing good.

The film also shows how Maslow's hierarchy is undermined by those in power, destroying all wellbeing. Ryker is stopping everyone from having their biological needs met, and he's also damaging their security and safety. This disruption at the lower levels of the hierarchy stops people from ever being content, which also stops them from being able to fulfil their potential and use all their abilities.

Shane is also strong when it comes to judgement.

Key takeaways:

- Greed corrupts.
- The powerful exploit others to increase their power.
- Not everyone can be bought off.

There is a value to some psychopathy. Psychopaths are very effective at getting things done. They can be very single-minded. It's well known that many people with psychopathic tendencies work in the finance sector, the media, politics, sales and as CEOs. There's no cure for psychopathy, but if you are one or know one, developing self-awareness is a good place to start. This can help to limit the damage. Psychopaths in the corporate world and organisations can do good, but you must set them the right objectives.

CHAPTER 11:
TRAUMA

25: *Death of a Salesman* (1985)

The storyline

This film dives into the territory of what life is all about and how our actions impact on others. It stars Dustin Hoffman as Willy Loman and John Malkovich as his son, Biff. The movie is fine, but the play, written in 1949 by Arthur Miller, who was at one stage married to Marilyn Monroe, might just be the best play ever written.

Willy's wife is worried about him. He works too hard, is clearly stressed and a little distressed, and has been in a car crash too. She convinces him to ask his boss to let him work in the Greater New York area. He lives in Brooklyn, so this will save him from doing so much travelling.

Willy's sons, Biff and Happy, are both visiting home. Willy is unimpressed with Biff, whom he views as a loser for failing his maths finals and not going to college and wasting his abilities.

Willy goes to see his boss, but he gets angry and ends

up being sacked. Biff goes to meet someone too, to raise money for a business idea, but he's turned down.

Willy bumps into a young neighbour, a successful lawyer who used to be a school mate of Biff's. He explains that Biff had ability and ambition, but that something happened many years ago when he went to visit Willy, who was working in Boston, which appeared to sap Biff's motivation. Willy reflects on this time, and we learn that the incident that caused the change in Biff was him catching his father, whom he idolised, with his mistress.

Willy meets his sons for dinner in a restaurant. Biff tries to explain that he didn't get the investment money, but Willy constantly interrupts him, as he doesn't want to hear any of this. Biff walks out on his dad, and Happy follows. They head home, and eventually Willy does too. He remains outside and is distressed, so Biff goes out to him. After a while they start to argue.

Biff tries to convey to his dad that he, Biff, is an ordinary bloke and that he's happy with this and wants his dad to accept him as this. They hug and cry, and Biff tells his father that he loves him.

Willy clearly misunderstands all of this. He knows he has been forgiven, which is true, but somehow he believes that Biff is still interested in a business career but just needs to get funding for it.

Willy deliberately crashes his car, killing himself, so that Biff will have the insurance money to use to start up his business. However, Biff is still clear that he doesn't want to be a businessman.

Leadership lessons

In *Death of a Salesman*, Willy is very unsatisfied in life. He's in his 60s and is unhappy that he didn't make it big. He achieved lots of things, but he wasn't a big hitter. He unfairly compares himself to his mega-successful brother, a diamond tycoon who got lucky by chance, and berates himself for not making it in the same way. Willy is also frustrated by his sons, whom he views as losers who've achieved very little. The big lessons here are in regard to grandiosity, in that Willy lacks humility and self-awareness, and as a result he doesn't accurately assess his strengths or factor in the role pure good luck plays, like with his brother's success. He creates a false perception and unrealistic expectations of others.

Willy's radar is way off in terms of interpreting what doing good really is. His true purpose appears confused or missing throughout his life. He lacks self-awareness of his strengths, but also many of the qualities that make Rocky Balboa, from *Rocky*, a solid person of character, such as humility. Willy can't unite his people and doesn't learn from the past.

The way Willy constantly compares himself to his brother is a great lesson in why we shouldn't compare ourselves to others. His brother got lucky, and Willy could never achieve that level of success without major luck, which he never got. Willy can never recognise that he's great in his own way, as he's always consumed with not being able to achieve what's actually unachievable success. He creates the sense of failure and the unhappiness that becomes his whole life.

In the modern world, the success his brother achieved in finding diamonds in Africa reminds me of the dot-com boom, when many started to see that as the way to riches and success, and these days, we're in the era where being part of a start-up fills that gap.

We can have Willy types in our teams, and they can be hard workers, but they can also be very hard on themselves and sometimes others, with this constant need to not feel like a failure. Maybe this is the territory of imposter syndrome. It's so important for leaders to create a space where recognition exists and is given to everyone, as it won't always be obvious who in the team is struggling. Some can create a veneer of being fine and in control, but behind the mask, they can be desperate.

Key takeaways:

- Our actions have consequences.
- Desperation arrives when hope is lost.
- Listening is key.
- Don't compare yourself to others.
- Don't waste your life.

26: *The Green Mile* (1999)

The storyline

The Green Mile is based on a novel by Stephen King. Paul Edgecomb (played by Tom Hanks) is a prison guard working on death row in Louisiana, and one of his prisoners is John Coffey (played by Michael Clarke

Duncan), a giant black man who's been convicted of raping and murdering two young white girls.

Edgecomb has a number of men reporting to him, and all of them are decent apart for one, Percy Wetmore, played by Doug Hutchison. He's sadistic and bad, but is a nephew of the state governor and he uses this to make it difficult for others to manage him or hold him to account.

Edgecomb has a severe bladder infection, and Coffey heals him just by touching him. Edgecomb also sees Coffey bring a mouse back from the dead. He realises Coffey has special powers, and this makes him question if someone with the desire to heal and help could really have committed the crimes that he's been convicted of.

Wetmore supervises the execution of an inmate, and deliberately does it wrong to make the electrocution an extremely painful death. As punishment, and to get Wetmore out of the way, Edgecomb and his men lock Wetmore in a padded cell. Then they take Coffey out of the prison to the house of a friend, who's dying from a brain tumour. Coffey heals their friend and they bring him back to death row.

The badness/disease from the tumour has to go somewhere, and this is held within Coffey for a short while. He releases this badness from himself and it's transferred into Wetmore, who then shoots the prisoner Wharton. Edgecomb doesn't understand why Coffey would do this, but through his special powers, Coffey is able to show Edgecomb a visual story that makes it clear that it was really Wharton who killed the little girls that Coffey has been convicted of killing.

Edgecomb and the others are now very troubled as they know Coffey is innocent and a very decent and important person who will be executed. Coffey accepts his fate and tries to help the others accept it too, but when he is executed, they're all upset and never come to terms with the event.

Leadership lessons

The Green Mile conveys a lesson relating to appearance and prejudice. Coffey is clearly a decent human and full of goodness and good actions, but bias and ignorance and racism stop nearly everyone from seeing this. In the workplace, self-awareness is always a good place to start, as by developing this, you start to understand your strengths and weaknesses, and this enables you to accept the same in others.

The biggest failure in the movie relates to failing systems and failing cultures, in that the innocent Coffey ends up being executed. There clearly aren't opportunities to speak up, there aren't whistleblowing policies – although sometimes these aren't enough, as other behaviours block these anyway. If Coffey were a white woman, he wouldn't have been suspected of being a child killer, but just because he was in the vicinity of the dead children and was a black male, he was the suspect. Clearly, within these institutions and communities, the general culture is one of not listening, not evolving, not growing.

A non-evil version of the Wetmore character does

turn up in organisations and teams every now and again. They rarely get their opportunities by merit, and this always ends up having a negative impact on the team spirit. It can also harm the organisational values, as when those who are connected to the owners or board are treated differently to others, it can create a sense of organisational hypocrisy and damage to psychological safety. This steps into the territory of establishing open and honest selection processes.

Edgecomb is a decent leader in this movie, and creates a good team spirit, and in some ways Coffey is another example of someone who doesn't get any recognition.

Key takeaways:

- Prejudice is real.
- There are bad people, but don't forget there are good people too.

27: *The Deer Hunter* (1978)

The storyline

The Deer Hunter is a film written and directed by Michael Cimino and the main players are Robert De Niro as Michael, Christopher Walken as Nick, John Savage as Steven and Meryl Streep as Linda.

Michael, Nick and Steven work in a Pennsylvanian steel mill and they're part of a tight-knit group of men who live a normal life of work, booze, romantic relationships etc. The three friends are heading off to fight in Vietnam. Before they go, Nick gets engaged to Linda, and the men, together with some other friends, take a final hunting trip, during which Michael stalks and kills a deer.

In Vietnam, Michael is unexpectedly reunited with Nick and Steven during a mission. All three are captured by the Viet Cong and imprisoned. All the prisoners are forced to play Russian roulette or be killed. Nick is clearly struggling with his mental health. They come up with a plan to escape, and during this Nick is wounded, shot in the leg. The trio end up floating down the river, but then an American helicopter sees them. They all manage to get a grip of the helicopter and are being whisked away when the physically weak Steven falls back into the river. Michael sacrifices his own rescue by jumping back into the river, as he knows his friend has no chance of survival without him, meaning only Nick escapes. Steven breaks his legs in the fall, so Michael now has to physically carry him. Michael manages to get him as far as a group of refugees with a vehicle, who agree to give Steven passage to American medics.

When his tour is over, the traumatised Michael returns home, but is very different now following his experiences in war and avoids many of his old friends and acquaintances. Michael tracks down his pal Steven, who is in a veterans' hospital, and Steven refuses to return to his family and hometown. He's had his legs amputated and only has the use of one arm, and he feels like a failure and knows he doesn't fit in anywhere but there now. Nick has been missing since Vietnam, but Steven makes Michael aware that he's been receiving money from Vietnam. Michael correctly assumes it must be from Nick.

Michael heads back to Vietnam to find his old friend and convince him to come home. Nick, suffering from severe PTSD, is now a professional Russian roulette player on the illegal underground scene. Michael finds him while he's playing Russian roulette, and before he's able to convince him to give up the game and return home, Nick's luck runs out, and he's killed by his own shot to the head.

Leadership lessons

A big lesson in *The Deer Hunter* is the naivety or arrogance of thinking you know things when you really don't. At the start of the film, the main characters have an impression of what war is going to be like and see it as some sort of jolly that's going to somehow be good for their country and community. Michael is certainly guilty of this and gets annoyed and a bit aggressive towards a returning soldier, who's probably traumatised by what he encountered in the war. Michael takes issue with him because he isn't positive about the war, and because he isn't bigging up Michael and the others for signing up and being ready to head off on their missions.

This happens a lot in organisations, where some groups can have incorrect perceptions of other groups, and incorrect opinions on what others do or should be doing. This can be at the heart of many team conflicts.

Where it's most damaging is with decision makers. If the decision maker is making decisions on matters they know nothing about, then it becomes potluck as to whether the decision will lead to a good outcome or not. Sometimes the decision makers are never impacted by these outcomes, but the impact is felt by many elsewhere in the organisation. At the heart of this is a lack of humility, a lack of self-awareness, a lack of curiosity and a lack of listening. This can go on for years and years and be quite cyclical. It's not always the case that the decision makers are bad or corrupt and are making the decisions just to benefit themselves. On the contrary, they can be good people, but they lack the self-awareness and insight to understand that they don't know everything, and have bias, sometimes conscious, sometimes unconscious.

The film is also an exploration of trauma, physical and mental, and how this impacts people – how those on the receiving end feel stuck and misunderstood and then isolate themselves from others. There's a big emphasis on inclusion and wellbeing, especially the emotional, but obviously the physical and financial too. Michael carries scars, but not to the same degree as the others. He's a great example of someone who takes his responsibilities for others very seriously, and he tries to reach out and help his traumatised pals, but sadly without success, leaving himself out of pocket and increasingly more traumatised too.

The film is a story of how geopolitical leadership impacts individuals, families, marriages and communities. There's also an element of live and let live, which is demonstrated by Michael: early on in the movie he kills a deer, but later in the film when out on a hunt, he decides not to take the life of a deer. Obviously, his wartime experiences have changed him and he has more respect for life now.

In your organisation, your actions and inactions have an impact. Also, the people you work with always have a backstory, which you mostly won't know. Don't forget this. Finally, try to involve the right people when making decisions and be mindful of all your biases.

Key takeaways:

- Trauma is nothing to be ashamed of and can be treated.
- Don't minimise the impact of war on people.
- Some really do go the extra mile and make sacrifices for others.
- Friendship is essential for happiness in life.

28: *Unforgiven* (1992)

The storyline

This is a Western, produced and directed by Clint Eastwood. It stars Eastwood, along with Morgan Freeman and Gene Hackman.

In the 1800s, in a town in Wyoming called Big Whiskey, a cowboy named Mike scars the face of a prostitute, Delilah, using a knife, because she laughed at him. The sheriff, Bill Daggett (Hackman), orders that Mike should give several horses to the owner of the brothel for his financial loss. This infuriates the prostitutes, who pool a thousand dollars to take out a contract/hit to have Mike killed.

A youngish man going by the name of the Schofield Kid turns up at Will Munny's farm. The Kid says he's an experienced bounty hunter and is looking for Munny's help to kill Mike. Munny (played by Eastwood) is a retired gunfighter and notoriously violent outlaw who's now a poor farmer, a widower with two children, and he needs the money, so agrees. He brings along another outlaw, Ned Logan (Freeman).

Richard Harris plays a gunfighter called English Bob, who turns up in Big Whiskey to kill cowboy Mike and claim the money. Sheriff Daggett takes the gun from English Bob and savagely attacks him. The following day, English Bob leaves, but the writer who was with him stays, and is considering writing an article about Daggett instead.

Munny, the Kid and Logan turn up at the saloon where the prostitutes work. Munny stays downstairs in the saloon, while the other two go upstairs with the prostitutes. Daggett rightly guesses that the feverish Munny is in town to kill Mike, and he and his men easily disarm him, and then Daggett gives him a very bad beating. The Kid and Logan pick up the injured and ill Munny from the street, and they hide out in a barn while the prostitutes nurse Munny.

When Munny is well, the trio come across one of

Mike's friends who was also involved in the attack on the prostitute. Munny steps in and kills him when it becomes clear that Logan no longer has the stomach for killing. Logan decides to quit, but on his way home he's caught by Daggett and his deputies and is whipped to death for information regarding the whereabouts of Munny.

Munny and the Kid track down cowboy Mike, and the Kid kills him. Later that night, the Kid is drunk and feels huge guilt about killing Mike and admits that this was the first person he'd ever killed and that he never wants to kill again.

The following day, one of the prostitutes turns up with the money for the contract on Mike. She also tells them that Logan was captured and killed and his body is now on display in a coffin outside the saloon. Munny is shocked and angry. The Kid heads home, but that night Munny heads to Big Whiskey to exact revenge.

When he enters the saloon, Daggett and his deputies are there organising a posse to go after Munny. Munny kills the saloon owner for having Logan on display outside. A gunfight ensues, and Munny kills them all and then rides out of town.

Leadership lessons

One thing leads to another, which leads to another. Bad actions create more bad actions and so on, and the trauma cycle continues and continues and continues. This happens in *Unforgiven* and in real life too.

The Kid pretends to be something he's not, he's

inauthentic, and it eventually catches up with him. He needlessly damages himself, through a lack of self-awareness, and he's to blame for ending up in the situations he finds himself in. However, he gets insight and clarity on who he is and how he wants to live going forward.

Munny is a former killer who gave it up years ago to go into farming, but he can't make a living and he's under further pressure because his wife has died, leaving him to raise their two kids on his own. He returns to contract killing, just one, a supposedly easy one, to make some big money for the sake of his kids. From an *expertise* perspective, he's really good at it. His justification is that he's doing good by killing bad people who have done bad things. But is this really doing good? You can make a utilitarian argument in terms of the greater good, but...!

At this time, this town is ruled by a sheriff, Daggett, who's corrupt and has taken on the duties of judge and executioner too. Autocratic styles are the leading styles here and dominate all others. There's no positive *raison d'êtres* in place for anyone, and the lack of *independence*, i.e. voice, creates the need for rebellion and revenge from the sex worker group, which is at the centre of the story.

Wellbeing is bad for everyone in town apart from Daggett. As long as the townsfolk, and strangers in the town, align with him, they'll be okay to a degree, and may benefit. But if they don't, all aspects of their wellbeing will diminish and wither. The film is an example of how, in order to flourish, autocrats damage the security and safety of others, damaging all pillars of wellbeing.

Munny is totally authentic, feels secure in himself, has *raison d'être, independence* and *expertise*, and is capable of *unite*, and ultimately, he's the only winner, but it comes at a serious cost.

It's fascinating to see Daggett's ego and narcissism kick in when the opportunity arises for him to have his life story told by the writer, who was only there to tell English Bob's story in the first place.

Key takeaways:

- Voice – many are afraid to use theirs for fear of reprisal.
- Listening to others has a huge positive impact on their self-worth.
- Revenge, is it worth it? I won't answer this one.
- Trauma is nothing to be ashamed of and can be treated.

29: *Taxi Driver* (1976)

The storyline

Taxi Driver is another Scorsese film and it stars some big names. Robert De Niro plays Travis Bickle, an ex-army veteran traumatised by the Vietnam War who, with a deteriorating mental state, is making his living in New York as a driver of one of the famous yellow taxis. Cybil Shepherd is Betsy, a campaign worker for a senator who's running for president, and Jodie Foster is Iris, a child prostitute who's controlled by her pimp, Sport (Harvey Keitel).

Travis is lonely and an insomniac and is really frustrated with how scummy New York is, and he thinks about cleaning the place up by dealing with all the undesirables. He starts to obsess about Betsy and she agrees to go on a couple of dates with him. The second date freaks her out and shows how De Niro doesn't understand women, as he takes her to see a porn film in a dodgy cinema. She initially liked him, but this is a major turn-off, and she starts to avoid him. He angrily confronts her at her workplace and is told to get out.

To manage his anger, he starts to work out, and then for no explicable reason, other than possible violent thoughts and a desire to rid the city of scum, he buys a number of guns. He starts to monitor the security people protecting the senator Betsy is working for at a number of rallies, but it's unclear to what end. One night he shoots and kills an armed robber who's holding up a shop that's owned by a friend of his.

Travis befriends Iris and tries to convince her to stop working as a prostitute. His mental state then deteriorates, and he styles his hair to have a mohawk. He attends another rally and intends to assassinate the senator, but the Secret Service clocks him. They chase but fail to apprehend him.

That night, Travis goes to the brothel where Iris works, to kill her pimp and rescue her. He shoots Sport dead and also a couple of others, but in doing so is shot a number of times himself. He then tries to kill himself but has run out of bullets.

He recovers and is deemed a hero by the media. Iris's parents write to him, thanking him, and he bumps into Betsy, who's positive and pleasant towards him now that he's a bit of a celebrity as a local vigilante hero.

Leadership lessons

Travis is isolated. He's alone and striving to find a place in the world. His financial and physical wellbeing are okay, but he becomes more and more emotionally damaged. He feels safe and secure to a degree, but he lacks love and belonging, and his self-esteem is low. His *raison d'être* is always for the wrong thing, perhaps until towards the end, when he saves the girl. But in truth he is mentally ill at this time, so his *raison d'être* is distorted and what he's trying to achieve is unclear, as he tries to kill himself too at this time.

The biggest theme in *Taxi Driver* is about not fitting in, not belonging, feeling isolated. Travis pursues Betsy, but he doesn't understand her and completely misreads the social situation, which has everything to do with a lack of self-awareness. He doesn't feel like he has *independence* and autonomy in his life. He has *expertise*, but is clearly unable to *unite* anyone around him, and alignment isn't a gift that he possesses, which may be due to the psychological trauma of Vietnam, but we never find this out. Maybe he was different before the war, and in some ways what we're seeing is the trauma from then, changing him for the worse and stopping him from getting balance with Maslow, wellbeing and

RISE UP, to the extent that his story was always going to end with a big bang. Leadership-wise, he is great for effort and commitment, but fails in all other areas, and he isn't someone you would follow.

Iris is trapped and from a wellbeing perspective isn't in a good place either, though she might dispute this. Again, we don't know the complete backstory here, but can assume trauma of some kind comes into it. As a child prostitute she's experiencing continuous trauma, but she's too young to understand this.

Key takeaways:

- Trauma exists; it's all around us.
- Understand how it impacts you and others.

> Sadly, many people have experienced trauma. They're traumatised by deliberate acts, accidental acts and sometimes in a secondary way, through the behaviours of traumatised people they're connected to. People pass trauma on to others and also down through the generations. The good news is that there are ways to treat trauma, usually via a range of different types of talking therapies.

CHAPTER 12:
INTEGRITY

30: *Jerry Maguire* (1996)

The storyline

In this film the lead roles are played by Tom Cruise, Cuba Gooding Jr and Renee Zellweger.

Cruise plays Jerry Maguire, a polished sports agent working for a big-brand sports-management agency. Maguire writes a public letter in response to criticism that the big sports agencies are dishonest and uncaring, advising that he'll work with fewer clients moving forward so that he can ensure he'll deliver meaningful and more caring outcomes for his clients. His employers sack him, and he ends up retaining only one of his current clients, footballer Rod Tidwell (played by Gooding). As he leaves the office, he declares that he'll set up his own business and asks those who want to join him to come with him now. The only person who joins him is secretary Dorothy Boyd, a single mother (played by Zellweger).

To make matters worse, his girlfriend dumps him. But he starts a relationship with Boyd and it gets very serious very quickly, and they end up getting married.

On the work front, Maguire puts all his efforts into helping Tidwell, who is nearly out of contract. He needs a big one, as it's likely to be his last, given his age, and he's worried about making sure he's able to provide for his family. He's also frustrated that he's never had a really big contract.

Maguire and Tidwell have a very fiery and combative relationship, and they frequently argue. Tidwell argues that Maguire isn't working hard enough for him, and Maguire retorts that Tidwell isn't delivering enough on the field, and the media and fans view him negatively and consider him unlikeable. They both take on board the other's opinion. This leads to Tidwell playing better and his team winning more, but Maguire neglects his marriage and the couple split up.

One night during a live game, Tidwell scores a touchdown, winning the game for his team and sending them to the playoffs. However, he's concussed and isn't moving and appears to have a very serious injury. Maguire calls Tidwell's wife to reassure her and is by Tidwell's side. After some time, Tidwell gets to his feet and dances with joy that he hasn't been badly injured. He and Maguire hug it out, and the positivity of their relationship shines out to the world, which is watching. It's clear that Maguire is achieving what he wanted, which was to be a person-centred agent.

Maguire flies to where his wife is and they rekindle their love. He wins a big contract for Tidwell, the biggest of his career, and the details of this are relayed live to

Tidwell on a TV show. Tidwell thanks everyone, but has the biggest regard for his agent, Jerry Maguire. This proves to be the hook that leads other elite athletes to want to work with Maguire.

Leadership lessons

In *Jerry Maguire*, Cruise's character shows us the trouble that ethics and the right values can get you into. Once he decides he wants to work in a different way, his company tries to destroy him, and nearly all his clients, for whom he's worked hard, show no loyalty to him, ditching him without discussing anything with him. People leave organisations all the time because they feel like their values don't align with the company's, or indeed that the company isn't delivering on the values that they're saying are important to them, meaning there's an integrity gap.

Many organisations and management articles big up the importance of trust, but the only trust on show in this film is between Maguire and Dorothy, and Maguire and Tidwell. There's also huge honesty between Tidwell and Maguire, with Maguire able to call him out, saying that he isn't delivering the goods on the field and that this is making it harder for Maguire to broker him a big deal. Trust and honesty go hand in hand.

Maguire also shows that he sees the big picture and the whole person, not just the talented bit of the person. He demonstrates this when he phones Tidwell's wife when she's worried about her husband.

In many ways the movie is telling us that we should

be brave and only work with the right people, whose values and actions align with our own. True *raison d'être* is evident here, as is the use of *unite*.

Key takeaways:

- Integrity is a leadership trait worth having.
- Listening to others makes them feel valued.
- Loyalty – have someone's back.
- Effort is essential to achieve results.

> Integrity and loyalty are synonymous with doing good. They are values everyone should aspire to and live by. They play a huge role in the building of trust, and as a result, relationships. How do you get good at these or where do you start? Well, you just get on with it: be honest, be straight with people, be a person of your word. Do what is right and good.

CHAPTER 13:
INSTITUTIONAL ABUSE

31: *One Flew Over the Cuckoo's Nest* (1975)

The storyline

This film, based on the novel by Ken Kesey and set in 1963, was produced by Michael Douglas and stars Jack Nicholson, Louise Fletcher, Danny DeVito and Christopher Lloyd.

Jack plays Randle McMurphy, who's jailed for the statutory rape of a 15-year-old. To get out of doing hard labour, he pretends to be mentally unwell, and is transferred to an asylum. The ward he's living on is run by Nurse Ratched (played by Fletcher), and she's a dominant, bullying, negative woman whom many of the patients are afraid of.

Two of the other patients are Billy, who has a stutter, and the deaf-mute Native American Chief Bromden. All of the patients apart from Nicholson and Chief are there on a voluntary basis and they're united by their lack of confidence.

Ratched correctly views McMurphy as a threat to her dominance and status on the ward. She demonstrates her power to him by rationing the patients' cigarettes and banning their card games. McMurphy, bored, but also wanting to broaden the patients' experience of life, escapes to meet his girlfriend, taking several patients with him. He steals a bus and they head to the ocean for a day out fishing.

On their return to the hospital, Ratched is very annoyed. After a while, one of the patients has a shouting argument with Ratched about cigarettes, and this spills into McMurphy fighting with the orderlies, and Chief joins in to support him. All three are sent down to the high-dependency ward. There, Chief reveals to McMurphy that he's able to speak and can hear; his behaviour is all an act. While in the HDU, McMurphy is administered ECT, electroconvulsive therapy. On his return to his ward, he pretends to be subdued and brain-damaged, and just as Ratched and the others start to believe this, he reveals that he's fine and laughs at her.

McMurphy realises that he really needs to move on and plans an escape with Chief. On the night that they are to escape, before they leave, they throw a party for the others. His girlfriend and another woman get access to the ward, and they bring loads of alcohol. McMurphy organises for Billy to have sex with his girlfriend's friend. It's a great party, but due to getting carried away with the occasion and the booze, McMurphy falls asleep and doesn't get to escape. He awakes when Ratched and the other staff members arrive to start their shift in the morning.

Ratched is furious and starts to berate Billy, trying to embarrass him in front of everyone. When he stands up for himself, she beats him down by saying she will tell his mother that he had sex with someone, which makes him fearful and subdues him.

McMurphy and Chief try to escape, but this is foiled and they end up fighting with the orderlies again.

Unexpectedly, Billy kills himself by using a piece of glass to cut his throat. McMurphy interprets Ratched's reaction as callous and disrespectful, and he almost strangles her to death, but is prevented from doing so by the orderlies.

After this McMurphy is missing from the ward for a short while, and Chief is disappointed, as he thinks he has escaped without him. Then Chief spots McMurphy being wheeled into his room. He's delighted, and once the orderly leaves, he goes in to see him. McMurphy clearly isn't himself. He's been lobotomised. Chief is devastated for his friend. As he cries, he uses a pillow to smother his McMurphy d to death. Then he smashes a window and escapes from the hospital, as the patients cheer him for doing so.

Leadership lessons

Everything about this hospital shouts controlling. It's a terrible place that belittles and humiliates the patients. The style of leadership here shouldn't be found in any organisation anywhere. It's all about power over those who are vulnerable and weak, and who shouldn't actually be there in the first place.

The idea of not judging a book by its cover is alive here, mostly with Chief, who's hiding out in the hospital and isn't mentally unwell in any way, which is one of the big reveals in the film.

The movie is also a great example of how leaders create culture, in that Ratched has it exactly how she wants it. She sets the tone and gets everyone to behave how she wants, and she reinforces this with bullying and psychological abuse, but also with physical punishments, such as the electric shock therapy for McMurphy and then the criminal lobotomy, which completely neutralises him, stupefying him. The film shows how those in control will keep cranking it up, to keep things how they want them to be.

There's also an element of being careful what you wish for, in that McMurphy thought the hospital would be an easy, soft option in comparison to doing hard labour in prison, which is why he pretended to be mentally ill in the first place.

Judgement, arguably poor, is evident when out of boredom, McMurphy starts to challenge Ratched, he might actually have been better served by keeping his head down and coming up with a strategic way of toppling her instead. He completely underestimates her, maybe because he can't see past the femininity and the nurse uniform. So, a bias in that regard. *One Flew over the Cuckoo's Nest* also shows us that sometimes in life all it takes is for someone to believe in a person for them to find their zest, self-esteem or confidence to live, which McMurphy ignites in the other patients. In that regard he's good at *unite*, and he can create a followership through influence, as opposed to Ratched, whose influence comes from her position of power.

Key takeaways:

- Control your emotions and thoughts and not others.
- Power in the wrong hands is dangerous.
- Culture is shaped. People decide whether it is positive or negative.
- Humiliation embarrasses and hurts people, by design.
- Fear can be overcome.
- Don't judge a book by its cover.

32: *Dead Poets Society* (1989)

The storyline

This film was directed by Peter Weir and stars Robin Williams. It's set in 1950s Vermont, in a boys' secondary boarding school. Williams plays the unorthodox English teacher John Keating, who's a graduate of Cambridge University, England. Now back as a teacher at his old secondary school, Keating tries to inspire his students by using the Latin phrase '*carpe diem*', which means 'seize the day'. To encourage them to see and understand life differently and from other perspectives, he gets the students to stand on their desks. He encourages them to be authentic by finding their own style of walking in the grounds of the school. He stops them reading the scholarly introduction to the poems in their books, which has a formulaic way of appraising the poems, instead getting them to think about what the meanings of the poems are and why the poets wrote them. This teaching style puts Keating in conflict with the ultra-conservative headmaster, Gale Nolan.

One of the new students finds out that when Keating was a student at their school, he ran a semi-rebellious underground reading club called the Dead Poets Society. This student, Neil, gets his friends to restart it. The society impacts the students in terms of gaining confidence and using their voices to question why things are the way they are. Neil, as it turns out, loves acting and gets a part in a Shakespearean play. His father is against this, as he wants him to put 100 per cent into doing what's needed to get into Harvard. Keating helps another student, Todd, to be more in the moment and engage with his creative being by composing a poem live in front of the whole class. Another boy, Charlie, publishes a letter in the school newspaper about letting girls be admitted to their school.

Nolan wants to regain control, and beats Charlie, trying to get him to reveal the names of everyone in the Dead Poets Society, but Charlie doesn't give them up. Nolan also confronts Keating, who then speaks with all the boys and makes it clear to them that before they do something, they need to assess all the potential outcomes and consequences of the action.

The night before the play, Neil's dad tells him in the strongest of ways to drop out. Neil doesn't want to. Keating urges him to stand up to his father, so that he can show his father how much he's interested in acting. Neil defies his father, and his father retaliates by immediately removing him from the school and sending him to a military school. Feeling isolated, distressed and stuck, Neil takes his own life.

Neil's parents demand an investigation. Nolan leads this. Another student, Richard, to lessen the guilt he feels about what happened, but also to avoid being punished by Nolan, blames Keating and the Dead Poets Society and names all the members. Charlie is angry with Richard for this betrayal, and when Richard suggests the others should do the same and let Keating take the blame, Charlie punches him and is expelled.

Nolan calls each boy to his office, to get them to sign the false accusation that Richard has made against Keating. Todd doesn't want to sign it, but his parents force him to do so. As a result of all this, Keating is fired.

Nolan takes over teaching the English class. When Keating comes in to collect his things, Todd speaks up, saying he was forced to sign the letter. Nolan shouts at the boys, saying they'll all be expelled if they don't hold their tongues. Despite this, Todd and some of the other boys, but not Richard, stand on their desks and respectfully call out to Keating the now famous line, 'O Captain, my Captain!' A proud Keating thanks the boys, and leaves.

Leadership lessons

Dead Poets Society demonstrates the damage caused by lacking the freedom to be who you are. It shows how some people are controlled by others to their own detriment, and where only the controller benefits. We've seen this since the beginning of time, where people are persecuted for reasons of sexuality, religious beliefs, gender etc. etc. etc. This story demonstrates the dreadful consequences of creating environments where people are forced to conform and be inauthentic; it shows what can happen when people feel truly stuck with nowhere to go or breathe. At the same time, the film shows us that by creating a safe place and implementing measures that enable psychological safety, people can become positive, creative and happy.

The movie also highlights the dark lengths that some people will go to because there isn't an open, honest or logical way for them to keep the status quo that they want to hold on to.

Key takeaways:

- Institutional power has a dark history of wrongdoing.
- Authoritarianism benefits a very small minority.
- Listening to others makes them feel valued.
- Voice – some are afraid to use theirs for fear of reprisal.
- Toxic cultures are created, but so are positive ones.

33: *Sleepers* (1996)

The storyline

This movie, directed by Barry Levinson, stars some big names, including Brad Pitt, Robert De Niro, Kevin Bacon, Jason Patric, Dustin Hoffman and Minnie Driver.

In the summer of 1967, four boys steal a hot dog stand as a prank. They hold it at the top of the steps to a subway but underestimate its weight, and it crashes down the steps, crushing a man against a wall and killing him. The four boys are sentenced to detention at the Wilkinson Home for Boys in Upstate New York. While there, they're subjected to torture as well as physical, emotional and sexual abuse from some of the guards.

The boys convince a bigger boy whom everyone respects to join the boys' football team in their annual game against the guards. This boy is Rizzo and he's an excellent player. The boys win the game, but it comes at a great cost, as the guards lock them in solitary for weeks, beating them regularly. Rizzo is beaten to death, but his family are told he died from pneumonia.

The night before the boys leave, they're brutally raped by the guards, more so than before. Once out, the boys agree not to tell anyone, as they wouldn't be believed.

Now, the film moves to the 80s. Two of the boys, John and Tommy, are criminals. They bump into one of the guards from the home and they kill him, in front of a number of witnesses. One of the other boys, Michael (played by Brad Pitt), is now the assistant district attorney, and he ensures the case is assigned to him. He plans to sabotage the case and use it to expose the evil at the home, while also getting his boyhood friends off. He will need help from the fourth boy, Shakes (played by Jason Patric), who works for the *New York Times*; King Benny, an elderly hoodlum whom the boys used to run errands for when they were young; and Carol (played by Minnie Driver), who was a childhood friend of theirs.

Michael orchestrates it that an alcoholic lawyer, Danny Snyder (Hoffman), will defend his friends. Michael secretly provides the questions that Snyder is to ask all the witnesses, and he also arranges for the guards who abused them way back to be called as witnesses, as character references for the murdered guard.

The witnesses to the murder are either easily discounted or scared off. Through Snyder, Michael gets one of the guards to admit all the evil acts carried out at the home, and Shakes is able to manoeuvre Father Bobby, a priest played by Robert De Niro, to perjure himself and give John and Tommy an alibi for the time of the shooting. The friends are acquitted. All the guards get punished in one way or another.

One of the more satisfying outcomes is for prison guard Nokes, the Kevin Bacon character. He has gambling debts, which King Benny buys. He tries to sell them to a big-time drug dealer, who isn't interested, until Benny explains that Nokes was the guard who killed his brother, Rizzo. The dealer buys the debt and has Nokes killed.

After all of this, Michael stops working as a lawyer,

Shakes remains a journalist, Carol continues to be a social worker, John dies from alcohol poisoning, and Tommy is killed by another criminal.

Leadership lessons

A great message in *Sleepers* is that even if you suffer in life and are very badly traumatised as a child, you can come out the other side and live a reasonably positive and happy life. The examples are Michael and Shakes, but of course the other two main characters are sucked into a life of crime and their lives are cut short by booze and the bullet. Trauma again.

Pitt gives a great performance as Michael, someone who's brilliantly strategic, who's mapped out every single chess move possible and in his head is already in a position of checkmate. He's also warm and compassionate and therefore has many of the attributes of a useful leader, and he makes great decisions, which shows he has sound judgement.

Father Bobby offers us someone who does good, and whose actions always add value for others.

Key takeaways:

- Institutional power has a dark history of wrongdoing.
- Physical and sexual abuse is so wrong wrong wrong.
- Trauma damages us, but we can see a therapist and survive.

We need to acknowledge that institutional abuse is something that happens, and we must put time into preventing and detecting it, and also supporting those who have been abused. This is really about the abuse of power; those who carry out the abuse have the power and the opportunity to do so. We need to protect the vulnerable by encouraging and supporting whistleblowing, by creating opportunities to speak up, and by uncovering and preventing the protection of organisational reputation by stopping the cover-ups, so the truth can come out.

To drive home the point about how horrendous institutional abuse is we just need to remind ourselves of some of the words used to represent it, such as physical and sexual abuse, trauma, institutional power, authoritarianism, toxic cultures, control, power, humiliation and fear.

CHAPTER 14:
THE LOST

34: *Trainspotting* (1996)

The storyline

This film is based on the novel by Irvine Welsh and directed by Danny Boyle. Leading roles are played by Ewan McGregor and Robert Carlyle.

Mark Renton (McGregor) is an unemployed heroin addict who lives with his parents and has a group of friends he scores with a lot. He decides to try to get off the smack and live a more positive life. He has a host of adventures while clean, but he eventually relapses back to heroin. Much of the film shows the social deprivation and the horror of life on heroin, including the death of one of the group's baby because of parental negligence due to being under the influence.

A shoplifting incident leads to Renton having to go to rehab to avoid going to jail. He relapses again, but his concerned parents lock him in his room, forcing him to go cold turkey and get off the heroin again. Clean now but bored with life, Renton ends up in London working for an estate agent. One of his friends from Edinburgh, the wildly violent Begbie (Carlyle), who's wanted by the police for armed robbery, finds Renton and hides out at his place. Begbie and another friend of Renton's get him sacked from his job, and the three of them move back to Edinburgh.

The original friend group, some still using smack, get involved in a scam to buy heroin at a knockdown price. They return to London with it and make four times what they spent on the heroin and retire to a hotel room to sleep after partying hard. Renton wakes and leaves with all the money, to start a new life. Begbie is volcanic when he awakes and realises that this has happened. This results in the hotel staff calling the police because of the disturbance, leading to Begbie's arrest.

Leadership lessons

Trainspotting shows the dangers and chaos that come from not having a useful *raison d'être*. All of these guys are lost, and it's due to their missing a positive *raison d'être*. Sadly, their *raisons d'être* and lives have been hijacked by highly addictive heroin. The film shows that when *raison d'être* is hijacked to this extent, you can't really have friends. They all just have acquaintances and are brought together by their addictive need for heroin.

This poor *raison d'être* makes it difficult for them to have *expertise*; they do have some, but it's massively diluted and hidden by heroin, as is their ability to have a say, with *independence*. They don't have a say in their own lives. *Unite* doesn't exist; they can't really unite apart from when it comes to scoring or sharing heroin.

The film is a great example of Maslow's hierarchy of needs, in that none of them can self-actualise, as they can't meet their own biological needs and can't be secure and safe.

Also, Renton cheats Begbie out of money, showing that there's no honour amongst thieves. On the other hand, Renton doesn't like him, so maybe he thinks that this makes it okay.

No one does good, no one. They have strengths, but we don't get to see them; we just get to see their weaknesses, and they all play to these weaknesses.

Their culture is clear. The artefacts, espoused values and basic underlying assumptions are all aligned: it's all about drugs.

Key takeaways:

- You can be totally lost.
- There is a rock bottom.

> The best thing to do is to support people and prevent them from ever finding themselves in the position where they need to try the drugs that will bring about their downfall. To do this, we need to recognise trauma and damaged self-esteem early, and then treat these, so that people aren't tempted to use these substances to deal with the emotional pain they're suffering. For those who find themselves stuck on these substances, it's about talking to addiction experts and seeking the necessary support to help them get their lives back.

CHAPTER 15:

DON'T JUDGE A BOOK BY ITS COVER

35: *Die Hard* (1988)

The storyline

This is an action movie directed by John McTiernan, starring Bruce Willis as a detective and Alan Rickman as the leader of an Eastern European terrorist group.

John McClane, (Willis), an NYPD cop, is in LA to try to win back Holly, his wife, (played by Bonnie Bedelia) who's now living in LA and working for a large company. He goes to the company's Christmas party, being held in an office tower block. While McClane is using the toilet to freshen up, the terrorist group takes all the people at the party hostage.

Hans Gruber (Rickman) intends to break into the company's vault and steal over $600 million in untraceable bearer bonds. However, he's unable to get the codes to open the vault, so has to drill it open. Gruber realises that they haven't got everyone in the building hostage, as someone is causing them problems from other parts of the building, and we know this someone is McClane.

McClane is able to notify the LAPD by radio that there are crimes happening in the office. They think he's pranking them but agree to send a car round anyway. McClane continues to spoil Gruber's plans and manages to kill a few terrorists and steal some of their C4 explosives and all their detonators.

The LAPD cop who comes to investigate what he thinks is a prank call has a look around the reception of the office tower block, and finds the terrorists there, who are dressed as reception security, to be helpful. He leaves satisfied that everything is okay. McClane sees that he's departing and has an outrageous idea to raise the alarm. He drops the dead body of a terrorist, tied to a chair, from more than twenty storeys up, and it lands on the bonnet of the police car, shocking the cop.

The terrorists quickly react and fire on the cop car with machine guns, hoping to kill the cop before he reports back to his department that there is indeed a major criminal event taking place at the tower block. The cop car is destroyed, but the cop is unwounded and he's able to raise the alarm.

The police then send a SWAT team to storm the building, against the advice and warnings of McClane and the cop from the destroyed car. The SWAT team are repelled by the terrorists, who have heavy weaponry including shoulder-held missile launchers.

The FBI turns up and takes control of the law

enforcement response. They immediately turn off the power, which actually opens the vault. Gruber had predicted this, and now the terrorists can access what they came for.

To divert the FBI's attention, Gruber gives them a list of fake requests. As part of this, he wants helicopters to take everyone, including the hostages, to the airport, where he can take a jet to freedom. However, his actual plan is to blow up the roof using the C4, killing everyone in the helicopters, and faking his death, which will allow him to slip away unnoticed with the bearer bonds.

A news report alerts him to the fact that McClane's wife is present, so he keeps her close to him, in case she becomes useful at a later stage. McClane manages to intervene and move everyone from the rooftop, meaning that when Gruber blows it up, all the hostages are saved.

McClane, who has been avoiding Gruber, has to go to him to negotiate for the release of his wife. Gruber can now personally exact revenge on McClane for all the problems he's caused him. Apparently unarmed, McClane surrenders himself to Gruber, and he's about to be killed, but then he surprises Gruber by snatching hold of a pistol that he had taped to his back. This element of surprise is all that McClane requires, as he's able to shoot Gruber, who falls out of a window and to his death.

Once McClane is outside, the cop from the destroyed car is alert and kills one of the captured terrorists, who was about to kill McClane.

Leadership lessons

Arrogance is at play in *Die Hard*, as is the underestimation of others. The LAPD think they can just turn up with their armoured vehicles and they discount what they're told. The FBI then arrive and do the exact same thing, and the consequences for both agencies are serious. They completely ignore what the LAPD patrol cop is trying to tell them. Arrogance is their Achilles' heel and is predicted by Gruber. Individuals and teams can be arrogant and complacent and make errors. That's why individual- and team-level self-awareness is important.

Gruber is a precision planner, and it's only by chance that he's foiled and fails. McClane wasn't supposed to be in LA at all. The other piece of bad luck for Gruber is how strong an opponent McClane is. He has huge motivation, in terms of wanting to save his wife, and he has the skill set, knowledge and resourcefulness to do so.

Also at play here is the danger of judging a book by its cover, which leads to dismissing a person and not recognising their abilities. As previously mentioned, the LAPD patrol cop isn't taken seriously by his superiors at the LAPD or the FBI, because he's just a patrol man, and not as shiny and important as them. Frequently in organisations there are brilliant people who aren't in senior positions because they don't want to be, not because of a lack of ability or aptitude. They just love what they do. Some people in leadership positions wrongly believe that staff in lower positions are there due to reasons of aptitude or ability, and therefore they don't listen to those staff members, dismissing anything they say very quickly. This is a huge error and is very damaging to the organisation.

McClane proves that motivation is one of the greatest attributes. He achieves so much, which is mostly down to motivation. Individuals and teams with high levels of motivation do this all the time, and where we get to see it most easily is in sport, with team sports and individual sports. We see what McClane achieves by getting stuck in and being resilient, and in that regard, he makes his own luck; as many successful people point out, by keeping at it, you increase the chances of good things happening to you. McClane also shows that he has good judgement throughout.

Key takeaways:

- Don't judge a book by its cover.
- Arrogance can be blinding, so do develop your self-awareness.

36: *My Left Foot* (1989)

The storyline

This is a film based on the life of Christy Brown, who was born with cerebral palsy in 1932. It was directed by Jim Sheridan and stars Daniel Day-Lewis as Christy and Brenda Fricker as his mother

Christy is unable to walk or talk. He's loved by his large family, and exists there, existing being the right word. Christy is in the house while his pregnant mother falls down the stairs. She's incapacitated and at risk as she's also in labour. Christy stretches every sinew he possesses to raise the alarm and his neighbours arrive on the scene. He's a hero.

The family have low expectations of Christy given his cerebral palsy, and his father is proud as punch and celebrates with exhilaration Christy's achievement of writing the word 'MOTHER' on the floor with a piece of chalk, using his left foot, the only part of his body he can control. He hoists him up and carries him to the local pub, telling everyone what's happened. Christy takes up painting, using this left foot, and becomes really good at it.

He's popular in his community and gets included in things that boys his age do, like having a kickabout. He shows his determination when in goal, making a save by trapping the ball between his head and the ground, and not giving up despite the striker repeatedly kicking the ball and Christy. In fact, he shows an ability to adapt and distract, by biting the striker on the ankle. A highlight of the film is Christy being given the responsibility to take a penalty kick and being carried to and laid down next to the ball, where he summons his left foot to do the necessary, and blasts the ball past the goalie, scoring.

Money becomes even tighter for the family when his dad is laid off, but his mother, who is his saviour, has been saving a little bit each week for years. She finally comes up with enough to buy Christy a wheelchair, granting him more independence and dignity.

Christy starts attending a school for people with cerebral palsy. He's championed by the owner, Eileen Cole, who helps get his paintings into an exhibition. Christy falls in love with her and is devastated when she gets engaged to someone. He feels suicidal, but he manages to overcome these feelings and get on with his life. The death of his father is another major blow for him, but it inspires him to write his life story, which is called *My Left Foot*.

Leadership lessons

A massive theme in *My Left Foot* is how individuals can overcome the biggest obstacles, and how despite massive disadvantages, an individual can do more than just survive, but actually thrive. Christy is resilient and tough, as evidenced when he puts his head in harm's way and traps the football, and despite getting kicked, won't back down. His disability is severe, but he won't give way, not an inch, to the able-bodied boy.

Christy is backed by his mother to the nth degree, and for all of us, knowing that someone has your back in this way is hugely important. This gives him strength and a foundation to build from. It's worth pointing out that this is something each of us has the ability to do for someone else. We can be that rock, be that safety and security layer for them, which we know is vital from a Maslow perspective. Christy also knows that his siblings love him and his dad is proud of him, and all of this must congregate in his psyche in a good, strong, positive way, and motivate him.

From an EDI and bias perspective, the film reminds us not to make assumptions or prejudge people – and if you did, Christy would prove you wrong all the time. The film allows us to see the levels of prejudice he encounters. It also reminds us to see the full person, and to not assume that a person with a disability is unable to fall in love or feel the huge disappointment and emotional dive that can sometimes come with rejection. Everyone has a part to play in a family, in a team, in a society, if we let them.

Key takeaways:

- Never give up.
- Resilience keeps us afloat in choppy waters.
- Support the disadvantaged.
- Don't judge a book by its cover.
- Sometimes blood is thicker than water.

> Judging a book by its cover is very damaging to others. It destroys people and communities. Avoiding this is about recognising your bias and prejudice. It's about recognising the concepts of conscious and unconscious bias. It's about educating people, so they can change their thinking and behaviours. From there we need to accept and support others.

CHAPTER 16:
GOOD AND EVIL

37: *Schindler's List* (1993)

The storyline

This is a film set during World War II and directed by Steven Spielberg. The film is based on the true story of Oskar Schindler (played by Liam Neeson), a wealthy German businessman who owned a number of factories in Krakow. He saved about a thousand Jews from certain death, by giving them jobs in his businesses.

At the beginning of the film, Schindler is money mad and sees the war as an opportunity to get rich, and he does. However, he quietly disagrees with the hatred and killing and starts to employ as many Jews as he can to prevent them from being killed, under the guise that they're vitally important to the German war effort. At the same time, Schindler, a member of the Nazi Party, tries to build some influence with Nazi officials and officers, mostly by paying them bribes.

SS officer Goth (played by Ralph Fiennes) has orders to manage the building of a concentration camp. He also oversees the murder of thousands of Jews and appears to get great enjoyment from shooting some of them himself.

Schindler puts a lot of effort into building a relationship with Goth as he recognises Goth has a certain amount of power, and is also quite brutal, so he needs to stay on the right side of him, if he wants to achieve his goal. To try to protect the Jews who work for him, Schindler pays Goth a lot of money to allow him to use them to build a small camp at his factory, which will be a safer place for them to live than their current camp. Schindler spends more and more money on bribes to try to keep the Jews who work for him safe.

The Allies start to win the war, and orders arrive from Berlin to move the Jews in Krakow to Auschwitz. Schindler is extremely worried, as he knows this is a death sentence. He comes up with another idea: to move the Jews who work for him to a town in Czechoslovakia where he's going to build a factory that makes weapons. Goth agrees following another big bribe. Schindler prepares a list of 1,100 people to go.

The male workers are transported by train to Czechoslovakia as planned, but an error of some kind means all the women and girls are transported to Auschwitz. Schindler goes there and has to pay another huge bribe to the SS officer there to have his original agreement with Goth upheld.

At his new factory in his hometown, he continues to bribe the Nazis to keep his Jewish workers safe. He runs out of money just as the Allies win the war. As a

Nazi Party member, Schindler now has to flee west to surrender to the Americans, as waiting for the Russians to arrive would mean certain death for him. Before he flees, he convinces the Nazi guards at his factory to disobey their orders, which are to kill every Jew at the factory. As he departs, the Jews at his factory present him with a letter signed by them that highlights his goodness and all that he's done for them.

Leadership lessons

The characters played by Neeson and Fiennes in *Schindler's List* are great case studies. One is doing his utmost to do good; the other is an excellent representation of evil in its worst form. Schindler is full of positive values and wellbeing as a saviour of others, and someone who despairs that he can't do more or save more people, and Goth is a selfish exterminator who sees Jews as nothing more than cockroaches. As a leader, Schindler has total followership, whereas Goth only gets followership through his rank and the fear he generates.

The film raises the questions of how we become who we are as people and leaders, and whether evil exists because of nature or nurture. There's also an interesting representation of hierarchy and values in an organisation, where Hitler, Himmler and the rest of those evil Nazis create structures and systems that enable and reward people like Goth to carry out acts of evil. But we see that even in the most horrendous of circumstances, good can survive as long as people have the courage to persevere, as Schindler does.

Returning to Edgar Schein, you can clearly see the culture here. It's a culture of hate and evil in which there's perfect alignment between the artefacts, espoused values and the results, and the basic underlying assumptions aren't hidden either – they're brazenly championed in public with pride, and without shame.

Key takeaways:

- Love of others and oneself is essential for peace.
- Effort can help to move mountains.
- Doing good is the meaning of life and small acts of good count.
- Evil wants to destroy all that is good in the world.

38: The *Lord of the Rings* series (2001–2003)

The storyline

This series consists of over nine hours of film time and comprises *The Fellowship of the Ring*, *The Two Towers* and *The Return of the King*. All the films are directed by Peter Jackson and based on the novel *The Lord of the Rings* by JRR Tolkien. The films are set in a place called Middle-earth and are a great example of the forces for good doing battle with the forces of evil.

Evil is represented by the dark lord Sauron. He needs to get hold of a Ring of Power (the One Ring), which he once created, in order to regain his physical form and become all-conquering, all-powerful and undefeatable, ensuring a world of danger and hate.

The ring is in the possession of a hobbit called Frodo. He's part of a fellowship that consists of three other hobbits, an elf, a dwarf, a ranger who's descended from the last overking of mankind, a champion warrior and the good wizard Gandalf. They take on the task of destroying the ring in the volcano where it was created, and throughout their quest they're hunted by evil wizards, orcs, goblins and other mythical creatures under the power of Sauron, while Sauron's armies attack the various tribes of mankind.

Frodo achieves the goal of destroying the ring and Sauron, but only because all the forces for good align: the different tribes of mankind, the elves and the dwarfs, who all resent and dislike each other, rebuild their relationships of old, taking a risk and starting to trust each other, and they sacrifice and die for each other.

Leadership lessons

One of the lessons in the *Lord of the Rings* series is not to judge a book by its cover. There are all these brilliant warriors and wizards on both sides, but it's two small hobbits, Frodo and Sam, who are the real heroes of the piece, showing huge bravery. In some ways, this happens in organisations too, where most of the attention is focused on the board, the CEO, the CFO, the COO etc., and other professional types like architects, accountants, lawyers and doctors, and the majority of the staff, usually in lower-paying positions, who deliver the products or services that the company exists to deliver, are invisible unsung heroes.

Another theme in the films is conflict, where different powers are fighting for control. Here, it's good versus evil, but in companies there are frequent power games too, which are rarely in the best interest of the shareholders, customers or staff.

The series also shows that alone, we have very little power, but when we combine with other like-minded people, we become a force to be reckoned with. This presents itself in industry in terms of learning to compromise and collaborate with others to achieve something. It's also important when it comes to workers' rights: being part of a union gives those without a voice or a say the opportunity to safeguard their positions.

A big message in the movies is that in times of war, life is terrible for everyone; no one wins from a wellbeing perspective, no one.

Two quotes really resonated with me. King Théoden asks, **'What can men do against such reckless hate?'** And Sam states: **'There is some good in the world and it's worth fighting for.'**

But the most poignant quote for me is from a conversation between Gandalf and Frodo, where Gandalf attempts to soothe the isolated, worried and distressed hobbit by saying, **'All we have to do is decide what to do with the time that is given to us.'** This might be the greatest piece of advice for all of humankind ever and might help us to chill out and stop making an absolute arse of everything. It might just enable us all to focus on what's important, and to add real value to the world, as opposed to all the negative and terrible things we see happening in the world today.

Key takeaways:

- Evil exists.
- Choose to do good.
- All we have to do in life is decide what to do with the time that's given to us.

39: The *Harry Potter* series (2001–2011)

The storyline

There are eight films based on seven novels by JK Rowling. Similar to the *Lord of the Rings* series, this is a great example of the epic battle between good and evil, where good is represented by the boy wizard Harry Potter, and evil by the extremely powerful wizard Voldemort.

Harry (played by Daniel Radcliffe) is an orphan being raised by his horrible uncle and aunt. At age 11, he's made aware that he's a wizard and is to attend a school of magic, Hogwarts. As Harry grows up, he has several adventures, and he learns that Voldemort (played by Ralph Fiennes) used to be a Hogwarts student called Tom Riddle, but he chose a path of evil. In his quest for almighty power, he killed Harry's parents, but failed to kill Harry, due to an old-magic spell cast by his mother. This created a small link between the minds of Harry and Voldemort.

The headteacher of Hogwarts, Professor Dumbledore, is the leader of the powers of good. He understands that Voldemort can't be killed because he has used dark magic to split his soul into several parts and hidden these parts in horcruxes. The horcruxes could be anywhere, but until all of these are found and destroyed, Voldemort can't be physically killed.

Against the odds, Harry and his friends find and destroy the horcruxes, meaning that Harry can actually kill Voldemort – and Harry achieves this in a battle. Now Harry has the elder wand, the most powerful wand in the world, making him all-powerful, but he deliberately breaks it, as he doesn't want himself or anyone else to have such unlimited power ever again.

Leadership lessons

There are many positive insights that we can take from these movies. One important one relates to individual choice. Tom Riddle chose to go down the path of evil, going on to become Voldemort. Every day, we all have choices to make. Are we choosing to do good, or to do bad, or to do something in between? The choice really is ours.

The series also shows the importance of friends and friendship, and of being there for each other when times are good, but especially when they're not.

Leadership is striking in the films, Voldemort's style

contrasting with that of Harry and Dumbledore. We see the difference between leadership by force, which does not create real followership, versus leadership by choice, which creates authentic followership, and is far more useful and powerful.

There are a number of brilliant quotes from Dumbledore that are meaningful and inspiring, and arguably wisdom that we should all live by, to be the best versions of ourselves. Two key ones are: **'It is our choices, Harry, that show who we truly are, far more than our abilities'** and **'It matters not what someone is born, but what they grow to be'.** The latter should take us away from being prejudiced against others just because they're born a particular way, be that of a certain race or gender or sexuality or disability, and this is a lesson for every individual, family, school, community and organisation to live by.

Another true insight from Dumbledore: **'Perhaps those who are best suited to power are those who have never sought it'.** This gives rise to questions of how best to select people for leadership positions in companies and communities, as we frequently see people who are clearly in certain jobs for the wrong reasons and are clearly doing a bad job. Remember: Mind the Gap.

Key takeaways:

- Power corrupts.
- Choose to do good.
- Equality is about giving everyone a chance, everyone.

40: *Macbeth* (2015)

The storyline

The movie is directed by Justin Kurzel. Michael Fassbender takes the role of Macbeth, and Marion Cotillard is Lady Macbeth.

Obviously, the source of this film is the play by Shakespeare from 1605, which is viewed as one of the best plays ever, and as a result is much better than any *Macbeth* movie can ever be. It's believed that Shakespeare wrote the play to court favour with the new king, James I. This was around the time of the Gunpowder Plot, and Shakespeare wanted to create a piece that warned people about the disastrous consequences, physical and psychological, that awaited any person who would try to harm a king. He had been in contact with Queen Elizabeth I to a degree, but didn't have a standing with James, and James was a bit paranoid – but then both his parents had been assassinated, so he had every reason to feel that way. *Macbeth* was well received by the king, who viewed it as supportive, and this allowed Shakespeare to be seen in a very positive light at a time when he'd been in the spotlight for the wrong reasons due to his daughter's anti-monarchy views.

In the movie, Macbeth is a popular and well-respected general and leader. He has a chance meeting with three witches, who prophesises that he'll become the thane of Cawdor and the king. Macbeth begins to wonder if what the witches said could be true when, soon after, he does indeed become the thane of Cawdor.

Macbeth, who has won the war on behalf of King Duncan, is to be honoured by the king, who will stay the night at Macbeth's castle. He shares all of this with his wife, who is very excited by what she hears. She puts all her energy into convincing Macbeth that he shouldn't leave anything to chance and should grab the opportunity to kill King Duncan and declare himself king. They hatch a plan.

The king's servants are drugged, to the extent they black out and won't remember anything. Then Macbeth kills Duncan with a dagger and smears the servants with his blood, so it looks like they killed the king. However Macbeth is distracted by a hallucination and the realisation of what he's done, so his wife has to take over the staging of the scene.

The next day, the king is found dead, and Macbeth kills the servants, apparently in a fit of rage, but really to prevent them from saying anything. Both of King Duncan's sons flee, out of fear for their own lives. This makes them look guilty, and in their absence, Macbeth declares himself king. Banquo, who was present when the witches told Macbeth about his future, starts to become suspicious of Macbeth.

The witches also made a prophecy about Banquo: that his sons would become kings. Macbeth heard this and knowing that all the prophecies about him have come true, he decides he has to kill Banquo and his son, so that he will remain as king.

Macbeth hires some assassins to kill Banquo and his son. They end Banquo, but his son escapes. This makes Macbeth more agitated, more paranoid, and he's having hallucinations. To preserve his position, Macbeth consults with the witches again, and commits a number of other murders, including the wife and children of Macduff.

All of this badness has a tremendous negative impact on Lady Macbeth's mental state. She appears distressed and is seen sleepwalking at night, and while in a trance she talks about all the heinous things she's got her husband to do and is seen trying to wash imaginary blood from her clean hands. She ends up completely losing her mind and killing herself.

Macduff raises an army, and he and Macbeth end up in combat against each other. Macbeth realises the game is up, but rather than surrender as requested by Macduff, he continues to fight and is killed and beheaded by Macduff.

Leadership lessons

The biggest theme in *Macbeth* relates to darkness. Lady Macbeth is the dark thinker and is always pushing her husband to commit dangerous and dark acts. She convinces him to kill the king, place the blame elsewhere and take the throne for himself. We see conniving like this frequently in the workplace, where people plot to get promotions by courting favour, by doing huge amounts of brown-nosing, while trying to damage their competitors' standing in the company.

Another major lesson here relates to the consequences of choosing a dark path, in that once you start down this road, it really never ends. This is similar to when someone does something wrong in a company, or in life, and then to keep it from coming out and thus harming them, they tell more and more lies or take other actions to cover up whatever they did in the first place. You can see this in companies sometimes, when a director or CEO appears to be supporting the poor behaviours of some people, or promoting people who don't seem good enough, or not sacking people who deserve to be sacked. More often than not, the CEO can't take action against the person because at an earlier stage of their career, the CEO did something to compromise themselves and they can't afford for it to come out. Or they didn't take the right action against a person when they should have, and as a result they condoned their poor behaviour, and now they can't reprimand the person as it's way too late, as they've enabled the behaviour for years.

Macbeth also presents a narrative in which those who do wrong get their comeuppance and get caught in the end. This is a positive narrative, but it doesn't always ring true in life.

Emotional wellbeing is sacrificed by the couple, and their actions impact their physical wellbeing too, all in the pursuit of enhancing their social and financial wellbeing, even though socially and financially their standing was already great. In terms of Maslow's hierarchy, all their needs were met, but they take actions that impede their wellbeing and pay the biggest price that can be paid, with their lives.

Like other dictator types, to get what they want they impede and actively damage the safety and security of others, and also the love and belonging of others. In addition, their *raison d'être* changes to become damaging and toxic. They already had *independence* and *expertise* and had *united* the people around them. They actually undo everything that was good in their lives. Both Macbeth and Lady Macbeth display poor decision-making capabilities.

Key takeaway:

- Doing bad changes you and actually damages you.

Evil exists. We need to understand this fact. That's a starting point. We need to hold those who commit evil acts to account via whatever structures and systems exist to enable this, and where they don't exist, we need to create them.

People do lots of good things for others. Lovely acts of kindness and goodness. Things that make a difference.

We don't always realise the value of doing small acts of kindness. We think they're small and don't matter, but they all add up. I do a lot of hiking and sometimes I use maps. And on the map, one degree looks like it's tiny and meaningless, but in reality it's huge, especially if you try to walk that one degree, because in reality it's sixty-nine miles.

CHAPTER 17:

EQUALITY, DIVERSITY AND INCLUSION (EDI)

41: *Dances with Wolves* (1990)

The storyline

Dances with Wolves is an American Western, produced by, directed by and starring Kevin Costner.

In the 1860s, John Dunbar (played by Costner) is a lieutenant in the Union army. He's wounded at a battle in Tennessee. The surgeon is set to amputate his leg, but Dunbar decides to die in battle instead. He creates a furore by riding a horse along the enemy lines. This distracts the Confederates, and the Union army use this to their advantage and win the battle. Dunbar survives, his leg is saved and he's viewed as hero. He's rewarded by a choice of posting for his next job. He requests and is given the American Frontier.

Dunbar is given Fort Sedgwick by the commander of Fort Hays, Major Fambrough. He's accompanied there by Timmons, a wagon driver. When they get there, it's rundown and deserted. Dunbar decides to stay and build it back up. However, because Major Fambrough kills himself and Timmons is murdered by Pawnees on the journey back, no one in the army knows that Dunbar is out there.

After a while, Dunbar becomes friendly with his Sioux neighbours. This eventually becomes a very close relationship, and he's accepted into the tribe, and is given the name 'Dances with Wolves' due to his rapport with a wolf cub called Two Socks. Dunbar learns the language of the tribe and marries into the tribe and lives in their camp.

The Sioux chief, Ten Bears, is worried about the amount of new white settlers in their region, so he decides that they should all decamp to their winter base. Dunbar will go with them, but first he needs to go back to Fort Sedgwick to retrieve his diary, for if it were to fall into army hands, the information in it would allow the army to track the Sioux tribe and he doesn't want this.

When he gets back to the fort, the army is there, and because he's in Sioux clothing, the soldiers attack and capture Dunbar. His diary has been stolen and he's unable to prove his story. Because he refuses to help the army track down the Native American tribe, they charge him with desertion, shoot his wolf and start to transport him back east as a prisoner.

The Sioux tribe, who now view Dunbar as family, are tracking Dunbar and his captors. They attack the convoy, kill the soldiers and free Dunbar.

Once at the winter camp, Dunbar decides to leave with his Sioux wife, Stands with a Fist, as he fears his being there will endanger them all. He has a number of meaningful exchanges with Kicking Bird, Smiles a Lot and Wind in His Hair, and then departs.

Leadership lessons

Dances with Wolves is a very clear example of good versus evil, and evil here is the white man's imperialistic exploitation of America and the genocide of its indigenous people, which makes the film a striking exploration of EDI too.

The performances of Costner and his Native American co-stars show that difference does exist, but that we're also very, very alike in many ways, which is a good thing (a point made by Shakespeare as far back as 1598 in his Shylock speech in *The Merchant of Venice*). In this film, Dunbar and the Native Americans share much and live side by side, and they come together to do good. What links Dunbar and the Native Americans is their decency and goodness, their honour and desire to be good. This heavily contrasts with the bad and evil acts carried out by many of the army characters in the film, who lie, cheat and kill.

While *raison d'être* is strong in all characters, the soldiers are aligned with doing bad. All characters have an *expertise* in killing and survival, but the voice of the Native Americans diminishes, and they have very little *independence*. Dunbar and the senior Native Americans have the ability to create followership, but that doesn't extend to their enemies in the army. This film is a great example of what happens in situations with a complete lack of EDI.

Key takeaways:

- Voice – some are afraid to use theirs for fear of reprisal.
- Listening to others makes them feel valued.
- Recognise the similarities, celebrate the differences.
- Hate is easy, it is better to understand and accept others and yourself instead.
- Loyalty – have someone's back.

42: *Chariots of Fire* (1981)

The storyline

Chariots of Fire is a film set in the UK that was produced by David Puttnam. It's based on the true story of British sprinters Eric Liddell, a very godly Scottish Christian, and Harold Abrahams, an English Jew. Ben Cross plays Abrahams and Ian Charleson plays Liddell. Other stars include Nigel Havers, Ian Holm and John Gielgud.

The film has become synonymous with an amazing musical score by Vangelis, which is used to great effect when a number of the athletes are running in slow motion on the beach at St Andrews.

In 1919, Abrahams is a student at Cambridge University. He experiences antisemitism from staff there, but focuses on his sprinting, winning a number of national competitions, while also falling in love.

Liddell loves running and views it as a way of celebrating and honouring God. He and Abrahams end up meeting on the track in a 100-metres race, with Liddell winning. Abrahams, who was unbeaten until that point, is devastated.

A professional trainer, Mussabini, explains how he can help him to improve, and they team up. The Cambridge seniors criticise Abrahams as 'ungentlemanly' for hiring a professional trainer of Italian heritage. Abrahams interprets this as antisemitism and class elitism and ignores it.

Liddell is criticised by his sister, an extremely devout Christian, for neglecting his duty to God because he misses some prayers, but he tries to reassure her by being adamant that he runs for God.

Abrahams and Liddell get selected to represent Great Britain at the 1924 Olympics in Paris. While on the boat to France, Liddell finds out that the heats for the 100-metres race are on a Sunday, and he refuses to race on the Christian sabbath, despite pressure from the Prince of Wales and the British Olympic Committee.

A solution is presented by another athlete, Lord Lindsay (played by Havers), who wins a silver in the 400-metres hurdles. He suggests that Liddell take his place in the 400 metres, which doesn't have any heats on a Sunday. Liddell is delighted and accepts. Liddell's refusal to run on the sabbath gets worldwide newspaper coverage.

Abrahams loses the 200-metres race, as expected, to the Americans, but he achieves his ultimate goal and wins the 100-metres final. Both he and his coach Mussabini, who isn't allowed into the grounds to watch the race, are delighted.

The Americans are also favourites for the 400-metres race, and their coach dismisses Liddell as having no chance of winning. Liddell wins the gold, and the British team returns home triumphant.

At the end of the film, we learn that Abrahams lived a long life, but Liddell went to China to do missionary work and died in a Japanese prison camp towards the end of World War II.

Leadership lessons

In *Chariots of Fire*, Abrahams and Liddell are very different types of people, but they're united by their love for sprinting, their ability, and the fact that they both have obstacles blocking them from achieving what they want, and these obstacles are the bias of others. For Liddell, it's his family and how the Church are treating him, even though he's clear that he's abiding by his faith and he makes a huge sacrifice in not running the 100-metres race to prove this. For Abrahams, it's the snobbish elite and closed culture that he encounters at Cambridge.

What also unites them is their willingness to listen and reflect: they take on board and analyse what's said to them, and then reflect and decide the best way forward, and which aspects of the criticisms are valid and which are not. These are serious leadership traits.

Abrahams also shows that he has an ability to see and think beyond the traditional ways of doing things, and he displays this by hiring the trainer Mussabini when others with more positional power are telling him not to.

We see a range of silos in play in terms of how different people and groups are divided off – Liddell from his family, from the elite running athletics, from the prince and other officials. But we also see how the people in different silos can be connected to create solutions that unite and bring success for all, and that's down to Lord Lindsay, who seems to have the knack for engaging and winning over people in the different silos and strata. Lord Lindsay is a connector of people. Some people have this talent, and it's a brilliant leadership ability to have.

There are also great examples of how natural talent plus hard work and smart thinking can lead to success, as Liddell, Lindsay and Abrahams all win medals.

For all the main characters, *raison d'être* is strong, which gives them huge focus. They have *expertise* too, as they clearly play to their strengths, and they make *independence* happen by finding ways to make others hear them. The film is a presentation of personal leadership and of taking responsibility for oneself. It also demonstrates how exclusion and bias help to create poor emotional wellbeing, which is something we need to remember.

Key takeaways:

- Innovation is a positive energy.
- Skill + effort = winning.
- Bias and prejudice have no place in a modern world.
- Closed cultures damage everyone in the ecosystem.
- A people connector can turn on the light for those who are stuck in the dark.

43: *Green Book* (2018)

The storyline

This American biographical film stars Viggo Mortensen as Italian-American bouncer Frank Vallelonga, and Mahershala Ali as the black American pianist Don Shirley. The film tells the true story of a music tour Don took to the racist Deep South in 1962 accompanied by Frank, whom he hired as his driver, but also to do personal security for him.

The story starts in the Bronx, with Frank looking for new work as the club he works for is closing for building repairs. He ends up going for an interview and is hired by Don for his eight-week tour. The tour is supposed to end in time for them to make it back to New York for Christmas.

In 1962, black people weren't allowed to stay at certain hotels or eat in certain restaurants, which were for white people only. Frank is given a copy of the Green

Book, a guide book which lists places where black people are allowed to stay and eat.

Frank and Don don't initially hit it off. There's a big class difference between the men: though Don is black, he's highly educated and learned, and comes across as snooty and reserved, while Frank is blue collar, working class and rough around the edges. However, once Frank hears Don playing the piano, he softens towards him a little, as he realises he has talent. He also becomes an ally and a protector, as he's shocked by the level of racism Don encounters in the Deep South and worries about him.

Don warms to Frank too and wants to help him. He's appalled by the one-dimensional letters Frank is writing to his wife, so he tells Frank exactly what to write. Frank's wife loves his very romantic letters, and by the end Frank has mastered this new writing style.

Frank saves Don when he's taking a beating from some white men in a whites-only bar, and on another occasion, he bribes the cops to turn a blind eye after they hold Don for committing an act of homosexuality. Without Frank's intervention this may have badly damaged Don's career.

Frank starts to struggle with the level of racism Don is subjected to. Late one night they're pulled over by some traffic cops, and after being insulted, Frank punches one of the cops, which leads to them both being arrested. Don asks to make a call to his lawyer, and he phones the Attorney General, Robert F. Kennedy, who gets the two men released, much to the incredulity of the cops. This gives us an indication of the echelons of society Don plays music for and his true talent.

Later, Don tells Frank off for hitting the cop over an anti-Italian racist remark, which is fair, given the huge amount of racism Don encounters and has to put up with. Frank returns serve and states that Don ignores his black culture and black people and is arrogant, and he does come across this way. Don points out that he's isolated, as white people accept him as a musical talent but reject him as a black man, and black people reject him because of the adaptions he's had to make to survive in white circles. But in reality his talent has given him opportunities that have enabled him to evolve and develop, and this makes him different from the average black person at the time, who's denied such opportunities. They make peace quite quickly, and it's clearly the beginning of a friendship, as they're able to be honest with each other and help each other to see other perspectives.

On the last night of the tour, Don is refused entry into the whites-only dining room of the hotel where he is to play. Don then refuses to play. They leave and end up at a black club, where Don joins the band there on piano and they play the blues.

Frank and Don then leave to try to get home by Christmas Eve but are caught in a blizzard. They worry when they're pulled over by the cops, but this cop is okay; he's just making them aware they have a flat tyre. The cop helps them fix the tyre, and they eventually make it home, with Don taking on the driving duties while the exhausted Frank sleeps in the back seat.

Frank invites Don to have dinner with his family, but Don says no and goes back to his own home. However, sitting there alone he has a change of heart, and goes back to Frank's, where he's warmly welcomed by Frank and his wife (who admits she knows Don was helping her husband with his letters), and then the wider extended family.

The film ends with a biographical note telling us that Don continued to tour and play music, while Frank went back to the club he used to work for, and that they were good friends until 2013, when they both passed away.

Leadership lessons

Green Book is huge in terms of EDI. Early in the film we see that Frank feels uncomfortable with black people and he has some bias against them, which is probably based on difference and a lack of understanding, or misunderstanding, which his wife doesn't appear to share. He struggles with the fact Don isn't doing the things that he believes a black man should do, like eating fried chicken, and he views this as Don being disrespectful to his own culture and people. But of course, Don doesn't understand the point that Frank is making, as Don behaves the way he does because he's used to living a particular way, which is according to the norms associated with affluent white people. This demonstrates a degree of stereotyping of black people by Frank, but he's being honest and authentic, and for me what this really is, is clear evidence of the narrow thinking that is driven by a lack of education around cultural intelligence.

Another barrier between the two men is that Frank is a blue-collar worker and has nothing in common with the rich apart from skin colour, while Don is of a higher social class, with more intelligence, academically and artistically, than Frank. Don's life in many ways is counter to what many might expect in the 60s, 70s and possibly the 80s, which shows our bias too, in that maybe we don't expect black people of the time to be like him: intelligent and financially rewarded for it. But the film also demonstrates to us that it's environment and access to money and opportunities that shape who we can become, as these things afford us education, housing, healthcare etc., which are the things that sit at the base of the Maslow hierarchy and are what everything else is built on.

Don and Frank also show us the solution to problems where difference, bias and racism exist. Through spending time together, they get to see the other person's similarities, personal challenges and humanity. They become inclined to help each other because they have the actual knowhow to do so, and this assists them in connecting with each other. Then as time goes on, they become each other's supporter, then ally, then friend. It gives us all hope.

Independence is evident in this film as many are isolated – the black people of course, but also Frank's family. His family are isolated due to social class, and aren't listened to and don't have a say, and much of this is to do with the barriers created by wealth, and on a deeper level, power, imperialism and greed. *Expertise* is evident with both men as they both have clear talents which means they're self-sufficient and in demand in their different careers. *Unite* is there with both men too, in how they learn to team up together.

Key takeaways:

- Racism is a form of evil.
- Culture can be created, it is up to us to make it positive.
- Friendship is essential for happiness in life.
- Overcome our biases.
- Recognise the similarities.
- Celebrate the differences.

> Be self-aware. Recognise your biases. Recognise your weaknesses as a person and do something about them. Accept others. Support others. Help others. Do small things; they will all add up to something meaningful and big.

CHAPTER 18:
LOVE

44: *Groundhog Day* (1993)

The storyline

This comedy stars Bill Murray and Andie MacDowell and is directed by Harold Ramis.

Murray is an unhappy TV weather man, Phil Connors, and MacDowell his new producer, Rita Hanson. They're attending an annual event called Groundhog Day in a town called Punxsutawney. The behaviour of the groundhog there is said to predict the weather for the year. Everyone ends up stuck in the town because of a blizzard.

On Groundhog Day, Phil is woken by his radio alarm playing the song 'I Got You Babe'. He does a TV report on the groundhog, and then tries to leave town, but can't because the blizzard has blocked all the routes. It means he has to stay another night.

The following morning, the radio alarm clock wakes him with the same song as the day before, and all his conversations and everything that happens to him are exactly the same as the day before, which he puts down to everyone being backward and stupid. Again, he tries to leave town, but the routes are still blocked, and he's forced to stay another night.

The following day, the same song awakens him, and all his conversations and everything that happens to him are again exactly the same as the previous two days. He realises that he's in a time loop of some kind. No one else seems to know. He speaks to Rita, his boss, about this, but she thinks he's losing his mind and refers him to some health professionals, who are unable to help him.

That night he goes out and gets drunk, and is involved in a car chase, arrested and put in a cell. The following morning, he awakens back in his hotel room with the same song playing again. He now understands that there are no consequences to any of his actions, and he takes it to the limit by sleeping around and even commits crimes. Then he starts to use his knowledge of what happens on this constantly recurring day to manipulate a range of things to benefit him. He then attempts to use his knowledge to seduce Rita, but it doesn't work. He becomes more depressed and distressed and just wants to leave the loop but can't. He kills himself in different ways, but each morning he wakes in his hotel room, to the same song on the radio.

He convinces Rita to spend the day with him, and he proves to her that he can predict everything that happens and that they're stuck in a loop. They fall asleep together on the same bed that night, and the following day, he's again woken by the same song and is alone, but he himself is a little different. He realises that his interest in Rita has changed. Instead of just wanting her for sex, he realises that he really, really likes her, and might actually be in love with her.

He starts to focus on being more positive and helping others, using his knowledge of each day to look out for and save others, while developing himself by learning new skills like how to play the piano and speak French. Still, he remains stuck in the loop.

One day, as he does his report on the groundhog event, he speaks with such positivity and beauty that everyone stops what they're doing and focuses on him, including Rita. Then he gets on with the day, helping others. That evening Rita realises she has feelings for him, after watching him entertain everyone with the piano and hearing from the townspeople about all the helpful things he's done that day. They spend some time together and he explains he's no longer worried about being stuck in this town in a loop, as he's here with her and he loves her. They retire to bed for the night.

The following morning, he's awakened by that same song, but the narrative from the people on the radio is different, and he's not alone in bed, Rita is there with him. Groundhog Day is over.

Leadership lessons

Groundhog Day emphasises the importance of doing good more than any other film in this book, but also the importance of finding your *raison d'être*, so that you can attain happiness, or in Maslow's language, self-actualise. Falseness and cynicism are really holding Phil back; it's quite damaging. The other characters, including Rita, are vehicles to make this point, and are quite one-dimensional. However, they do all change too, in that they become more positive towards Phil and actually start to enjoy and follow him, but only when he becomes positive, helpful and authentic. He takes a risk and lets his guard down, mainly because he's totally exasperated with his life as it is.

However, a true test of character is how you behave when you believe no one is watching you, i.e. you can't get caught and therefore there are zero consequences. Murray fails in this, as he becomes self-serving and doesn't protect others. Worse still, he becomes exploitative of others and the law, because he can't be held to account. It's a little reminder to us that there are people in positions of power in the workplace and community who have knowledge of how to take advantage of the system and others, and who do take advantage, just because they can. This is a form of darkness.

The film also shows how an individual, a single individual, can change and have the positive ability to do good and create harmony all around them. When he decides to change and do good, Phil has a hugely positive impact on everyone around him and makes their lives more meaningful.

This film is also very much about emotional wellbeing. From a RISE UP perspective, *raison d'être* is huge: Phil

Connor finds his and then inspires everyone else to find theirs too. This *raison d'être* in the film seems to activate and link in very well with *expertise* and ultimately leads to a very powerful *unite*. Maybe the lesson is to stop putting all our energy into resisting doing good and get with the programme of doing good earlier, and then we can reap the benefits.

Key takeaways:

- Find your raison d'être.
- Impact positively on others.
- Reap the benefits.
- Don't waste time.

45: *Four Weddings and a Funeral* (1994)

The storyline

This is a romantic comedy written by Richard Curtis and directed by Mike Newell. It stars Andie MacDowell, and it made a star out of the male lead, Hugh Grant.

Charles, played by Grant, bumps into Carrie (MacDowell) at a wedding in Somerset and they spend the night together. The following day, Carrie flies back to America. Three months later, they bump into each other again at a wedding in London (the wedding of a couple who met and got together at the wedding in Somerset). Charles is delighted to see Carrie, and to hear that she's moved to England. However, this is short lived when he understands that she's engaged to someone else, who's present at the wedding. Very late that night, the pair happen to find themselves alone in an area of the hotel. One thing leads to another and they end up in bed again.

A couple of months later, Charles attends Carrie's wedding, to which he was invited. He's devastated that she's married someone who isn't him. At the wedding, a friend of his collapses and dies. At the funeral, Charles and Carrie bump into each other again and exchange pleasantries.

Nearly a year later, it's Charles's own wedding day. He's settling for someone who loves him, but he doesn't love her. Before the ceremony starts, he bumps into Carrie, who's attending by herself, and she tells Charles that she's single, as her marriage didn't work out.

The wedding doesn't happen, as when it gets to the 'Does anyone know of any reason why these people shouldn't marry?' part, everyone becomes aware that Charles isn't in love with his wife-to-be but is in love with someone else. This brings the ceremony to a violent end, with Charles being knocked out by his fiancée's punch

Later that evening, Carrie comes to Charles, and they declare their love for each other and decide to get engaged. A year later, they have a baby.

Leadership lessons

Four Weddings and a Funeral gives us a lesson in timing, destiny and fate. Charles thinks he has feelings for Carrie, and maybe she thinks he might be a good guy for her, but she isn't emotionally available as she's getting married. Eventually, things happen, and she becomes available. But by then he's in the church and about to get married himself. He knows he's just following the herd, and that his wife-to-be isn't really the right one for him, but he also believes that he'll be happier hitched. What he does, in my opinion, isn't ruthless, because that isn't in his character. When he ditches his fiancée at the altar, he does it because he knows that Carrie is 100 per cent right for him, and this proves to be the case. He trusts his gut, and if Carrie had the same instinct and level of bravery, she might not have married the wrong person, and may have saved herself a lot of emotional turmoil and a divorce etc.

The funeral represents the theme of life being short: we don't know when it will all come to an end, so we should make the most of our time, do the things that we want to do, be with the people who add value to us.

By the end, Charles is being totally authentic, and so is Carrie, and this brings about what is right for them both. In our organisations, authenticity can lead to better connectivity and the creation of a sense of belonging.

Key takeaways:

- Don't waste time – act today.
- Listen to yourself; you do really know.
- Trust yourself.

46: *When Harry Met Sally* (1989)

The storyline

This is a romantic comedy that stars Billy Crystal and Meg Ryan, as Harry and Sally.

In the late 1970s, they both graduate from university in Chicago. They're only acquainted because Harry is dating Sally's friend, but they both need to get to New York City, so they agree to travel by car together. On the journey, they talk about relationships in general, and Sally disagrees with Harry's view that men and women can't be friends as sex gets in the way. Harry also expresses that he thinks she's very good-looking, which she's offended by, as she thinks he's making a move on her. Once they arrive in New York, they part company.

About five years later, they bump into each other on a flight. Harry suggests that they become friends, but it doesn't happen.

Another five years pass and they bump into each other in a bookshop. They have a coffee together and discuss their failed romantic relationships with others. They agree to become friends, and end up spending a lot of time phoning each other and meeting, etc. At a New Year's Eve party, they share a kiss, but it doesn't lead to anything more.

They then decide to set each other up on a date with their best friends, and they all go out as a foursome. The double date ends with their two friends getting together, and soon enough, their friends end up getting engaged.

Not long after this, Sally is upset that her ex is engaged to someone else. She feels like a failure. To support her, Harry goes round to her place, and they end up having sex. They both feel awkward about this, and it doesn't lead to a romantic relationship, but it does put pressure on their friendship and they become distanced from each other. A short while after this, they have an argument at their friends' wedding. Sally decides firmly that their friendship is over.

Another New Year arrives. Sally is at a party and Harry is at home watching TV. He goes for a walk and has an epiphany of sorts, realising that he loves Sally. He rushes to the party she's at. He declares his love for her, and a few months later they get married.

Leadership lessons

The biggest lesson in *When Harry Met Sally* is the inability of humans to recognise what's under their nose. Harry and Sally fail to see that the best person for them in life in terms of partnership and belonging has been there all along, they just couldn't see it, and then they actually deny it to themselves.

This could be termed poor self-awareness, and the impact is very destructive, as they're denying each other true happiness. Their best friends have huge self-awareness, and when that pair meet each other for the first time, they immediately realise that they're made for each other, and very soon afterwards they get married and have a long, happy marriage.

There's also a point to be made about being

courageous, and in the end, Harry displays this, by being vulnerable and declaring his love for Sally, even though he knows she's annoyed with him and may reject him. He takes the chance. He knows it's a chance worth taking, and it works out. Sometimes we're our own worst enemy. Anxiety and fear can be very damaging. Sometimes to get people to trust you, you have to take a step that puts you in a vulnerable position.

This can present itself in companies between colleagues, between managers and staff members, and between the managers. Can you make the first move? Can you be totally transparent? It can also be found between board and union members. All of this can be overcome by collaboration and compromise, and by doing something that shows some vulnerability or a willingness to take a risk. By doing so we create an opportunity for reciprocity, and then solutions can be found. Solutions that create trust improve all elements of wellbeing. To find the right solution will also require a person to be an accomplished listener, so that they can understand exactly what's actually happening and respond appropriately.

Key takeaways:

- Listen to others, you will learn something.
- See what's under your nose.
- Take a chance. Trust your gut.
- It's okay to be vulnerable.
- Be courageous.
- Trust people.

Sometimes love embarrasses us. Sometimes it feels cheesy and awkward. But it does sit at the heart of all things good. If the word is a block for you, then substitute it with 'doing good'. Everything we've covered so far connects here. If we're delivering on everything in the book so far, then what we're really doing is giving love to ourselves, others and the planet we live on, which is just doing good, lots of it, and all the time.

CHAPTER 19:
FRIENDSHIP

47: *Toy Story* (1995)

The storyline

Toy Story is an animated movie in which all toys come to life when humans aren't around. The two main characters are a toy cowboy called Woody (played by Tom Hanks) and a spaceman toy, Buzz Lightyear (played by Tim Allen).

Woody belongs to a child called Andy and has always been his favourite toy. But new toy Buzz has taken on that mantle, and this causes friction between the pair because Woody is jealous. He's the leader of the toys and is frustrated by Buzz, who's delusional, for want of a better word, as he doesn't realise, he's a toy at all but thinks he's really a spaceman. This happens just as Andy's family are getting ready to move to a new house.

A couple of days before the move, Andy's family are going to dinner at a restaurant. Woody needs to make sure Andy brings him and not Buzz, so using a remote-controlled car, he tries to knock Buzz off the desk and out of view, but Buzz ends up falling out of the window. Most of the other toys think Woody tried to kill Buzz, but of course that wasn't his intention.

Andy takes Woody, but a very angry Buzz joins him in the car. The pair fight and fall out of the car. They end up getting to the restaurant another way, but are taken by Andy's bad neighbour, a boy called Sid. Sid is going to either destroy them or injure them like he has hundreds of other toys in his room.

Buzz becomes depressed after seeing a TV advert that helps him realise that he is indeed a toy and not a spaceman. He's so depressed that he doesn't care that he will die on Sid's exploding rocket. Woody puts great effort into trying to save Buzz, and introduces Buzz to their purpose in life, or *raison d'être*, which is to create enjoyment and happiness for Andy.

This inspires Buzz, but he's still tied to the rocket. Sid takes him to the garden to launch the rocket. Woody manages to convince the damaged, broken, scary and weird toys to help, and they come to life in front of Sid, scaring him so badly that he will never harm another toy.

Woody and Buzz have now been left behind by Andy, as he's just moved, so to catch up with the car he's in, they light the rocket that was tied to Buzz. They manage to free themselves from it just before it explodes, and they fall through the sunroof of Andy's car and land right next to him.

Leadership lessons

Toy Story gives us many lessons. One relates to jealousy. Woody becomes jealous of Buzz, which affects his emotions and his thinking, and gets him thinking dark thoughts about how to dispose of Buzz. His dark plan goes wrong and leads most of his friends to think poorly of Woody. We need to manage our jealousy and control our emotions.

Woody ostracises himself from the group with the clumsiness of his plan, and there's another lesson here: if you're going to go dark, make sure you don't get caught, because there'll be a consequence if you do. So, don't go dark, engage with your feelings and manage your emotions.

Another lesson in the film is that in the workplace and/or your friendship groups, new people will arrive, and it can impact your standing in these circles and sometimes your identity. You have to deal with this by being confident in who you are and accepting this change as reality – accepting that change will always occur and that relationships evolve.

A hugely significant lesson here is found in the two sides to the toys. The toys are only seen by humans as one-dimensional, pretty useless, inanimate objects that are there for the purpose of play. But what the humans don't get to see is that there's much, much more to them. The toys are actually real and alive with ideas and thoughts, feelings and plans.

Don't forget that how some people present themselves to you isn't how they really are. Some will hide who they really are to manipulate you, to gain from you in some way – it can be deceitful, a con. Others present themselves differently to how they are out of fear. They know that they don't fit in, and they worry that this will put them at risk in some way, such as not getting their work-day preferences on the rota or being demoted or blocked from being promoted. Authenticity is at play here too. Is there a cost to being authentic? Should there be?

Another big lesson is the power of friendship. Buzz becomes depressed when he gets the shock of his life, realising something he believes is hugely negative about himself. When this happens, it's Woody who helps him to see his true value, and who saves him from his pain. Everyone needs friends. Everyone at some stage will have a difficult time in life, so be prepared to offer help and support to others when you can. And when it's you who's stuck in life, be prepared to accept the help offered – you will need it.

Key takeaways:

- Emotions exist in the workplace and they need to be managed.
- Jealousy and fear can lead to poor behaviour.
- Everyone needs a friend.
- Help someone.

48: *The Full Monty* (1997)

The storyline

This is a comedy set in Sheffield in the UK. It's directed by Peter Cattaneo and stars a number of people including Robert Carlyle, Tom Wilkinson and Mark Addy. The story centres on six unemployed men attempting to change their fortunes by putting on a striptease show.

Carlyle plays Gaz, who is in conflict with his ex-wife, Mandy, who's annoyed and frustrated that he isn't paying any maintenance for their son, Nathan. This fuels her desire to seek sole custody of Nathan, with her respectable partner, who has a professional job.

The Chippendales are in town, and Gaz notes how many women go to the show and how much money is made. He sees an opportunity to do better than the Chippendales by doing something they don't: going totally naked.

Carlyle convinces his pal Dave (Mark Addy) to form a striptease troupe, and they bring in Lomper, a guy they save from suicide, and Gerald (Wilkinson), who hasn't told his wife that he's unemployed yet. They hold auditions to get two more men to join, and settle on a guy who's a great dancer (Horse) and another (Guy) who's a terrible dancer and appears a bit boring, but who has a long penis.

They start practising at a disused mill. They settle on a date to put on the show, but they need £100 to book the hall and haven't got the money. Nathan agrees to loan it to his dad.

One day when they're rehearsing, a passing policeman sees them stripping and arrests them for indecent exposure. This creates additional trouble for Gaz as Nathan is present, which means the police have to engage and tell Mandy about what's been going on. This increases the conflict between the estranged parents and is exactly what she needed to block him from seeing Nathan.

It looks like the show will have to be cancelled as some of the guys aren't interested or have a build-up of other problems in their lives, and there's been so much hassle because of the police too. However, the notoriety of the arrests has led to a sellout show, which is enough for Gaz to convince all the men to give it a go, for one night only.

On the night, Gaz has butterflies, and then Nathan turns up to tell him that Mandy is present, and they're also aware the cop who arrested them is in for the entertainment factor too. The men rally and take to the stage. The show is packed and a huge success, and the men do what they said they would and let it all hang out.

Leadership lessons

The Full Monty is a great example of the importance of friendship. A number of the characters are stuck in depressing situations and have a lot of fear and anxiety. Gaz feels stuck and Dave feels stuck, but they have each other. Dave also has a supportive wife, though he doesn't confide in her enough and as a result feels even more lonely, self-conscious and a failure.

Gaz's inability to communicate honestly with his ex-wife is probably what brought that relationship to an end, but also his lack of maturity. He starts to find this maturity by the end of the film, which means he can have a friendship of sorts with her, and possibly her new partner, and he might just be more capable of having a better romantic relationship with a new person too, if he were to meet someone.

Wilkinson, who plays a middle-class character while the others are working class, shows fear and desperation too, and this effectively makes the point that lack of income and financial worry affect everyone who needs an income. Like Dave, he has a supportive wife, but he withholds information from her so that she doesn't have to worry, but also so he can play the macho provider role. This puts him under more and more stress, which isn't actually required, as when he tells her the truth, they team up to find solutions.

Another lesson for men in this film is that men are generally supportive of each other, once they get past the bravado and falseness of pretending to be okay. Be authentic with yourself first. Then you can be authentic with others.

This film is a good example of the importance of authenticity and how damaging it is to have to present a facade of being someone other than who you are. It takes us into the territory of EDI and psychological safety, where people don't feel they can be who they are for fear of being harmed or discriminated against.

The film is also an example of how poor financial

wellbeing very negatively impacts on emotional wellbeing.

Key takeaways:

- Support each other.
- Be authentic.
- Be honest.

49: *Forrest Gump* (1994)

The storyline

Forrest Gump is a 1994 film written by Eric Roth. It stars Tom Hanks, Robin Wright and Gary Sinise.

As a boy, Forrest (played by Hanks) becomes friends with Jenny (Robin Wright), who lives nearby. She's supportive of him in contrast to many others, who badly bully and belittle him because he has intellectual problems.

Forrest is a strong and fast runner, which leads to his getting an American football scholarship to go to university. He excels in the game at university.

After he finishes university, he joins the army and makes a friend, Bubba, and they decide to open a shrimping business together once their tour of Vietnam comes to an end. In Nam, Forrest's group are ambushed while on patrol. Many are killed, including Bubba, but Forrest saves several men, including Lieutenant Dan (Gary Sinise). He wins a Medal of Honour for this.

While in rehab, he starts playing ping-pong and

is excellent at it. Forrest then plays international tournaments for the army, which leads to his getting invited onto a national TV show. He gets a sponsorship deal on his discharge from the army, and he uses this money to set up a shrimping business. Dan joins him in the business as his first employee.

Luck intervenes when a storm destroys all the ships of their competitors, meaning they're the only ones trading, and they have great success. With the continuous profits, Dan makes shrewd investments on their behalf, and they both become millionaires.

Dan, who's struggled with being a double amputee and has a serious drink problem, eventually finds peace, and thanks Forrest for everything he's done for him. Forrest gives a load of money to Bubba's family, because even though legally Bubba was never involved in the business, it was both Bubba's and Forrest's idea.

Forrest cares for his dying mum and buries her and doesn't go back to shrimping. Jenny comes back into his life, and they become as close as when they were children. She appears to have dealt with the drink, drugs and trauma that have blighted her life. Forrest proposes to her, but it turns out that she's still quite damaged and doesn't feel like she's deserving of happiness and love with Forrest, so she leaves in the night. As a result of this, Forrest sinks into a mild depression.

Years later, Jenny re-enters Forrest's life. She's psychologically sorted now but has a terminal illness. She introduces Forrest to their young son, who was conceived just before she previously vanished. They marry and are happy, but of course she dies, and Forrest raises their son.

Leadership lessons

Forrest Gump is a gift, and the characters played by Hanks, Wright and Sinise give us much to think about.

Forrest displays kindness, integrity and loyalty throughout. He has many of the attributes that create followership. But because he has some intellectual disability, many don't give him the recognition that he deserves.

At the start of the film, Sinese's character doesn't actually think for himself. He's a lieutenant in the army because that's what his father and grandfather did etc. The shame and sense of responsibility he feels because some of his men died on his watch make him suicidal – maybe in a similar way to Willy in *Death of a Salesman*, he feels he's failed to live up to the expectations or achievements of others. The trauma of losing his legs, the disability he now has, and how he's viewed negatively by society fuel his alcohol abuse, anger and unhappiness. His physical and emotional wellbeing are poor, and his social wellbeing has been impacted, with a lack of belonging.

His saviour is his one and only friend, Forrest s. Perhaps the lesson for us here is that if we make an extra effort with just one person in our circle of acquaintances, it can add a lot of value to them, and make a serious difference, in the end.

Jenny is another example of why we shouldn't give

up on people. She's damaged by sexual and physical abuse in childhood, and this leads to a continuous cycle of self-harm, self-doubt and feelings of worthlessness. Again, time and true friendship from Forrest help her immensely.

Dan and Jenny both find *raison d'être*, Dan in running Forrest's business and learning to accept himself, and Jenny with the birth of her son. This also connects with *expertise*, in that they get to do things they're good at.

Don't forget everyone is on a journey in life and some of these journeys are difficult ones. Don't be too quick to judge others in a negative way; instead, be quick to help.

Back to Forrest. In the business world today, would we hire and promote someone with his level of disability, even though he's a constant success and achieves and achieves and achieves? He's positive and decent, but if he attended an interview for a senior job, do you think he would get it? Would you give it to him? Would people be happy to follow him?

We know many people are judgemental and biased, and I think it's likely that despite all of his ability and success, people wouldn't be able to see past his disability and probably wouldn't give him the job or the responsibility.

In this film, is Forrest a good decision-maker with sound judgement, or is he just lucky? I don't think anyone can get that lucky all the time by accident, and he has to overcome a lot throughout, so he has his fair share of bad luck too. I think Forrest is a values-based decision-maker, and it's his convictions that bring him success.

Key takeaways:

- Friendship is something we can all give to at least one person.
- Decency is a great quality to possess and helps to build trust.
- Goodness is the essence of life.
- Bias is something we all have, what are yours?
- Trauma isn't your fault, but you can control your response and go and get help and support.

> Just be a friend to others as much as you can. Remind yourself of what we covered in the love, EDI, and good and evil chapters. If you're doing those things, you'll be a great friend to many. Well done.

CHAPTER 20:
TRUST

50: *Good Will Hunting* (1997)

The storyline

This is a movie written by and starring Ben Affleck and Matt Damon, and it also stars Robin Williams, Stellan Skarsgard and Minnie Driver.

Matt Damon plays Will Hunting, a 22-year-old who works as a janitor at Massachusetts Institute of Technology (MIT). He's recently come out of prison after being in trouble with the law. He's a maths genius but has never been schooled in maths.

Professor Lambeau (played by Skarsgard) puts an impossible maths problem on a blackboard to challenge his brilliant students. Will, who enters the classroom to do some cleaning, solves the problem anonymously, which bewilders everyone.

Lambeau puts an even more challenging maths problem on the board. Will solves it, and while he's admiring his work, Lambeau catches him. He shouts at him and chases him away, thinking he's a thief or someone who's there to do damage.

After a short while, Lambeau realises Will was actually the guy who solved it and asks for him at the maintenance department, but they advise that he's missing. Lambeau does some digging and learns that Will was placed at MIT by his parole officer.

Will gets in a fight with a gang that includes someone who used to bully him in the past. He lays into the guy but ends up exchanging punches with a cop who tries to break up the fight. Will gets arrested. Luckily for him, Lambeau has been in touch with his parole officer, and turns up at court. He tells the judge that he'll take responsibility for Will and asks that he's spared prison in exchange for Will going to therapy and learning maths under Lambeau.

Will is very disrespectful to the therapists in their sessions, meaning that they all refuse to continue to work with him. Lambeau is at his wits' end and doesn't know what to do, but then remembers an old friend of his, a decent guy with an inner toughness who now teaches psychology at a community college. This is Dr Sean Maguire (played by Robin Williams).

These sessions are different. Maguire takes little notice of Will's attempts to throw him off the scent, or his mocking of him, and is happy to engage in games of silence. But when Will starts mocking his dead wife, Maguire angrily responds and tells him he will bust his face if he ever insults his wife's memory again, and he means it. Will can see that Maguire is a different kind of therapist, and a different kind of man to the others.

Eventually, after several sessions, they develop a bit of a rapport. Will buys into Maguire, because Maguire is real with him and shares his deepest personal experiences with Will. Stories that make an impact, like how he met his wife, how he knew she was the one, how he cared for her when she was dying from cancer.

This encourages Will to engage properly and in an adult way with his on-off girlfriend, who really loves him – Skylar (played by Minnie Driver). But he's still cautious and is also ashamed of his past and his neighbourhood, so he doesn't tell her the truth about these things.

Lambeau sets up some big career opportunities for Will with companies and contacts he knows well, but Will sabotages these interviews, including one with the NSA.

Skylar needs to head to California and asks Will to join her. Will is extra vulnerable at this time as he's trying to make sense of the things that have happened to him in life, and he refuses to join her. He also insults Lambeau, telling him he's a joke and can't even do baby maths in comparison to what Will can do. However, he does divulge to Skylar some of the trauma from his childhood, at the hands of his foster father, and that he's an orphan, which helps Skylar to understand why Will is the way he is. This is all too much for Will and he dumps Skylar.

Maguire explains to Will that he's deliberately breaking these relationships to avoid the emotional pain that he thinks will come his way when these relationships end up failing, when he ends up being rejected.

Affleck, playing Chuckie, Will's best friend in the film, questions why he deliberately flunks these great job opportunities, which Chuckie and the other guys would absolutely love to get but never could. He shocks Will by telling him that when he turns up at Will's house in the morning to collect him for work, he waits and hopes that Will won't show because he's taken one of the great opportunities, which will take him out of their deprived area and off to better parts of the country, where he can live the good life.

Will challenges Maguire to take an objective look at his own life, since he can't move on from his wife's death.

Will walks in on a serious argument between Maguire and Lambeau, and Lambeau leaves. Will and Maguire have a deep conversation during which Maguire tells Will about the terrible abuse he suffered from his own father. Their bond is very strong now. Maguire helps Will to accept the past and the present and accept that he didn't do anything wrong and didn't deserve the abuse he experienced.

Will accepts one of the job offers organised by Lambeau but then doesn't take it. He leaves a note for Maguire to explain why he has left for California, to try to make a go of his relationship with Skylar.

Leadership lessons

Trauma is a major theme in *Good Will Hunting*, with the two most traumatised characters being Will and Maguire. What separates them is that Maguire has figured out a way to live with his trauma and not let it derail his life, whereas Will is seriously stuck and is repeatedly doing things that actually harm him, things that are probably a defence mechanism, to ensure that others can't hurt him. The only person he trusts is Chuckie, but by the end he trusts Maguire and also Skylar.

Maguire is the only therapist capable of connecting with Will, which is to do with authenticity. The other therapists were probably being authentic, but Maguire takes it to a different level with what's known these days as compassionate leadership. He genuinely listens, in a way that the others couldn't, and he perhaps understands Will better than anyone else too, because as it turns out, he had similar toxic childhood experiences. Maguire is able to acknowledge what Will is saying but also the things that Will hasn't told him, and this only happens because Maguire is a brilliant listener; he sees and hears everything, and fills in the blanks himself. The final aspect of compassionate leadership is that he tries to collaborate with Will to find solutions.

Another theme relates to the inequalities in society and how those with money get more opportunities, which means they earn more, which makes their lives easier and better.

Will is incredibly intelligent, but because he grows up on the wrong side of the tracks, he doesn't get to attend tertiary education, even though his mathematical mind is superior to even that of the award-winning mathematics professor.

Another major lesson here is that if we help those

who have suffered in life, the traumatised, then we're giving them that opportunity to heal, which enables them to have a more pleasant, fulfilling, happy life, and to create and be part of a warmer society.

Lambeau, Maguire, Chuckie and Skylar are great in that they're resilient, and in their own different ways they don't give up on Will when perhaps it would have been easy to do so. The lesson for us here is to follow their lead and be more patient and supportive of others.

All the characters are strong on *raison d'être* and *expertise*, but it's really only Maguire who enables the *independence* in others.

Maguire might also have a message for all of us in terms of how we spend our time and what we choose to chase in life. He isn't part of the rat race. He bowed out of that when he found something more meaningful, which was love. Will learns this exact life lesson from him, which is something the other characters haven't learnt yet, especially Lambeau.

Key takeaways:

- Trauma isn't your fault, but you can control your responses and go and get help and support.
- Trust is a platform upon which many good things are built.
- Friendship is something we can all give to at least one person.
- Helping others encourages others to do the same.
- Choosing the road to happiness is in your control.

- Love others and yourself and the positive difference you can make.

51: *28 Days Later* (2002)

The storyline

This is more a post-apocalyptic movie than a zombie horror movie. It stars a young Cillian Murphy and Christopher Eccleston and was directed by Danny Boyle.

At a Cambridge University lab, a monkey infected with a virus is set free from a cage, and bites one of the activists who broke him free. The activist immediately transforms into a highly aggressive zombie type whose sole purpose is to attack people. The activist starts attacking others, and the virus quickly spreads across the country, turning nearly everyone into a high-energy, fast-paced, violent zombie, and devastating society as we know it.

Twenty-eight days after the outbreak, Jim (Murphy) wakes up in a deserted London hospital, having been in an induced coma following an accident. Judging by the empty streets, something seismic has happened. Jim has no idea what, though, as he wanders around London. He finds himself being chased down by these zombies-on-amphetamine types, and is saved by a couple of people, Selena (Naomie Harris) and Mark (Noah Huntley), who bring him to their hideout.

Worried about his family, he convinces them to take him to his parents' house in South London. He finds them dead, and the note they left behind shows it was suicide. It's too late to head back to the hideout, so Selena, Mark and Jim stay at his parents' house.

In the middle of the night, Jim is awake and lights a candle to look at family photos. This light attracts the zombies, and while the trio manage to escape, Mark is bitten. Now he will obviously turn into a zombie, but before that can happen, Selena kills him.

Shortly after this, they come across a taxi driver, Frank, and his daughter, Hannah. Frank makes them aware that the military have achieved a zombie free safe zone near Manchester. The four of them decide to travel to Manchester and seek the protection that will be on offer up there.

They reach what they believe to be the rendezvous point on the road, which is a blockade point that was broadcast by the military, however when they get there, there's no one about. Tragically, some infected blood from a dead zombie drops from a height, making contact with Frank's eyes. He hasn't transformed yet, but when some soldiers arrive on the scene, they see no option but to kill him, and they shoot him, causing his daughter, Hannah, huge distress.

Jim, Selena and Hannah are brought to a mansion fortress which is being controlled by an army officer, Major West, played by Christopher Eccleston. Jim finds out from West that the broadcast they put out, which Frank heard, was partly a lie. The reason for it wasn't to offer safety, but to get access to females, and force them into a programme to repopulate the country against their will.

Jim disagrees with this, so is taken away to be executed. He manages to escape from his executioners but is being pursued. He decides that his chances of survival are better if he frees an incarcerated and infected soldier zombie. This zombie runs amok, killing all of the soldiers in the secure mansion apart from West.

Jim frees Selena and Hannah, and their escape is nearly foiled by West, who shoots Jim. However, the trio manage to escape after the zombie soldier kills West, and the wounded Jim doesn't die.

Leadership lessons

Raison d'être is strong with the zombies. They have complete clarity on what their purpose is, and they achieve it with a zest that psychopaths could only dream of. Jim, Frank and Selena are a great example of how difficult it is to survive on your own and how important it is to unite with other like-minded people. Their individual and collective *raison d'être* is strong.

Another thing that this film triggers is the thought that some managers and leaders can be a bit like zombies (not the manic types here, but more the slower ones represented in the usual zombie movies). These leaders are there in your company not adding value and having a detrimental impact on everyone, and your only chance for good wellbeing is to stay well away from them.

We always need to try to trust others, and the Jim/

Selena group trust that West and his army colleagues are honest and supportive. It turns out that they aren't trustworthy. Obviously, if you know someone is dodgy, you need to take appropriate action to keep yourself safe from them, but at that point they don't know the truth about West. They're right to take the risk, they need to – what else can they do at that time? But when it becomes clear that he's bad, they're then right to remove themselves from his clutches.

28 Days Later also demonstrates Maslow's hierarchy, and the perilous position you can find yourself in when you don't have safety and security.

Key takeaways:

- You will have to trust someone.
- Sometimes people you trust will let you down.
- Some managers and leaders are zombies.

> Do the things that will enable others to trust you. Be honest, have integrity, listen, do good things, be self-aware, be authentic. Trust others; give them a chance.

CHAPTER 21:

WE ARE ALL SPECIAL

52: *Kung Fu Panda* (2008)

The storyline

Jack Black plays Po, a clumsy panda bear who's crazy about kung fu. He works in his father's noodle shop. A kung fu exhibition is held in his town, and at this event the identity of the mythical dragon warrior will be revealed – the one kung fu leader capable of understanding the secret of the dragon scroll, which is believed to lead to ultimate power.

Everyone expects it will be one of the famous kung fu experts, but Po, who accidentally gets into the exhibition, is chosen by the elderly, maybe senile person who allegedly has the knowledge and ability to recognise the dragon warrior.

The local kung fu master is asked to train and prepare Po, alongside the established kung fu experts. They don't believe he's the dragon warrior, and bully and belittle him to force him to quit. He doesn't, but his self-belief remains low.

Ian McShane plays the part of Tai Lung, a seriously evil but absolutely brilliant king fu expert, maybe the best there's ever been. He's broken out of prison and is on a revenge mission to acquire the dragon scroll, something that was promised to him when he too was led to believe that he was the dragon warrior. He attacks and defeats the kung fu leader and all the kung fu experts, meaning the only person standing between him and the achievement of his evil plans is Po.

Po has a huge battle with Tai Lung, and it turns out that he's the perfect nemesis for Tai Lung and defeats him. Tai Lung mocks him as just being 'a fat panda', but Po retorts before defeating him that actually he's 'THE fat panda'.

Another major point is that the dragon scroll is actually blank and has a mirror-like quality that shows you your reflection, which helps Po to appreciate that true power is within, in accepting yourself and being you, which is good enough.

Leadership lessons

Kung Fu Panda takes us into the territory of imposter syndrome, and feeling like we aren't good enough, or that we don't belong, or that we're useless. It's a good example of how low self-esteem can grab hold of you and make you feel unworthy or worthless.

The film also shows mobbing, where the local kung fu master and the people he trains mock and undermine Po. This is something that happens in teams and organisations all the time. It can happen because an individual stands out, not generally for a negative reason, and because of this their working life is made a misery, until they leave. It's bullying, it's mobbing, it's the antithesis of inclusion and it's wrong. The people who behave like this are very damaging but are also probably damaged themselves.

Po gives us all hope as individuals, but this film is also a good case study for wider teams too, to demonstrate closedness, rudeness and general awfulness. It shows how team leaders enable the poor behaviour, and it can also be an example of poor selection processes – go and revisit Mind the Gap.

I want you to remember that you're unique, and that you are good enough.

Key takeaway:

- You are good enough.

> Don't ever forget that you are good enough. Don't forget others are too. Build your self-awareness. Help others to build their self-awareness. Accept yourself. Accept others.

And now a word of warning.

CHAPTER 22:

ARTIFICIAL INTELLIGENCE/ THE FUTURE

53: *Mad Max* (1979)

The storyline

Mad Max is a movie set in Australia, and Mel Gibson plays the lead, a cop who becomes a vigilante.

As Australia falls into societal breakdown, it's certainly well on the way to a dystopian future. A motorbike gang member, Nightrider, kills a young cop, and is able to evade the police, so the toughest cop, Max Rockatansky (Gibson), is tasked with dealing with him. This results in a high-speed road chase, which ends with Nightrider crashing and being burned alive.

Nightrider's gang causes a lot of trouble in town, and it leads to Max and another cop, Goose, arresting a young psychopath known as Johnny. No witnesses turn up in court, and the court deems that Johnny is mentally unfit to stand trial anyway, so he's released, to the frustration of Max and Goose.

Johnny messes with Goose's motorbike, causing him to crash at high speed. Goose isn't badly hurt and uses a van to take his bike back to police HQ to have it repaired. Again, Johnny causes problems for Goose by throwing an object at the windscreen, which leads to Goose crashing again, and being trapped in the van. Encouraged by other gang members, Johnny sets fire to the van, burning Goose alive.

This trauma devastates Max, and he's discouraged from resigning and instead is convinced to take a short break. Max heads off with his wife and child.

They stop at a remote village, so Max can fix the spare tyre. While he's doing that, his wife and child go for some ice cream. She's accosted by the motorcycle gang and threatened by them. She escapes with her son to a farm owned by an elderly friend. The gang chase after her. Her farmer friend helps her to rescue her baby from the gang, and the three of them drive down the road, but they don't get far, as the vehicle breaks down. She tries to escape on foot but is run over by the gang. The child is killed, and she ends up in intensive care and is expected to die.

This tips Max over the edge. He returns to work, puts on his uniform and takes the turbo-charged police car. He's hell-bent on revenge, and manages to kill several of the gang members, before he's wounded in the leg by the people who killed his family and Goose. He somehow manages to chase after them again, before killing the remaining three.

Leadership lessons

In *Mad Max* we see societal breakdown, failure of the rule of law and the bad acts that can follow from this. The film also shows the impact of the bad acts, the trauma they cause. People change from being rule-abiding, the cops, into law breakers and killers themselves, with the only difference now being that they target the types of people who made them this way, the bad guys. We don't get to see why the bad guys are antisocial and psychopathic, but we can assume that it's probably trauma-related too.

In the workplace, there are always people who have suffered trauma and we need to be mindful of this. Of course they don't always identify themselves to us, but they're there and they do exist, so we should always be kind to colleagues. There are also some jobs that expose staff to trauma: the armed forces, the police, paramedics, prison staff, mental health hospital staff. This can impact on their wellbeing, and as a result substance abuse and suicide rates can be higher amongst some of these groups.

At the beginning of the film, Max appears to have balanced wellbeing pillars, and to be doing well in all the Maslow areas, and with the *raison d'être*, *independence*, *expertise* and *unite* elements of RISE UP. Some of the people on his side appear to be okay with these markers too, but all of these markers are changed by exposure to the trauma caused by the criminals. By the end, Max's *raison d'être* has stepped into a dangerous area, and it could be argued it's now a form of badness. His emotional wellbeing is gone, as is his social wellbeing, and his physical wellbeing is damaged. From a Maslow perspective, his safety and security, love and belonging are all gone too.

Maybe the big lesson for us here is to avoid societal destruction, as the impact will be dreadful for us all, but we can see this in reality already, in several war-torn countries across the world.

Key takeaway:

- Everyone loses, very badly, when societies are harmed.

54: *Alien* (1979)

The storyline

This film was directed by Ridley Scott and stars Sigourney Weaver.

The spaceship *Nostromo* is returning to Earth when the ship's computer, called Mother, receives a transmission from a small planet nearby. Mother wakes the crew, one of whom is Warrant Officer Ellen Ripley, played by Sigourney.

They land on the planet, and a party of three – Captain Dallas, Executive Officer Kane and Navigator Lambert – leave the ship to investigate. The trio realise that the communication came from a derelict spaceship. Inside, they find a dead alien with a big hole in its body. Mother finally interprets the communication that she received and Ripley believes it to be a warning of some kind.

Kane comes across a room with hundreds of large eggs in it. He touches one, and a small octopus-type creature pops out, gets inside his helmet and attaches itself to his face. The other two carry him back to the ship, but Ripley, who is now the most senior officer on board the ship, refuses to let them enter, quoting quarantine rules. However, another crew member, Ash, takes it upon himself to open the door and let them in.

Ash tries to remove the creature from Kane's face but stops when he understands that the creature has corrosive acidic blood, which could kill Kane. Luckily, after a while, the creature dies and falls off Kane's face.

When Kane awakens, the ship is back travelling in space. He's fine but can't remember anything about the incident. A little while later, Kane starts to have convulsions, and a small alien creature bursts from his chest, killing him. Before the team can react, the alien escapes into the main part of the spaceship. The team set out to capture it.

Another crew member, Brett, is isolated, and is attacked by the now full-size alien, who takes his body away with it. Dallas, who has a flame-thrower, is outmanoeuvred by the alien, and is killed.

An emotional Lambert rallies the team to flee in an escape shuttle, but Ripley, who's now the commanding officer, says no, as the shuttle can't carry four people. She says they should stick to the plan, which is to flush out the alien.

Using Mother, Ripley becomes aware that the

company that owns the spaceship has secretly ordered Ash to bring the alien back to Earth for research purposes and has told him that the crew are expendable. Ripley raises this with Ash, who attacks her, but crew member Parker saves her by bashing Ash with an implement, knocking his head off, which highlights that he's an android.

They're able to get Ash's head working again, and he tells them the truth about the company's orders, and that the alien can't be killed and they're doomed.

Ripley, Parker and Lambert agree to blow up the spaceship and escape on the shuttle. However, the alien corners the two men and kills them. Ripley programs the ship to self-destruct. Though the alien tries to block her from getting to the shuttle, she manages it and is clear of the spaceship when it explodes.

After a while on the shuttle, Ripley realises that the alien is aboard. She decides to flush it out and kill it. As it approaches her, she manages to trap it in an airlock and then opens the outer door and ejects it far into space.

Leadership lessons

Trust your gut instinct. In *Alien*, the leaders of the spaceship are far too inquisitive and it ultimately costs them their lives. It's healthy to have a fear of the unknown. Yes, have a look and take a risk, but when your sixth sense is telling you to back off, listen to it. It's trying to warn you and keep you safe and alive. Ripley's sixth sense is quite good and she listens to it. Some of the others don't, and it costs them.

When Ripley is thrust into the position of official leader due to others being dead or incapacitated, she's immediately undermined by subordinate Ash, who ignores her order, an order which would have saved all of them on the ship, and he stupidly opens the door. The emotion behind Ash doing this is powerful, as he wants to save his friends/colleagues, but if Ripley had been a male leader, Ash – a male – probably would have obeyed the order. This is something that many female leaders encounter from their male subordinates, who are incorrectly programmed by society to think that they're better than females. This film takes us back to the theme of male dominance and superiority, which is really just bias, prejudice and ignorance.

A theme of corporate corruption and deceit arises here too, when Ripley discovers that the company that owns her spaceship covertly planned everything and wants the alien brought to Earth for commercial reasons. We've encountered the power of greed in this book already, and we're very well acquainted with it in real life too; it's very powerful indeed.

Ripley is a great example of how drive and determination, and a willingness to change plans when they aren't working, can achieve big things.

We know a lot about Earth and the damage we've caused it and the consequences of this. We don't know that much about space, but we continue to put a huge amount of satellites and debris up there. As we know from Newton, there will be consequences, and therefore, perhaps we should be more respectful of space, as space is so vast and powerful, if we damage it, the consequences, given we are a mere speck in the universe, could be extreme.

Another point the film raises is to have the good sense to leave some things alone. The company and the spaceship crew should stay well away from the alien and they don't. We meddle a lot with AI, and there are positives with it, but we're meddling without regulation and without respect, and are we about to create something that we'll eventually regret? Ripley would probably say, leave AI alone. Have our old enemies greed and power already let the genie out of the bottle? Have they finally created a monster bigger than themselves – the ultimate monster, an all-conquering, mankind-ending monster called AI?

Ripley displays great decision-making ability, which tells us she has sound judgement.

Key takeaways:

- Greed is addictive and destructive.
- Corruption destroys equality and communities.
- Dishonesty breaks trust and creates division.
- Effort will lead to achievement.
- Know your limits.
- Listen to your gut.

55: *The Terminator* (1984)

The storyline

The Terminator is an American science-fiction action film directed by James Cameron, and starring Arnold Schwarzenegger as the Terminator, Linda Hamilton as Sarah Connor and Michael Biehn as Kyle Reese.

The Terminator is a cyborg that's been sent back from the future, approximately 2030, to 1984. He looks human, but underneath his skin he's effectively a robot. His objective is to kill a childless woman called Sarah Connor before she becomes the mother of John Connor, who in the future will be a significant rebel leader of mankind against the dominant AI military forces. The AI way of thinking is that if they kill Sarah before she has her child, the humans won't have his leadership in the future, meaning AI will have complete control.

In the future, John Connor sends back his most trusted lieutenant, Kyle Reese, to track down and save his mother from the Terminator. Both the Terminator and Kyle arrive in Los Angeles separately. Naked, their first task is to steal clothes, and then weapons.

The Terminator locates a phonebook and tears out the page with the addresses of everyone called Sarah Connor, and he starts to visit those addresses and kill those with that name. He tracks the Sarah Connor he's seeking to a nightclub, but she's rescued by Kyle. They steal a car but are pursued by the Terminator in a police car.

When he gets an opportunity, Kyle explains to Sarah

what's going on: that the Terminator is a cyborg sent back from the future to kill her and has been programmed to do this by the AI military network, Skynet, who have orchestrated a global nuclear war, bringing mankind close to extinction. That her not-yet-born son, John, is leading the resistance/fightback by the humans. And that the Terminator is a killing machine that probably can't be killed on Earth in 1984.

Sarah and Kyle are arrested by the police, and an undeterred Terminator bursts into the station, killing over 30 cops. But he doesn't get to Sarah, as Kyle helps her escape once again. They end up hiding out at a motel and the physical attraction between them leads to a sexual encounter, and the mind-bending reality is that this is the moment that John is conceived, as Kyle is his father.

The Terminator locates them again and another chase commences, with Sarah and Kyle in a pickup truck and the Terminator on a motorbike; and then the couple are on foot and the Terminator is in a truck. In both situations, Kyle throws pipe bombs, which damage the Terminator (he's now without skin and is clearly a metallic cyborg), but he's still functional, though slower.

The Terminator pursues them into a factory and Kyle uses his last pipe bomb to badly damage the Terminator but dies himself from the blast. The Terminator is now just a steel body without legs and is using his arms to drag himself towards Sarah, still intent on ending her. She lures him into a hydraulic crusher, and once out of it herself, she presses the appropriate button to crush the cyborg to death.

Months later, the visibly pregnant Sarah is buying petrol at a petrol station, and the attendant comments on the weather, saying a storm is coming. Her poignant response is that she knows, but she's referring to nuclear war, and future battles with AI and Skynet.

Leadership lessons

Both the Terminator and Kyle in have a strong *raison d'être*. In fact, it's very strong, as the stakes are so high for them both. They also have great *expertise*, especially the Terminator.

In this movie, Sarah Connor's role is subservient to the male characters, and as such she's not a leadership example, apart from in her ability to survive and be resilient. However, the character does evolve, and in *Terminator 2*, she's arguably one of **the strongest female leadership characters of all time**. (Even though it's a great movie, it didn't make the cut for this book.)

The biggest lesson for us in this film is to do with the type of future we're creating for ourselves, and the negative consequences of developing AI. The military may initially use it, but ultimately AI takes over and it then owns the military, and decides to end mankind.

I reflect on Eisenhower, whom I quoted earlier regarding the military-industrial complex. I also think of the godfather of AI, Geoffrey Hinton, who resigned from his commercial AI role so he could make us aware of his concerns about 'the existential threat' (Brown, 2023). Hinton calculates that there's a 20 per cent chance that humanity will be wiped out by AI within 30 years (Milmo, 2024).

Is it too late? Are we incapable of listening and being careful, and is this just another example of us causing our own demise, similar to what we may already have done with global warming and climate change?

Key takeaways:

- AI might be the end of us.
- Greed is addictive and destructive.

56: *The Matrix* (1999)

The storyline

The Matrix is a science-fiction movie. The big stars in this are Keanu Reeves, Laurence Fishburne, Carrie-Anne Moss and Hugo Weaving.

Thomas Anderson (Neo) is a computer programmer and hacker, played by Reeves. He's phoned by a person called Trinity (played by Moss) who says that a man called Morpheus (played by Fishburne) has the answers to all the questions that perturb Neo.

Special agents commanded by Agent Smith (played by Weaving) turn up at Neo's work office looking for him. This is all very worrying and confusing for Neo. Via a mobile phone, Morpheus tries to lead Neo away from the agents to a place of safety, but the route is too dangerous for Neo, and he also lacks confidence, and is captured. He refuses to cooperate with the agents, who are looking for information regarding the whereabouts of Morpheus, so they gag him and insert a tracking device into his stomach.

Neo wakes up thinking it was all a bad dream. However, Trinity soon turns up and brings Neo to meet Morpheus, and the tracking device is removed from his stomach and destroyed.

This leads to a famous scene where Morpheus offers Neo two pills to choose from. The blue one will wipe his memory clean of his ever-meeting Morpheus and Trinity, and allow him to return to his meaningless and fake/delusional life. The red one will enable him to know the truth about who he really is and about the real world, which is the Matrix.

Humanity is unaware that they're trapped inside the Matrix. It's a reality that AI has created that completely distracts humans from the real reality, which is that they are stored in liquid pods and are just an energy source.

Neo chooses the red pill, which kicks off a new, mind-blowing existence. He's transported into the real world, and onto Morpheus's spaceship. Morpheus explains that an energy war broke out between humans and AI. AI won this war by trapping mankind in a fake reality, which is the world as it was in 1999, while imprisoning them in liquid pods, where they're used for their bio energy. Some humans managed to avoid this fate and live in secret in a place called Zion, which the agents want to find and destroy.

Morpheus and his small team try to enter the real world and unplug and recruit humans. Morpheus is specifically targeting Neo because he believes that he's 'the One', who is prophesised to save all mankind and defeat the machines. The others are unsure if Neo is actually the One, and Neo doubts it himself, especially after interpreting what the Oracle, a person that predicts the future, says to him in a negative way.

The agents have special powers; they're machines that move way faster than humans and can't be physically defeated by humans.

Another famous scene has Neo downloading a huge amount of information and knowledge into his brain, which means he now has an immediate expertise in kung fu and the use of weapons. He is better than his new rebel colleagues at kung fu, who aren't a match for an agent, but will Neo be able to take on the agents?

Morpheus is betrayed by one of his team to the agents. The rest of the team would also have been captured if it weren't for Morpheus sacrificing himself so they can escape. During this time, even though Neo has physical abilities beyond his colleagues', he has an encounter with an agent which proves that he has much less ability than any single agent. This is a disappointment to him and the others.

Neo hatches a plan to re-enter the Matrix and help to save Morpheus. Either this will prove that he's the One, or he and the others will die. With newfound confidence, Neo rescues Morpheus. In saving Morpheus, Neo is trapped with Agent Smith, and he receives a bad beating which appears to have killed him. An intervention from Trinity, which is an act of love, reboots Neo, who now has abilities that are way beyond those of Agent Smith and all the other agents. Neo now clearly has a much higher level of superpowers. Morpheus was right. Neo is the One.

Leadership lessons

The Matrix cuts right to the heart of the meaning of life and what it is to live. We could argue that many people in the world aren't living, they're surviving – or working to exist and never getting to live. Do they get to rest, to learn, to develop, to think? Or are they just flogging themselves to put a roof over the heads of their loved ones, doing little more than working and sleeping?

The film is maybe a warning too about what lies ahead. Will AI enslave us all? Will AI, or the owners of AI, just let us live a peaceful life of enjoyment, a life of leisure, when there's no need for humans to work in jobs anymore?

The big positive message in the film is the power of love, as this is what ultimately kickstarts the opportunity to save mankind. Maybe this is an important lesson for our world, which seems hell-bent on destroying itself, and for what exactly? The right to be more powerful than others, to rule over others, to decide what inequality should exist and who's in and out! This is madness.

Key takeaways:

- Are we really living?
- Will AI be good or bad?

Be cautious. When I reflect on the warnings of Eisenhower and Geoffrey Hinton, of course I'm concerned. There are positives with AI, but very serious risks too. And of course, will AI, or the owners of AI, just let us live a peaceful life of enjoyment, a life of leisure, when there's no need for humans to work in jobs anymore?

CHAPTER 23:
FORGIVENESS

57: *Casablanca* (1942)

The storyline

This film was made and is set during World War II. It stars Humphrey Bogart as Rick, and Ingrid Bergman as Ilsa.

In Casablanca, Morocco, American expat Rick owns a nightclub/café which also has a casino function room. His establishment is well known, and his patrons are a mix of all sorts, such as Nazi officers, the Vichy French, and people who are looking to flee Africa and Europe for a safer life in the USA. Rick claims to be neutral in the war, and at this time America hasn't entered it yet, but there are things in Rick's past that suggest he's likely to be against the Nazis.

A local criminal kills two Germans and takes their letters of transit, which will allow the bearer to travel around Nazi-occupied Europe and into neutral Portugal, from where they can go to the USA, which is an opportunity that many want. The criminal gives them to Rick for safe-keeping while he meets someone who's looking to buy them from him. This turns out to be a smart thing, as the criminal is arrested by the police and killed in custody, and he hasn't revealed that he gave the papers to Rick.

Rick is an edgy and bitter man. This is due to a failed relationship. He was madly in love with Ilsa when they decided to escape Paris to avoid the invading Nazis, but she didn't turn up as agreed, so he had to leave alone. She arrives at the café with her husband, Laszlo, a renowned Czechoslovakian freedom fighter whom the Nazis view as an enemy. They're looking to meet the criminal with the letters of transit, so they can escape to America, but a Nazi major has arrived in Casablanca to prevent that from happening, and ultimately to arrest and kill Laszlo.

An underworld fixer advises Laszlo that Rick might have the letters. He asks Rick to sell them to him, but he refuses. At night, Ilsa comes to see Rick and asks for the letters, but he refuses to give them to her. She threatens him with a gun, to no avail, and then she fills in some of the blanks for Rick. When she was in a relationship with Rick, she believed she was a widow – that her husband had been killed by the Nazis. But on the day she was due to leave Paris with Rick, she became aware that Laszlo was still alive, but very ill, and in hiding, just outside Paris, and she felt obligated to go and care for him.

Rick's hatred of her melts away now that he knows the truth, and it's clear that there's still love between them. Rick agrees to get her husband out, but with her remaining in Casablanca with him. Laszlo now realises that Rick and Ilsa have a history, and fearing for her safety, he asks Rick to use the letters and take her to safety himself. The police arrest Laszlo on trumped-up charges, to avoid a confrontation with the powerful Nazi major. Rick is now very worried for Laszlo's safety and fears he will be executed once handed over to the Nazis. He hatches a plan to try and save him. Rick has a strong working relationship with the local chief of police, who financially benefits from Rick. Rick presents an idea to the police chief which will make him look very favourable in the eyes of the Nazi major, which is to release Laszlo, so that Rick can give him the letters of passage. Then the police chief can arrest Laszlo in possession of the letters, which will be a much bigger prize, and will give Laszlo more favour with the Nazi leader. The police chief agrees.

Later, when the police chief attempts to arrest Laszlo when in possession of the letters, Rick pulls a gun on the chief, preventing him from doing so. The married couple get to escape, but at the last minute, the Nazi major arrives and tries to prevent them from doing so. Rick supports them further by shooting the Nazi major dead. The police chief understands that this doesn't look good for either him or Rick, and they decide to go on the run together, as friends, to the Congo.

Leadership lessons

In *Casablanca*, Rick is cynical and damaged following Ilsa letting him down in Paris; in fact, he's quite bitter about it, to the extent that he certainly now lacks trust. He clearly has some morals and values though, and is a bit of a romantic too, which he demonstrates when he allows a young husband to win big on a roulette wheel that he controls. This means he actually loses a lot of money, just so that this husband has the money to buy hugely expensive travel tickets for himself and his wife, which will allow them to flee Casablanca to safety. He does this because he's warmed to the man's young wife, and he's saving her from having to compromise herself and her marriage by having sex with someone predatory, who has power and who can provide them with safe passage but wants to use her body as payment.

This predatory person is the chief of police and for taking advantage and exploiting people in this way, in my opinion there is badness in him. It's also fair to say that at other times in the film, the chief comes across as reasonable, because he commits acts of goodness. He appears to be very agile and fluid when it comes to his morals. The chief does also succumb to the Nazi demands on every occasion without argument or discussion. Maybe this is because he has a great sense of how evil power behaves and knows this is what he has to do to survive. It later becomes clear that he actually despises the Nazis.

This film helps us to understand that people act differently when under pressure, especially when fearful, some cave in but others step up and do extraordinary things. Ilsa's husband in the film, Laszlo, demonstrates strong morals and bravery, and has a huge ability to inspire others. It's this ability that forces the Nazis to take action against him, as they can't afford for him to have a positive impact on the people they're repressing.

The power of an explanation and communication is also conveyed in this film. Rick realises that he wasn't actually jilted by Ilsa, and that she didn't break her word to him. This creates a spirit of forgiveness in Rick, and he chooses to support Ilsa and Laszlo as a couple, out of love for Ilsa, but also for the greater good, as he knows that Laszlo's survival is hugely important to those who are fighting the evil Nazis.

Very much like the chief of police, Rick initially appears to be neither for nor against the French and the Nazis. The lesson for us here is that perhaps there are times when we don't have to be transparent about our beliefs and values etc. The film was made before the USA joined World War II, and this is represented well by Rick, an American who's sitting on the fence – and then of course he isn't.

Raison d'être is huge in this movie, as is *unite*. The lack of *independence* is very apparent, which happens in companies and countries when people feel unsafe and don't have a say.

Key takeaways:

- Sometimes you have to hide your goodness to survive.
- Communicate as clearly as you can, it will prevent needless misunderstandings.
- Forgive people, it will help them, but also you.

- Help others when you can, it is good for your and their wellbeing.
- Do the right thing.

58: *Gandhi* (1982)

The storyline

This film is based on the life of Mahatma Gandhi. It was directed and produced by Richard Attenborough and stars Ben Kingsley as Gandhi.

The film starts with the 23-year-old Gandhi being booted off a train in South Africa in 1893 for sitting in a first-class compartment. As an Indian, he's not permitted to sit there, even though he has a first-class ticket. This triggers him to start a non-violent campaign for the rights of all Indians in South Africa, arguing that they should have the same rights as the white people there, as Indians are British subjects.

Eventually, after Gandhi is arrested many times and the international media put the South Africans in the spotlight, the Indians get additional rights. After this, in 1915, Gandhi is invited back to India as a hero. He's convinced by others to help fight for the country's independence from the British Empire. He starts a massive non-violent non-cooperation campaign across the whole of the British Indian Empire, involving millions of Indians. However, there are numerous setbacks, with Gandhi being regularly arrested and imprisoned, and there's also some terrible violence and deaths, including the dreadful Jallianwala Bagh Massacre in 1919.

Gandhi's campaign garners huge media interest across the globe and puts the British government under constant pressure. He attracts even more attention when he commits to the Salt March, which is a protest against the salt tax imposed by the British on all Indians. He's arrested and imprisoned again for most of World War II for disagreeing with India's involvement in it. Some of his self-sacrifice lies in not being with his wife, and this is felt more heavily when she dies while under house arrest.

After World War II, India gets its independence, but the peace that Gandhi had hoped this would allow does not come. The British Indian Empire is quickly partitioned by religion. It splits into India, a Hindu nation, as it is today on the map, and Pakistan, a Muslim nation, which then also included what's now known as Bangladesh. The Muslims at that time feared being a minority in a very large Hindu nation, and believed splitting off would give them real independence.

Before the partition, there's a massive amount of violence across the nation, and some now believe that the partition will reduce the violence and bring about peace. Gandhi is opposed to the partition, and in an effort to create inclusivity and unity, he proposes that a Muslim, Muhammad Ali Jinnah, become the first prime minister of the whole of India. His idea is rejected. The violence continues throughout the land, but it isn't quite a civil war. Devastated by all of this, Gandhi goes on hunger strike, declaring that he won't eat until the killing ends. After a while, his status has an impact and the needless violence comes to an end.

The elderly Gandhi tries to improve the relationship between India and Pakistan, because as a moderate he wants peace. This approach means extremists on both sides now view him as a problem and someone to be despised. One evening in 1948, on his way to a prayer meeting, Gandhi is shot dead at point-blank range by a man called Godse, a Hindu nationalist. Gandhi is cremated and his ashes are scattered in the Ganges River. His funeral procession is attended by millions.

Leadership lessons

Gandhi is an example of a film where the person the story is based on is way bigger than the film itself. You could write books about Gandhi as an example of leadership, and indeed many have. (This is also the case with the films *JFK* and *Mandela: Long Walk to Freedom.*)

Gandhi covers many important themes. Imperialism, where one race believes they're better than and can own another. Power and greed, and arguably evil. Trauma. And how peaceful protest can make big things happen.

Key takeaways:

- Followership is what you have to be able to create, to be a real leader.
- Power in the wrong hands is very dangerous.
- Imperialism is a form of evil; we are all equal.
- Culture is created, so create positive helpful cultures.

- Dividing people is easy to do, and it creates needless harm.
- Uniting people is true leadership and it adds value to the world.
- Peace, peace, peace.

> You don't have to forget. You don't have to expose your underbelly to those who have harmed you or may do so. Try to understand them. Understand the role trauma may have played in making them who they are. Stop holding on to grudges. Let it go. Forgive them. It will help you too, maybe more than it will help them.

CHAPTER 24:

HOPE

59: *It's a Wonderful Life* (1946)

The storyline

This movie is all about doing good, all about purpose. And it has a great line: 'Remember, no man is a failure who has friends.'

This is a film by Frank Capra, and stars Donna Reed and the great Jimmy Stewart. A movie that's shown on a number of channels most Christmases.

Jimmy plays George Bailey, who decides to travel the world before going to college, but his father dies suddenly, meaning George delays this until some decisions are made about the family business. It's a building and loans company, where his dad was the brains and his brother helped out – a well-meaning guy but not the sharpest tool in the box.

Most of the town and the bank is owned by a horrible and ruthless man, worse than Scrooge, called Henry Potter. Potter is on the board of directors of the Bailey brothers' business, and George quickly recognises what a nasty, selfish man he is. Potter is very keen to dissolve the company, but George understands that the townspeople would be at risk from this. This insight, coupled with the board of directors voting that George should take over from his dad, becomes a reason to stay for a couple of years. It also gives George the means to help support his younger brother, Harry, in school and then college. They agree that once Harry finishes college, he'll reciprocate and take over the running of the business and support George in going to college.

Life happens, and Harry gets a better offer. He marries, and on graduation from college accepts a job from his father-in-law. George accepts that his life is now in his hometown, running the building and loans company, which is the main competitor to Potter's bank, meaning Potter views George and his uncle as enemies.

George uncle misplaces $8,000, which Potter finds and keeps. The missing money means the building and loans company will go bust, and the scandal around it, be it alleged financial incompetence or possible theft by George, will lead to prison. A devastated George decides to kill himself and wishes he'd never existed, but is saved by his guardian angel, who shows him what his hometown would be like if George had never existed.

Harry would have drowned as a child, as George wasn't there to save him. The local pharmacist would have gone to prison for manslaughter, as George wasn't there to spot an error that led to an incorrect prescription being dispensed, which killed someone. His uncle would have been sent to a mental institution after losing his mind because he couldn't run the building and loans company after George's dad died. Potter would have owned the whole town, and everyone would be living in slums and in destitution. And because Harry would have died as a child, he wouldn't have become the fighter pilot who saved a ship from being sunk during the war, meaning hundreds of sailors would have died, and all their families suffered.

George sees the error of his thinking and thankfully doesn't kill himself. If he had, he wouldn't have seen how all the townspeople come together and put up the $8,000 to save George business and reputation. They do it because he's helped them all in different ways at different times, and they recognise his goodness and trust him – in other words, they love him.

Leadership lessons

Raison d'être is huge with George. The town is really a team with George as its captain. Everyone is doing good, except Potter. Community wellbeing is huge.

This movie brings me back to Newton's third law of motion: *for every action there is an equal but opposite reaction*. Here, there's a consequence for every action.

Hope is something that great leaders can create. If there isn't hope, then life becomes grey and energy-sapping, and every step is like walking in a bog or wading through treacle.

The film is also an example of the psychopathic behaviours of a leader, Potter, and the power and social consequences of greed. Note that people like Potter are excellent at finding their way into organisations and systems and causing negativity and hardship for others. We really need more of the George Bailey types in our organisations and the world.

Also, the film is a reminder that we all play an important part in some people's lives, and probably within our communities too, and we just don't realise it. You need to be kind to yourself and be kind to others.

Key takeaways:

- Do good. It's worth the risk.
- Hope is something we all need and the best people create it.

60: *Slumdog Millionaire* (2008)

The storyline

This is a film directed by Danny Boyle and set in Mumbai, India. It stars Dev Patel as Jamal Malik, Madhur Mittal as his older brother Salim, and Freido Pinto as Latika.

Jamal is an 18-year-old who's a contestant on the *Who Wants to Be a Millionaire?* TV show. He's answered the penultimate question correctly, but before he gets the chance to answer the final question and maybe win the huge prize, the show's producers, who believe he's been cheating, have him arrested by the police. Under torture from the police, he explains to them the story of his life, and how these experiences have enabled him to know the correct answer to each question so far.

As a young child, Jamal and his slightly older brother, Salim, are orphaned, and they start to hang out as a trio with another young child, a girl called Latika. A dangerous and serious gangster called Maman recruits them and trains them to be street beggars. Salim finds out that Maman blinds kids to increase the amount that they can earn as beggars, and he and his brother flee, leaving Latika behind.

The brothers travel around India on trains for a few years, earning a living doing a range of menial things including petty crime. They move back to Mumbai as Jamal wants them to find Latika. Maman is grooming her to be a prostitute. Salim kills Maman, freeing Latika, but treats her as his sexual property, which leads to a breakdown in the relationship between the brothers and the departure of Jamal. To avoid retribution from anyone loyal to Maman, Salim starts working for a much bigger criminal, Javed.

Many years later, Jamal tracks down Salim, who's now a senior member of Javed's criminal syndicate. Salim sneaks Jamal into Javed's compound, so he can meet Latika, who's now the property of Javed. Jamal tells her he loves her and convinces her to escape with him. She's captured by Javed's men before getting to the meeting point with Jamal.

Time passes again, and Jamal has no way of making contact with Latika, but he knows she watches *Who Wants to Be a Millionaire?* so he gets on the show in the hope that she will see him, and she does.

The police who arrested Jamal on suspicion of

cheating eventually realise that he's telling the truth and has achieved the answers in a legitimate way. They release him. He returns to the show.

Salim feels guilty for all the bad things he's done and has allowed to happen to Latika and his brother, and he encourages her to leave and make a life for herself with Jamal. He gives her his phone and car keys.

Javed becomes aware, and when he and his men turn up to kill Salim, Salim manages to kill Javed, before he's killed himself.

Jamal doesn't know the answer to the last question, but thinks his brother will, so he uses his 'phone a friend' lifeline to phone him. Latika answers the phone: she doesn't know the answer but is safe. Jamal guesses the right answer and wins the prize. He rushes to the place that they always agreed would be their meeting place if they were both free, and the film ends with them reunited and sharing a kiss.

Leadership lessons

Slumdog Millionaire tells a story of trauma, and how trauma creates more and more trauma. Trauma carries the children into the clutches of the criminal world (and those in the criminal world have all probably been traumatised themselves), and then they learn to comply with the culture of this world, which is their new reality.

In the movie, Jamal and Latika appear to be forces for good. Despite being traumatised and stuck in the criminal world, they somehow just about keep their chins above the toxicity that's drowned everyone else.

Maslow's hierarchy is evident here, as everyone is denied the lower tier, which comprises the basic biological needs, and this keeps them all insecure and compliant.

Everyone in the film has *raison d'être*, but for most it's rotten, and this is an example of how a rotten *raison d'être* can only create poison.

Resilience is alive in this film, and somehow Jamal and Latika have it, and it allows them to have hope, and ultimately to escape and survive.

The story of the gameshow and the fact that Jamal has all the answers because of the different journeys he's been on in life is a great reminder to us all that our time is never really wasted. We're always learning, and in many ways it's the accumulation of our experiences that makes us who we are today.

Jamal and Latika also represent the importance of keeping the dream alive, and that by doing so, you retain the possibility of making it happen. Despite everything and against all the odds, they make it.

The forces of darkness here are all strong on *expertise*. This reminds us that even though the RISE UP model is about goodness, expertise aligned with a rotten *raison d'être* can be very damaging and dangerous.

Finally, Salim shows that even if you've always done bad, it's never too late to turn your back on that way of being, and that if you're courageous, you can draw a line under the past and start doing good. Just because you behave a particular way today, that doesn't mean you have to behave that way tomorrow.

Key takeaways:

- Hope is important.
- Love is real.
- You can make it.
- Stick to your dreams.
- Be good.
- Evil targets your biological needs and your security and safety.

> We need hope. Don't we? Don't give up. Don't stop believing in the value of us making a difference, and us doing good.

So that is the Significant Sixty. I'm sure that you've heard of all these films and have probably seen many of them. I hope that now you're seeing the leadership patterns and are recognising my point about the films being easier to engage with from a leadership perspective than some books and articles on the topic, though I think it's worth reading those books and articles too.

Now let's step back from the films and focus on the themes.

PART 3:
YOU CAN DO IT

CHAPTER 25:

RECURRING THEMES, WARNINGS, ADVICE AND LEADERSHIP BEHAVIOURS IN THE SIGNIFICANT SIXTY

Let's start with the obstacles to leadership we've identified.

The major obstacles to great leadership

Greed

Greed is present in many films as a terrible trait in leaders and a major block to leadership. It has shown up in many of the films I've presented, but the ones I've specifically highlighted are *Wall Street*, *Trading Places*, *The Last of the Mohicans*, *The Untouchables*, *Raiders of the Lost Ark* and *Spartacus*. It's connected to some other negative aspects found in leaders such as psychopathy, toxicity, greed, lies and dishonesty. It's also an associated factor in matters like imperialism and can be connected to things that can be considered acts of evil.

What might help a person to manage the urges of greed is focusing on being good at or supporting the following: friendship, honesty, authenticity, loyalty, listening, integrity, honour, teamwork and freedom.

We need to have a heightened awareness of what a danger privilege can be, in that it can blindly take a person down the road to greed. And that power corrupts but so too does greed; they're interconnected. And that power in the wrong hands, a homogenous minority, can be dangerous for the heterogeneous majority.

Be a better person. Be a better leader.

> There's no real value to be had from greed. It's important to understand this. Evil, corruption, toxic cultures, lies, dishonesty, psychopathy, and imperialism: this is what greed creates. It's okay for us to have self-interest, which is something the Dalai Lama advised is essential to our survival as individuals, but there's obviously a line that gets crossed where self-interest becomes selfishness, and then greed kicks in.

Evil and good

Good and evil, as we know, do exist. They're present in many films, as terrible traits in some leaders and dreadful acts, but also in how good prevails. This theme has shown up in many of the films I've presented, but the ones I've specifically highlighted are *Schindler's List*,

Lord of the Rings, *Harry Potter* and *Macbeth*.

We need to be honest and recognise that evil does exist. That power corrupts. That what evil does is target and then damage equality. And, finally, that doing bad changes you and actually damages you.

We combat evil by choosing to do good. By putting effort into doing good and championing things like equality.

Love is important when it comes to choosing not to be evil, and in tackling evil. Love can sometimes feel like a cheesy thing for people to consider, but in many ways it's synonymous with being good and doing good, as you have to have that strong positive regard for others.

Remember, the most important quote I've ever come across in a film is from Gandalf in the *Lord of the Rings.* He says, 'All we have to decide is what to do with the time that is given to us.' We need to be mindful of this. It can really be as simple as this.

Be a better person. Be a better leader.

As I said earlier, evil exists. We need to accept this fact. We need to hold those who commit evil acts to account via whatever structures and systems exist to enable this, and where they don't exist, we need to create them.

Don't forget, people do lots of good things for others. Lovely acts of kindness and goodness. Things that make a difference.

Psychopathy

Psychopathic behaviour is present in many films as a terrible trait in leaders and a major block to good, decent leadership. It has shown up in many of the films I've presented, but the ones I've specifically highlighted are *Braveheart*, *Training Day*, *Goldfinger* and *Shane*.

The warnings to us are that the obsession with financial wellbeing of a minority can have a huge negative impact on the physical and emotional wellbeing of the many. That power corrupts. That greed corrupts. That the powerful exploit others to increase their power. There's also a warning that once you choose to do bad, then this is your lane, and getting out of it is extremely hard.

Of course, not everyone can be bought off, and living with the right values and having honour can assist you in keeping on the right path. Having an aim/objective to improve equality can help too.

Be a better person. Be a better leader.

> There is a value to some psychopathy. Psychopaths are very effective at getting things done. They can be very single-minded. It's well known that many people with psychopathic tendencies work in the finance sector, the media, politics, sales and as CEOs. There's no cure for psychopathy, but if you are one or know one, developing self-awareness is a good place to start. This can help to limit the damage.

Institutional abuse

Institutional abuse is evident in several of the films I've presented, and these illustrate the negative traits that we don't want to see in people in general and that are connected to poor leadership. The films are *One Flew Over the Cuckoo's Nest*, *Dead Poets Society* and *Sleepers*.

Control, power, humiliation, fear and authoritarianism are associated with institutional abuse, as are the crimes of physical and sexual abuse. It's all trauma and it creates toxic cultures.

Listening and ensuring voices that can be heard is hugely important.

<u>Be a better person. Be a better leader.</u>

We need to acknowledge that institutional abuse is something that does happen, and we must put time into preventing and detecting it, and also supporting those who have been abused. This is really about the abuse of power; those who carry out the abuse have the power and the opportunity to do so. We need to protect the vulnerable by encouraging and supporting whistleblowing, by creating opportunities to speak up, and by uncovering and preventing the protection of organisational reputation by stopping the cover-ups, so the truth can come out.

To drive home the point about how horrendous institutional abuse is we just need to remind ourselves of some of the words used to represent it, such as physical and sexual abuse, trauma, institutional power, authoritarianism, toxic cultures, control, power, humiliation and fear.

There's a strong link between institutional abuse and trauma, but support and a way forward exists today in the form of different therapies and psychological interventions.

Equality, diversity and inclusion (EDI)

The theme of EDI is raised in many films due to terrible acts and behaviours driven by terrible traits in terrible leaders. It has shown up in many of the films I've presented, but the ones I've specifically highlighted are *Dances with Wolves*, *Chariots of Fire* and *Green Book*.

Unfortunately, hate exists, and sometimes it presents itself as prejudice. We can all have biases and prejudices and recognising this can prevent us from acting on opinions of others that are based on ignorance of differences in areas like gender, religion, ethnicity, disability, age and a number of other protected factors.

It's hugely important to recognise the similarities and celebrate the differences. This can open the door to understanding others, which can create the green shoots of friendship.

Some people are brilliant people-connectors, and they can play a key role in helping all people everywhere to engage and find that something that helps a person to relate to another. It can be anything, but usually relates to finding commonalities, like a love of a particular sport or subject, or song, or brand of some kind, or type of food, or both being parents.

Be a better person. Be a better leader.

> Be self-aware. Recognise your biases. Recognise your weaknesses as a person and do something about them. Accept others. Support others. Help others. Do small things; they will all add up to something meaningful and big.

Bad leadership exists and has a terrible impact.

The damage caused by dangerous and poor leadership

Trauma

Trauma is evident in many of the films I've presented, but the ones I've specifically highlighted are *Death of a Salesman*, *The Green Mile*, *The Deer Hunter*, *Unforgiven* and *Taxi Driver*. These films show that trauma is real, that it's all around us and that it has a big impact on people.

Some of the behaviours that cause trauma come from a position of prejudice and the bad actions of others. In addition, we shouldn't minimise the impact of war on people.

Some people feel really desperate because of trauma.

We need to make sure we treat others well, knowing that our actions have an impact on others.

Listening helps, as does being a friend. And some people really do go the extra mile to support others. Also, people should try to recognise that they have a problem as early as they can and get the support they need.

<u>Be a better person. Be a better leader.</u>

Sadly, many people have experienced trauma. They're traumatised by deliberate acts, accidental acts and sometimes in a secondary way, through the behaviours of traumatised people they're connected to. People pass trauma on to others and also down through the generations. The good news is that there are ways to treat trauma, usually via a range of different types of talking therapies.

The lost

The film I have used to represent the lost is *Trainspotting*. The lesson here is that there is a rock bottom and you can be totally lost.

Be a better person. Be a better leader.

The best thing to do is to support people and prevent them from ever finding themselves in the position where they need to try the drugs that will bring about their downfall. To do this, we need to recognise trauma and damaged self-esteem early, and then treat these, so that people aren't tempted to use these substances to deal with the emotional pain they're suffering. For those who find themselves stuck on these substances, it's about talking to addiction experts and seeking the necessary support to help them get their lives back.

So, what should you focus on?

How to be a great leader

Integrity

The film I've used to represent this is *Jerry Maguire*. The types of behaviours synonymous with integrity are listening and loyalty. Ignatius (2019) points out that leaders who prioritise integrity achieve better employee engagement and more profitability. Chesnut (2020) says that leaders need to talk frequently about how essential integrity is, so that employees fully take on board that the company is serious about it and that it isn't just another company tick-box exercise.

You know yourself the value of integrity: you just don't trust people who don't have it. So, if you want people to trust you, you must have this.

Be a better person. Be a better leader.

> Integrity and loyalty are strongly ingrained with doing good. They're a matter of honour. They're values everyone should aspire to and live by. They play a huge role in the building of trust, and as a result, relationships. How do you get good at these or where do you start? Well, you just get on with it: be honest, be straight with people, be a person of your word. Do what's right and good.

Authenticity

Authenticity is present in many films as something

that's important in leaders and leadership. It has shown up in many of the films I've presented, but the ones I've specifically highlighted are *The Truman Show*, *Legally Blonde*, *Some Like It Hot* and *Grease*. The obstacles to authenticity include societal silos, toxic cultures, fickleness and deception.

To overcome these, you're going to have to be brave, trust your gut, be kind to others and yourself, put in effort, have skill, show integrity, show dignity, and build your self-awareness and the self-awareness of others.

Authenticity is connected to psychological safety, in that people won't always show this vulnerability and be themselves if the conditions aren't right. So help to build an environment that allows them to be authentic.

Don't forget that some people are inauthentic out of fear. Don't be too critical of them for behaving that way; there may be a good reason why.

Authenticity is a key part of great leadership. Goffee and Jones (2005) point out that if you try to lead like someone else, you will fail, as you won't come across as real. Ibarra (2023) suggests that you may have to balance authenticity with vulnerability when you engage with your team, as being truly authentic may feel uncomfortable, but you have to go with it, or you'll end up holding yourself back.

Be a better person. Be a better leader.

Authenticity is at the heart of transparency. It allows others to see who you are exactly. This helps them to make a judgement call on your character and whether you are their type of person or not. The opposite of authenticity might be that a person is fake or a fraud, so you can see that being authentic is important. Authenticity is key when it comes to having others trust you. And this plays a role in creating *true* followership (as opposed to just followership, as some people follow others who aren't authentic, but that says a lot about them, too).

First you need to find out who you are. Then you must practise telling the truth. Practise aligning your words with your actions.

Self-awareness

Self-awareness is present in many films as something that's important in leaders and leadership. It has shown up in many of the films I've presented, but the ones I've specifically highlighted are *Rocky* and *A Simple Plan*.

An obstacle to self-awareness can be the blinding power of greed. It can take effort to build self-awareness, and acceptance of yourself is an important aspect of achieving this too.

Some are afraid of self-awareness, because it means being really honest with yourself and sometimes, we don't like that level of self-truth. However, if you realise you are a particular way and you're unhappy with that trait, then you can do something about it and become a better version of yourself.

Self-awareness connects with humility too and is also a key building block for true happiness.

Dickerson (2024) advises that self-awareness is vital, as leaders with good self-awareness make better decisions as they know what their strengths and limitations are and therefore are able to manage tricky situations. Eurich (2018) maintains that the self-aware make better decisions and have stronger followership, which results in the staff being more content and the company delivering better financial results.

Be a better person. Be a better leader.

> Self-awareness is key to building strong relationships with others. It helps you avoid accidentally offending others. It helps you to understand others. It's a key to personal happiness, as you'll be able to get more from your relationship with yourself and with others. It's important when it comes to preventing and minimising conflict, and when you have to collaborate, compromise and negotiate. It's essential when trying to build teams.
>
> There are different ways to build self-awareness. It might be through reflection, 360-degree feedback, listing your strengths and weaknesses, or doing some tests like the Myers–Briggs Type Indicator or the DISC personality test.

Skill set

The theme of skill set features in many of the films I've

presented, but the ones I've specifically highlighted are *Pulp Fiction* and *Jaws*.

It's clear that having a skill set is useful, as is being an expert. Recognising the expertise of those around you and harnessing it is useful in all walks of life, from family life to communities, different clubs and of course large organisations.

Marone (2024) believes that we need to develop leaders to be flexible and adaptable, so that they're better able to use their skill set in a more complicated world. Stobierski (2021) believes that the best skill set to have is a leadership skill set, and he shares his view on what the six core skills are. As it turns out, we're addressing some of these here in this book, notably emotional intelligence and self-awareness, and touch on financial literacy later in the real leadership section of the book.

<u>Be a better person. Be a better leader.</u>

We all have a skill set, but the difference that comes from knowing you have one and not knowing can be the difference between having good self-esteem and poor self-esteem. There is a connection between skill set and self-awareness, in that if you're self-aware, you're likely to know what you're good at and what you're not good at. Knowing your skill set can enable you to play to your strengths. This can stop you playing to your weaknesses, so that you're perceived as competent and proficient rather than incompetent. And then there are the successes, failures and consequential feelings and emotions that come with feeling like either a winner or a loser.

Figure out your strengths. Figure out your weaknesses. Then decide if you want to strengthen your strengths or lessen your weaknesses. Build from there. Specialise or generalise, that's up to you – just know, and then decide.

Emotional intelligence

Emotional intelligence is present in many films as something that's important in leaders and leadership. It has shown up in many of the films I've presented, but the ones I've specifically highlighted are *Goodfellas*, *Heat*, and *Mrs Doubtfire*.

Emotions are very powerful and therefore shouldn't be misused or abused. In addition, we need to ensure we aren't emotionally out of control ourselves, as that damages others, our personal reputations and our ability to make a positive difference. Learn to manage your emotions and to manage stress in the right way. A good coach can make a serious impact and help you.

Be careful, because success can breed arrogance and become a block to understanding your emotions, and those of others. There's a relationship between emotional intelligence and humility.

Emotional intelligence is also key to being a great listener and collaborator. Stobierski (2021) views this as one of the six essential leadership skills, but also probably the most important of the six, as it influences the other five.

Landry (2019) says that emotional intelligence has become a must-have skill for leaders in executive positions, and that the best-performing leaders usually have it as a strength.

Be a better person. Be a better leader.

There are terrible pitfalls and consequences to not having emotional intelligence. Emotions are very powerful and needs to be controlled.

You need to understand what triggers you and also what triggers others, so you're not triggering them. It's important to recognise changes in others, to be able to read them. What is their body language telling you? What language are they using; is it different to how they usually speak? Get into the habit of pausing before you react to something, the old 'count to ten' advice. It's also good to develop your listening skills, and one way to get insights into other people is to ask them how they're feeling.

Don't judge a book by its cover

This theme is evident in many of the films I've presented, illustrating how we can misjudge, underestimate or undervalue others by not seeing beyond their appearance, or making a poor judgement based on nothing factual. The films I've chosen to represent this matter are *Die Hard* and *My Left Foot*.

Judging a book by its cover is sometimes associated with arrogance, or laziness, or unwillingness or inability to be curious. Be curious. Don't be superficial. Look under the bonnet. Don't be fooled by polish.

People who find themself unnoticed or underestimated can sometimes be quite resilient, with a 'never give up' attitude, which is a serious strength. We shouldn't misjudge others, but also, if we encounter someone who's struggling or plodding along in life and work, we should respect them and help them if we can. They have strengths. A kind and useful thing we can do is help them to play to their strengths.

Be a better person. Be a better leader.

> Judging a book by its cover is very damaging to others. It destroys people and communities. Avoiding this is about recognising your bias and prejudice. It's about recognising the concepts of conscious and unconscious bias. It's about educating people, so they can change their thinking and behaviours. From there we need to accept and support others.

Love

Love is present in many films. It has shown up in many of the films I've presented, but the ones I've specifically highlighted are *Groundhog Day*, *Four Weddings and a Funeral* and *When Harry Met Sally*.

The big lessons here are about listening to yourself, seeing what's under your nose, and trusting yourself and your gut instinct. There's a big warning about not wasting time. There's also a reminder that it's okay to feel and be vulnerable.

The theme of love relates to finding your *raison d'être* and then impacting positively on others and reaping the benefits. Be prepared to take a chance, to be courageous, and to trust both yourself and others.

We know that hate exists and we know that hate is

damaging, and that more hate can't lessen or defeat hate. We need something else and lots of it. And Newton's third law of motion helps us find the solution. We need an opposite but equal reaction, and that reaction is love. That positivity, that goodness, that decency – what it really is, is love. It's the most powerful force in the world and the most powerful thing we can ever do.

Don't be ambivalent. You can't sit on the fence. There's too much at stake. You have to actively step in the right direction. Reject hate. Choose love.

<u>Be a better person. Be a better leader.</u>

> Sometimes love embarrasses us. Sometimes it feels cheesy and awkward. But it does sit at the heart of all things good. If the word is a block for you, then substitute it with 'doing good'. Everything we've covered connects here. If we're delivering on everything in the book, then what we're really doing is giving love to ourselves, others and the planet we live on, which is just doing good, lots of it, and all the time.

Friendship

Friendship is present in many films. It has shown up in many of the films I've presented, but the ones I've specifically highlighted are *Toy Story*, *The Full Monty* and *Forrest Gump*.

A big message is that we all need a friend, all of us. A big part of being a friend is supporting each other, and friends always display behaviours associated with honesty and authenticity. Friendship is always about goodness and decency.

Some people, due to trauma and mistrust, don't always recognise who their genuine friends are. Don't give up on these people – they need you, and you just might be the sole person in their life who fits the definition of friend. Help someone, be a friend; it's a good thing to do.

And if you've ever been in a dark place, or going through a tough time, you know how invaluable your friends have been. They accept you. No effort is required. Sometimes nothing needs to be said, sometimes they don't have to be physically present. Just knowing you have that person and that they've got your back is hugely significant for your wellbeing and happiness.

Your friends are the people in your life who help you to survive when you're struggling, who celebrate with you when you're winning, and who just chill out with you through the mundane. Your friends are the people who are on your 'living life' team. Sometimes you pick them, and other times they pick you.

Be a better person. Be a better leader.

Just be a friend to others as much as you can. Remind yourself of what we covered in the love, EDI, and good and evil chapters. If you're doing those things, you'll be a great friend to many. Well done.

Trust

Trust is present in many films. It's a big enabler of good things happening. It has shown up in many of the films I've presented, but the ones I've specifically highlighted are *Good Will Hunting* and *28 Days Later*.

Things that block trust are fear and anxiety, which can be consequences of the impact of trauma. Trust and true friendship are connected. A way to build trust is by helping others.

We also need to be prepared and accept that some people will let us down and betray our trust. Despite this, not trusting others will prevent us from ever finding the road to happiness.

There's a connection between trust and love. Sometimes you have to love blindly before the trust can arrive, and other times the trust has to be there first and the love is then built on it.

The Wisdom of the Geese video is well worth watching, you will find it online, and its core point is highlighting the importance of trust when it comes to teamwork, but in the here and now, please note that Frei & Morriss (2020) make a similar point to the geese, which is that everything is built on trust, and they distil the building of trust down to being able to deliver on three things:

authenticity, logic and empathy. The authenticity we touched on in an earlier theme, and the logic fits with the acumen part of the REAL leadership model which I will discuss later in this book.

Zak (2017) takes it a step further and measures oxytocin levels in the brain, concluding that to build trust you have to be prepared to be vulnerable, develop others, share information, build a rapport, and deliver on recognition and autonomy.

Be a better person. Be a better leader.

> Do the things that will enable others to trust you. Be honest, have integrity, listen, do good things, be self-aware, be authentic. Trust others; give them a chance.

We are all special

Being special is represented by *Kung Fu Panda*. There's only one thing to remember, which is that you are good enough.

Some will target you to make you feel small and irrelevant, and sometimes that's because they have low esteem and putting others down is a tactic they use to feel better about themselves. Somehow you need to rise above it. Stay clear of them. Feel sorry for them, but don't let them get to you. They don't know you and they don't care about you. Just know that you are good enough.

And to those of you who misbehave towards others, learn to be kind and recognise the strengths and goodness in others. The 'we are all special' theme fits very nicely with the Grow Great Teams and Mind the Gap concepts I introduced to you early in this book. The 'we are all special' theme is also connected to equality and sits at the heart of humanity and what it is to be human. Accept that you're special and so are others.

Don't wish to be someone else and waste the opportunity to be the best you that will ever exist. Everyone is unique, , and that's why you're so special.

Tell yourself you're special. Know it, mean it and accept it about yourself, and others too.

Be a better person. Be a better leader.

> Don't ever forget that you are good enough. Don't forget others are too. Build your self-awareness. Help others to build their self-awareness. Accept yourself. Accept others.

Forgiveness

Forgiveness is an extremely important part of being a human. It gives us and others peace of mind. It's important in families, the workplace and in organisations, and is a key strength for any leader who wants to be able to create genuine followership. People who can forgive are viewed by others as being trustworthy. The films I have used to demonstrate forgiveness are *Casablanca* and *Gandhi*.

An inability to forgive can create division and allow it to occur and persist. Forgiveness can help others but also you, in terms of giving it and receiving it.

Forgiveness allows a person to redeem themselves, and it's generally the right thing to do. It doesn't mean that you have to trust a person – that's a totally different matter; and it doesn't mean you have to like a person. Forgiveness is essential when it comes to uniting others.

John Hopkins Medicine (2025) maintains that forgiveness can have a positive impact on a range of conditions such as anxiety, stress, sleep and blood pressure. The Mayo Clinic (2025) also supports that view, adding that practising forgiveness creates peacefulness, and that as you let go of anger, you find better emotional and physical wellbeing.

Be a better person. Be a better leader.

> You don't have to forget. You don't have to expose your underbelly to those who have harmed you or may do so. Try to understand them. Understand the role trauma may have played in making them who they are. Stop holding on to grudges. Let it go. Forgive them. It will help you too, maybe more than it will help them.

A warning – beware

Artificial intelligence/the future

AI and the future is a theme in many films with a warning attached. It has shown up in many of the films I've presented, but the ones I've specifically highlighted are *Mad Max*, *Alien*, *The Terminator* and *The Matrix*.

The warnings are stark. One is that when societies are harmed, everyone loses badly. What seems to be at the heart of the warnings are matters we've encountered in a number of other movies in the book, terrible things like greed, corruption and dishonesty. Knowing our limits and listening to our gut/sixth sense can help us. But the biggest warning is that AI might be the end of us.

Be a better person. Be a better leader.

> Be cautious. When I reflect on the warnings of Eisenhower and Geoffrey Hinton, of course I'm concerned. There are positives with AI, but very serious risks too. And of course, will AI, or the owners of AI, just let us live a peaceful life of enjoyment, a life of leisure, when there's no need for humans to work in jobs anymore?

Back to how to be a leader

Hope

Hope is something all humans need. It gives us

something to aim for, and the positivity that comes from thinking that things can get better. It's important for us as individuals, but also in our families, communities and companies.

The ability to build hope is a key, must-have strength for any leader who wants to create calmness and alignment and followership. People who can create hope are viewed by others as having vision, direction, knowledge and insights that others don't.

Films that I've used to demonstrate hope are *It's a Wonderful Life* and *Slumdog Millionaire*. They give hopeful messages that love is real, that if you stick to your dreams you can make it, and that to do good is worth the risk.

It's also worth noting that some people want to control and minimise you as a person, and worse, try to remove your hope, and they do this by targeting your biological, safety and security needs, which are the lower tiers of Maslow's hierarchy.

Brim (2021) believes that hope is a powerful thing, and he points out that in complex and confusing times, people can feel lost at work, and that it's hope created by leaders that shows them what's possible, which is vital for the company if it is to survive and thrive.

Llopis (2013) really believes that hope is significant, as it builds faith, creates confidence, pushes empowerment, forges connections and impacts positively on motivation. These are great things to have in your culture.

Be a better person. Be a better leader.

> We need hope. Don't we? Don't give up. Don't stop believing in the value of us making a difference, and us doing good.

CHAPTER 26:

MY TOP TEN LEADERS IN THIS BOOK AND WHY

I've excluded Michael Corleone (Al Pacino) from *The Godfather*. I don't deny his abilities, but because he does bad, he's out. I'm giving a special mention to the following five leaders, who don't make the top ten.

- Sylvester Stallone as Rocky Balboa in *Rocky* – self-awareness, honesty, drive
- Kirk Douglas as Spartacus in *Spartacus* – values, followership, strategy, unite
- Daniel Day-Lewis as Hawkeye in *Last of the Mohicans* – focus, values, integrity, honesty, clarity
- Tom Cruise as Jerry Maguire in *Jerry Maguire* – integrity, vision, honesty
- Daniel Day-Lewis as Christy Brown in *My Left Foot* – resilience, drive

Now, the top ten:

10: Jimmy Stewart (George Bailey), *It's a Wonderful Life*

What we get from George is brilliant leadership behaviours like decency, honesty, transparency, goodness, a desire to help, an ability to make a difference, perseverance, humility and selflessness. He gets buy-in, he's trusted and he creates followership.

9: Ben Kingsley, *Gandhi*

What we get from Gandhi is brilliant leadership behaviours like calmness, consideration, thoughtfulness, strategic thinking, decency, honesty, transparency, goodness, a desire to help, an ability to make a difference, perseverance, humility and selflessness. He gets buy-in, he's trusted and he creates followership.

8: Robin Williams (Sean Maguire), *Good Will Hunting*

What we get from Maguire is brilliant leadership behaviours like vulnerability, listening, a willingness to challenge and to argue at the appropriate time, but also gentleness, calmness, decency, honesty, transparency, goodness, a desire to help, an ability to make a difference, perseverance, humility and selflessness. He's more of a relationship-builder type of leader than the type that gets wider followership, but he probably could make that happen if he wanted to.

7: Sigourney Weaver (Ellen Ripley), *Alien*

What we get from Ripley is brilliant leadership behaviours like toughness, resilience, clarity, calmness, strategic thinking, transparency, perseverance, single-mindedness, and a willingness to challenge and to fight at the appropriate time. She has followership capability too but doesn't get the opportunity to prove it in the way that Gandhi and George Bailey do; but then she does get to show abilities that we don't see from them.

6: Sean Astin (Samwise Gamgee), *Lord of the Rings*

What we get from Sam is brilliant leadership behaviours like toughness, resilience, bravery, calmness, loyalty, transparency, perseverance, single-mindedness, a willingness to challenge and to fight at the appropriate time, and a desire to do good. He has a huge amount of selflessness and humility and is a leader who's prepared to support another leader without seeking wider recognition or additional compensation. These types of leaders are brilliant in organisations and communities and are great supporters of other leaders, which adds huge value.

5: Brad Pitt (Michael Sullivan), *Sleepers*

What we get from Sullivan is brilliant leadership behaviours like hidden toughness, resilience, calmness, loyalty, single-mindedness, a desire to do good, broad listening ability, a willingness to challenge, gentleness, decency, goodness, a desire to help and an ability to make a difference. He's very strong on selflessness, but his greatest attribute is his strategic thinking; this is huge with him.

4: Tom Hanks (Captain John Miller), *Saving Private Ryan*

What we get from Miller is brilliant leadership behaviours like genuine listening, empathy, resilience, calmness, loyalty, single-mindedness and a desire to do good. There's also bravery, gentleness, decency, goodness, a desire to help and an ability to make a difference.

He's very strong on selflessness and emotional intelligence, but his greatest attribute is that he won't ask anyone to do something he isn't prepared to do himself, regardless of the difficulty and danger. He's both a team player and a leader and creates genuine followership. His people completely believe in him. In some ways there's a case to be made for placing him at number one in this list.

3: Liam Neeson (Oskar Schindler), *Schindler's List*

What we get from Schindler is brilliant leadership behaviours like empathy, resilience, calmness, single-mindedness and a desire to do good. There's also bravery, decency, goodness and a desire to help.

He's a great improviser as well as being very strategic. He's a strong communicator, with a chameleonic ability to engage with very different types of people and be viewed positively by all sides. His high emotional intelligence helps here, but I think his strongest attribute is selflessness. Again, he could be my gold medallist, but in the end, I gave him bronze.

2: Julia Roberts, *Erin Brockovich*

There's something unique about Brockovich as a leader here. I can't quite put my finger on it. Maybe it's to do with the difficulties of being a single mum, being poor and stuck for money, working in an environment where her lack of qualifications is frowned upon, and her working-class status. Yet despite all of this, she makes some really big and important things happen.

What we get from Brockovich is brilliant leadership behaviours like resilience, single-mindedness and a desire to do good, but also genuine bravery, where she's prepared to fight the fight for herself and for others. She will do it, she will go for it. She also shows grit and determination to understand and get to the bottom of things, to find the dots and then actually join them all together. She does that more than any other leader in the book.

She has humility and selflessness, but her two biggest attributes are perseverance and empathy. It's the empathy that creates trust, and from this she gets massive followership, which enables the deserved success.

1: Tom Hanks, *Forrest Gump*

There's also something unique about Forrest as a leader here, which is the small disability he has coupled with his genuine and huge decency.

What we get from Forrest is brilliant leadership behaviours like empathy, warmth, calmness, resilience, a desire to do good and bravery. He never gives up on other people, he's a great believer in them and he's hugely loyal. He's prepared to fight for others and is kind and fair, maybe more so than anyone else in this book apart from Schindler in *Schindler's List*. He's also very disarming and unassuming.

He also has a knack for being in the right place at the right time, and he takes the opportunities that come his way. And he's very lucky. Being lucky in life and as a leader is great, regardless of whether or not it just comes your way by accident, or you attract good fortune through the good things you do.

Many of Forrest's behaviours are associated with being decent, kind and good, and this, coupled with the successes he achieves, means I have to give him the gold medal in this book.

Now I want to introduce you to REAL leadership.

CHAPTER 27:
REAL LEADERSHIP

REAL leadership is what it says – it's real. How we get to it is by understanding and doing the following.

I've already presented RISE UP, and we'll come back to that. The great leaders in the Significant Sixty are also able to *listen*, and they have great *acumen*. That's true of leaders in the real world too: they're strong on judgement and make great decisions. And – something we don't get to see in the films – they *engage* with and then understand facts, figures, intelligence and information, and use these to shape decisions.

Let's look at these key aspects of leadership in turn:

- **LISTEN:** These days in the workplace, listening is about much more than the definition of the word in the dictionary. It's about having a sixth sense about what's going on, an ability to read body language, an ability to join the dots and triangulate information – what you hear, what you see etc. You work to understand what people need and want, by gathering information, and then you try to meet their needs. What you're doing is acknowledging and recognising them, and making them feel valued. It isn't about having solutions or all the answers. It's about the simple act of demonstrating that you care. Listening is a major part of compassionate leadership, as described by West (2021), and is regularly promoted by the independent think tank, The King's Fund, which specialises in the healthcare system. This opinion is also supported by Itzchakov and Kluger in their article 'The power of listening in helping people change' (2018); Gallo in 'What is active listening?' (2024); and Abrahams and Groysberg in 'How to become a better listener' (2021).

- **ENGAGE:** Leaders need to engage with facts, figures and intelligence, and then actually understand them, so they can apply the knowledge in a meaningful way. This is supported in '10 important business skills every professional needs' by Gavin (2019); 'The advantages of data-driven decision-making' by Stobierski (2019); and 'Data and intuition: Good decisions need both' by Farrell (2023).
- **ACUMEN:** People with acumen make good decisions, and they have good judgement. Acumen is essential. This viewpoint is supported by the Harvard Business Publishing Corporate Learning article 'The three critical business acumen skills leaders need now' (2022); Horwath's article 'How to become a better

strategic thinker' (2023); and Hall's article 'Accelerate your strategy using strategic thinking, business acumen and resilience to change skills' (2020).

So, aligning everything:

RISE UP: Raison d'être. Independence. Stimulation. Expertise. Unite. Process-fixing.

Engage

Acumen

Listen

This is what you need to be a REAL leader and deliver in REAL leadership.

So, RISE UP, Engage, build your Acumen and Listen.

CHAPTER 28:
CONCLUSION

As I said at the start, there are many things wrong with the world today. Horrible acts are taking place in some countries, and other countries are behaving in ways that are inhumane and anti-humanity. There are things going wrong in families, in personal relationships and in communities. And of course, some institutions, organisations and companies are completely misbehaving, in ways that see them only working in the best interests of a few (often the owners or those in charge) while they make minimal or negative contributions to employees, the environment and humanity in general.

A common denominator across all of the above is people. It's people who are doing the bad things, and it's important to remember, the solutions are with people too.

Selfishness, power and greed appear to be at the heart of these issues, which cause so much damage. Badness is real, and its different levels of badness that create these issues, up to the furthest end of the spectrum, which takes us onto the path of evil.

Most people don't set out to do bad or haven't got 'doing bad' as their objective or goal, but that's what is being achieved. It is okay for us to have self-interest. Remember that, according to the Dalai Lama, it's essential to our survival as individuals. But there's obviously a line that gets crossed, where self-interest becomes selfishness, and then greed kicks in, and by then we are well down that road and into the territory of badness.

Finally

It's disgraceful, terrible and sad how it's the biological needs and safety and security tiers of Maslow's hierarchy that are targeted by those who are consumed with greed, evil, psychopathy and institutional abuse.

Many people do bad things out of ignorance or blindness, maybe because they haven't set their own personal compass. This lack of a specified positive goal or objective means they accidentally stray into the domain of doing bad, and then this becomes their norm. With some people maybe they never know otherwise; and with others, maybe they become too ashamed to admit who they have become; or maybe they now think they have too much to lose; or think that they are incapable of changing.

So how do we deal with all of this, how do we improve? For starters, **we need people to set themselves the goal of doing good. This will get them actively thinking in a positive way about what is good and about how to do good.** For many, this simple act will help to steer them down the right road and then keep on this road.

So, how can people understand what it is to do good? People aren't stupid, they know what good is. There are loads of ways to help here. A good start is understanding and drawing on utilitarianism, which is about delivering actions that bring the greatest good for the greatest number of people. With utilitarianism, you zone in on creating happiness and wellbeing, and you try to prevent harm and pain.

I want to remind you of something I said earlier. People do lots of good things for others. Lovely acts of kindness and goodness. Things that make a difference. But frequently we don't realise the impact because we don't always get to see the results. I've worked with people who do lots of small things for colleagues that will have helped those people in their relationships with their partners and children. But at work they don't get to see or know this. Healthcare staff do things that have a huge impact on their patients and the patients' families, which then changes how they think and behave towards those surrounding them in their personal and professional lives. These acts have a significant reach, and this is all doing good.

Take the five million people in Ireland. If they do one decent act every day, that's five million acts of kindness each day and 1.825 billion acts a year. That's a huge amount of goodness. The population of India in 2025 is approximately 1.5 billion. If every person in India does one act of kindness a day, that equates to 547 billion acts a year. Just one act a day very quickly becomes a huge amount of goodness.

We don't always realise the value of doing small acts of kindness. We think they're small and don't matter, but they all add up. I do a lot of hiking and sometimes I use maps. And on the map, one degree looks like it's tiny and meaningless, but in reality it's huge, especially if you try to walk that one degree, because in reality it's sixty-nine miles.

Schein (2010) makes the point that leaders shape and create the culture; in other words, leaders shape the values and behaviours of others. All of us are leaders of some kind, at the very least a personal leader who just leads ourselves. But we also have the power to shape behaviour within our families, in our friendship groups, in our communities and in the workplace. Each of us has the power to make all of these groupings and places positive. We can do this by behaving in ways that are good. We should do it.

Companies, and individuals, can work for the Triple Bottom Line of profit, people and planet (Elkington, 1999). We can't just focus on money and finances in isolation or as the only objective anymore; we have to consider people and the planet too. This means minding the environment and doing things that help it, while also focusing on people – and a good way to think about people might be through the prism of wellbeing, not just financial but also physical, emotional and social. This is taken a step further by Polman & Winston (2021) who believe that companies can actually make a profit by fixing the problems of the world such as climate change, inequality and our challenged biodiversity. In addition, De Neve, Kaats and Ward (2024) evidence from their Oxford University study, which was written about in the *Financial Times*, that there is a strong link between employee wellbeing and a company's financial performance, which seems obvious but for some reason workplaces ignore it.

One of the ways I want to help is by shaping how people think about the concept of leadership, in terms of personal leadership, leadership within communities and also with leadership in the more traditional sense – the people in leadership positions in companies and countries.

As I said earlier there are lots of journal articles and books about leadership, many of which I have read and enjoyed. Often, though, these texts on leadership focus on politicians and companies etc., and as a result we may struggle to engage. We may not be aligned with the political standpoint of the book, for example, or feel good about the brands or companies profiled. As people, we can be quite biased and tribal.

But with films, engagement is simpler. Generally, we align with the protagonist, the lead character, and understand them and their actions, even if that person commits negative acts. Therefore, I think films are an excellent medium for exploring leadership: because we're engaged and aligned with the film, we're more open to taking on any leadership lessons that it might contain. Much of this book looks at lessons learnt from films that I call my Significant Sixty.

To help you understand leadership in these films, and in life, I've used the following concepts and theories.

Ideas that belong to others:

- Brian O'Driscoll's new way of thinking
- Newton's third law of motion
- Maslow's hierarchy of needs
- Edgar Schein and culture
- The four pillars of wellbeing

Ideas from me:

- RISE UP
- The Sistine Chapel
- How to build self-awareness
- Grow Great Teams
- Mind the Gap
- One degree of longitude on a map is sixty-nine miles
- The Panama Canal

REAL leadership: I encourage you to RISE UP, to Grow Great Teams, to develop your self-awareness and to Mind the Gap.

The meaning of life

If you are yet to figure out the meaning of life, please try on the following for size and see how it fits for you. My personal view is that life is about doing good. It's as simple as that, and therefore we should all be trying to do as much good as we can. Simple. JUST DO GOOD.

Worth thinking about?

Eisenhower again, Nelson Mandela, Martin Luther King and John Hume.

Eisenhower

> Down the long lane of the history yet to be written America knows that this world of ours, ever growing smaller, must avoid becoming a community of dreadful fear and hate, and be, instead, a proud confederation of mutual trust and respect.
>
> Such a confederation must be one of equals. The weakest must come to the conference table with the same confidence as do we, protected as we are by our moral, economic, and military strength. That table, though scarred by many past frustrations, cannot be abandoned for the certain agony of the battlefield.
>
> Disarmament, with mutual honour and confidence, is a continuing imperative. Together we must learn how to compose difference, not with arms, but with intellect and decent purpose. Because this need is so sharp and apparent I confess that I lay down my official responsibilities in this field with a definite sense of disappointment. As one who has witnessed the horror and the lingering sadness of war – as one who knows that another war could utterly destroy this civilization which has been so slowly and painfully built over thousands of years – I wish I could say tonight that

a lasting peace is in sight.

[...]

So – in this my last good night to you as your President, I thank you for the many opportunities you have given me for public service in war and peace. I trust that in that service you find somethings worthy; as for the rest of it, I know you will find ways to improve performance in the future.

You and I – my fellow citizens – need to be strong in our faith that all nations, under God, will reach the goal of peace with justice. May we be ever unswerving in devotion to principle, confident but humble with power, diligent in pursuit of the Nation's great goals.

To all the peoples of the world, I once more give expression to America's prayerful and continuing inspiration:

We pray that peoples of all faiths, all races, all nations, may have their great human needs satisfied; that those now denied opportunity shall come to enjoy it to the full; that all who yearn for freedom may experience its spiritual blessings; that those who have freedom will understand, also, its heavy responsibilities; that all who are insensitive to the needs of others will learn charity; that the scourges of poverty, disease and ignorance will be made to disappear from the earth, and that, in the goodness of time, all peoples will come to live together in a peace guaranteed by the binding force of mutual respect and love. (Eisenhower, 1961)

Nelson Mandela

No one is born hating another person because of the colour of his skin or his background or his religion. (Mandela, 1994)

Martin Luther King

Darkness cannot drive out darkness; only light can do that. Hate cannot drive out hate; only love can do that. (King, 1957)

John Hume

Hume won the Nobel Prize in 1998. He said:

Difference is of the essence of humanity. Difference is an accident of birth and it should therefore never be the source of hatred or conflict. The answer to difference is to respect it. Therein lies a most fundamental principle of peace – respect for diversity. (Hume, 1998)

And finally, and in the spirit of the book, I quote from one film character, Gandalf, once again:

All we have to decide is what to do with the time that is given to us.

And of course, I have the final say and I only have one thing to add, which is, DO GOOD, JUST DO GOOD.

REFERENCES

Books and articles

Abrahams, Robin & Groysberg, Boris (2021). 'How to become a better listener'. *Harvard Business Review*, 21 December. Online at: https://hbr.org/2021/12/how-to-become-a-better-listener.

Brim, Brian J. (2021). 'Strengths-based leadership: Building hope in followers'. Gallup, 30 September. Online at: https://www.gallup.com/cliftonstrengths/en/250571/strengths-based-leadership-building-hope-followers.aspx.

Brown, Sara (2023). 'Why neural net pioneer Geoffrey Hinton is sounding the alarm on AI'. MIT Management Sloan School, 23 May. Online at: https://mitsloan.mit.edu/ideas-made-to-matter/why-neural-net-pioneer-geoffrey-hinton-sounding-alarm-ai.

Dickerson, Craig (2024). 'The ladder of inference: Building self-awareness to be a better human-centred leader'. Harvard Business Publishing Corporate Learning, 9 May. Online at: https://www.

harvardbusiness.org/the-ladder-of-inference-building-self-awareness-to-be-a-better-human-centered-leader.

Chesnut, Robert (2020). 'How to build a company that (actually) values integrity'. *Harvard Business Review*, 30 July. Online at: https://hbr.org/2020/07/how-to-build-a-company-that-actually-values-integrity.

Dalai Lama & Hougaard, Rasmus (2019). 'The Dalai Lama on why leaders should be mindful, selfless, and compassionate'. Harvard Business Review, 20 February. Online at: https://hbr.org/2019/02/the-dalai-lama-on-why-leaders-should-be-mindful-selfless-and-compassionate.

De Neve, J-E, Kaats, M. & Ward, G. (2024). *Workplace Wellbeing and Firm Performance*. University of Oxford Wellbeing Research Centre Working Paper 2304. doi.org/10.5287/ora-bpkbjayvk .

Eisenhower, Dwight D. (1961). 'President Dwight D. Eisenhower's farewell address', 17 January. National Archives, Milestone Documents (Archives.gov). Online at: https://www.archives.gov/milestone-documents/president-dwight-d-eisenhowers-farewell-address.

Elkington, John (1999). *Cannibals with Forks: The Triple Bottom Line of 21st Century Business*, 1st edition. Gabriola Island, BC: Capstone.

Eurich, Tasha (2018). 'What self-awareness really is (and how to cultivate it)'. *Harvard Business Review*, 4 January. Online at: https://hbr.org/2018/01/what-self-awareness-really-is-and-how-to-cultivate-it.

Farrell, Marcy (2023). 'Data and intuition: Good decisions need both'. Harvard Business Publishing Corporate Learning, 6 January. Online at: https://www.harvardbusiness.org/data-and-intuition-good-decisions-need-both.

Frei, Frances X. & Morriss, Anne (2020). 'Begin with trust'. *Harvard Business Review*, May–June. Online at: https://hbr.org/2020/05/begin-with-trust.

Gallo, Amy (2024). 'What is active listening?' *Harvard Business Review*, 2 January. Online at: https://hbr.org/2024/01/what-is-active-listening.

Gavin, Matt (2019). '10 important business skills every professional needs'. Harvard Business School Online, Business Insights, 23 May. Online at: https://online.hbs.edu/blog/post/business-skills-every-professional-needs.

Goffee, Rob & Jones, Gareth (2005). 'Managing authenticity: The paradox of great leadership'. *Harvard Business Review*, December. Online at: https://hbr.org/2005/12/managing-authenticity-the-paradox-of-great-leadership.

Hall, Bill (2020). 'Accelerate your strategy using strategic thinking, business acumen and resilience to change skills'. *Forbes*, 6 July. Online at: https://www.forbes.com/councils/forbescoachescouncil/2020/07/06/accelerate-your-strategy-using-strategic-thinking-business-acumen-and-resilience-to-change-skills.

Harvard Business Publishing Corporate Learning (2022). 'Level up your leaders: The three critical business acumen skills they need now'. Harvard Business School Publishing. Online at: https://www.harvardbusiness.org/wp-content/uploads/2022/08/Perspectives-Level-Up-Your-Leaders-The-Three-Critical-Business-Acumen-Skills-They-Need-Now.pdf.

Horwath, Rich (2023). 'How to become a better strategic thinker'. *Harvard Business Review*, 8 November. Online at: https://hbr.org/2023/11/how-to-become-a-better-strategic-thinker.

Hume, John (1998). 'Nobel Lecture'. Oslo, 10 December. Online at: https://www.nobelprize.org/prizes/peace/1998/hume/lecture.

Ibarra, Herminia (2023). 'What makes an "authentic" leader?' *Harvard Business Review*, HBR on Leadership podcast, episode 22, 6 September. Online at: https://hbr.org/podcast/2023/09/what-makes-an-authentic-leader.

Ignatius, Adi (2019). 'The thing about integrity'. *Harvard Business Review*, July–August. Online at: https://hbr.org/2019/07/the-thing-about-integrity.

Itzchakov, Guy & Kluger, Avraham (2018). 'The power of listening in helping people change'. *Harvard Business Review*, 17 May. Online at: https://hbr.org/2018/05/the-power-of-listening-in-helping-people-change.

John Hopkins Medicine (2025). 'Forgiveness: Your health depends on it'. John Hopkins Medicine. Online at: https://www.hopkinsmedicine.org/health/wellness-and-prevention/forgiveness-your-health-depends-on-it.

King, Martin Luther (1957). 'Loving your enemies'. Sermon. Dexter Avenue Baptist Church, Montgomery, Alabama, 17 November. Online at: https://kinginstitute.stanford.edu/king-papers/documents/loving-your-enemies-sermon-delivered-dexter-avenue-baptist-church.

Landry, Lauren (2019). 'Why emotional intelligence is important in leadership'. Harvard Business School Online, 3 April. Online at: https://online.hbs.edu/blog/post/emotional-intelligence-in-leadership.

Llopis, Glenn (2013). '5 ways leaders keep hope alive in difficult times'. *Forbes*, 19 August. Online at: https://www.forbes.com/sites/glennllopis/2013/08/19/5-ways-leaders-keep-hope-alive-in-difficult-times.

Mandela, Nelson (1994). *Long Walk to Freedom*. Johannesburg: Little, Brown and Company.

Marone, Mark (2024). 'Transforming leadership development: Why widening skill sets is crucial for today's leaders'. Harvard Business Publishing Corporate Learning, 29 July. Online at: https://www.harvardbusiness.org/transforming-leadership-development-why-widening-skill-sets-is-crucial-for-todays-leaders.

Maslow, A. H. (1943). 'A theory of human motivation'. *Psychological Review*, 50 (4), 370–96.

Mayo Clinic (2025). 'Forgiveness: Letting go of grudges and bitterness'. Mayo Clinic. Online at: https://www.mayoclinic.org/healthy-lifestyle/adult-health/in-depth/forgiveness/art-20047692.

McKinsey & Company (2024). 'What is leadership?' McKinsey & Company, 10 September. Online at: https://www.mckinsey.com/featured-insights/mckinsey-explainers/what-is-leadership.

Milmo, Dan (2024). '"Godfather of AI" shortens odds of the technology wiping out humanity over the next 30 years'. *The Guardian*, 27 December. Online at: https://www.theguardian.com/technology/2024/dec/27/godfather-of-ai-raises-odds-of-the-technology-wiping-out-humanity-over-next-30-years.

O'Driscoll, Brian (2014). *The Test: My Autobiography*. Dublin: Penguin.

O'Driscoll, Brian (2017). Brian O' Driscoll – Brian O' Driscoll's rugby motivation. Available at: https://www.youtube.com/watch?v=YZoGqx5wPgE. (Accessed 01 June 2025).

Pink, Daniel H. (2009). *Drive: The Surprising Truth About What Motivates Us*. New York: Riverhead Books.

Polman, P. & Winston, A.S. (2021). *Net positive: How Courageous Companies Thrive By Giving More Than They Take*. Boston. Harvard Business Review Press.

Schein, Edgar H. (2010). *Organizational Culture and Leadership*, 4th edition. San Francisco: Jossey-Bass.

Stobierski, Tim (2019). 'The advantages of data-driven decision-making'. Harvard Business School Online, 26 August. Online at: https://online.hbs.edu/blog/post/data-driven-decision-making.

Stobierski, Tim (2021). '6 leadership skills you need for business success'. Harvard Business School Online, 16 September. Online at: https://online.hbs.edu/blog/post/leadership-skills.

Storey, John & Holti, Richard (2013). 'Towards a new model of leadership for the NHS'. NHS Leadership

Academy. Online at: https://www.leadershipacademy.nhs.uk/wp-content/uploads/dlm_uploads/2014/10/Towards-a-New-Model-of-Leadership-2013.pdf.

West, Michael (2021). *Compassionate Leadership: Sustaining Wisdom, Humanity, and Presence in Health and Social Care*. London: The Swirling Leaf Press.

Zak, Paul J. (2017). 'The neuroscience of trust'. *Harvard Business Review*, January–February. Online at: https://hbr.org/2017/01/the-neuroscience-of-trust.

Films

28 Days Later (2002). Danny Boyle (Dir.). UK: DNA Films, UK Film Council.

Alien (1979). Ridley Scott (Dir.). UK/USA: 20th Century Fox, Brandywine Productions.

A Simple Plan (1998). Sam Raimi (Dir.). USA: Paramount Pictures.

Braveheart (1995). Mel Gibson (Dir.). USA: Icon Productions, The Ladd Company.

Casablanca (1942). Michael Curtiz (Dir.). USA: Warner Bros Pictures.

Chariots of Fire (1981). Hugh Hudson (Dir.). UK/USA:

Allied Star Ltd, Enigma Productions.

Dances with Wolves (1990). Kevin Costner (Dir.). USA: Tig Productions, Majestic Films International.

Dead Poets Society (1989). Peter Weir (Dir.). USA: Touchstone Pictures, Silver Screen Partners IV.

Death of a Salesman (1985). Volker Schlöndorff (Dir.). USA: Roxbury Productions, Punch Productions.

Die Hard (1988). John McTiernan (Dir.). USA: Gordon Company, Silver Pictures.

Erin Brockovich (2000). Steven Soderbergh (Dir.). USA: Universal Pictures, Columbia Pictures, Jersey Films.

Forrest Gump (1994). Robert Zemeckis (Dir.). USA: The Tisch Company.

Four Weddings and a Funeral (1994). Mike Newell (Dir.). UK: Channel Four Films, Working Title Films.

Gandhi (1982). Richard Attenborough (Dir.). UK/India: Goldcrest Films, National Film Development Corporation of India.

Goldfinger (1964). Guy Hamilton (Dir.). UK/USA: Eon Productions.

Goodfellas (1990). Martin Scorsese (Dir.). USA: Warner Bros, Irwin Winkler Productions.

Good Will Hunting (1997). Gus Van Sant (Dir.). USA: Be Gentlemen.

Grease (1978). Randal Kleiser (Dir.). USA: Allan Carr Enterprises, Stigwood Group.

Green Book (2018). Peter Farrelly (Dir.). USA: DreamWorks Pictures, Participant Media.

Groundhog Day (1993). Harold Ramis (Dir.). USA: Columbia Pictures.

Harry Potter series (2001–2011). Chris Columbus/ Alfonso Cuarón/Mike Newell/David Yates (Directors). UK/USA: Warner Bros Pictures, Heyday Films, 1492 Pictures.

Heat (1995). Michael Mann (Dir.). USA: Regency Enterprises Forward Pass.

It's a Wonderful Life (1946). Frank Capra (Dir.). USA: Liberty Films.

Jaws (1975). Steven Spielberg (Dir.). USA: Zanuck/Brown Company, Universal Pictures.

Jerry Maguire (1996). Cameron Crowe (Dir.). USA: TriStar

Pictures, Gracie Films, Vinyl Films.

Kung Fu Panda (2008). Mark Osborne & John Stevenson (Directors). USA: DreamWorks Animation.

Legally Blonde (2001). Robert Luketic (Dir.). USA: Metro-Goldwyn-Mayer Pictures, Mark Platt Productions, Type A Films.

Macbeth (2015). Justin Kurzel (Dir.). UK/France: StudioCanal, Film 4.

Mad Max (1979). George Miller (Dir.). Australia: Kennedy Miller Productions.

Mrs Doubtfire (1993). Chris Columbus (Dir.). USA: 20th Century Fox, Blue Wolf Productions.

My Left Foot (1989). Jim Sheridan (Dir.). Ireland/UK: RTE, Ferndale Films, Granada Film.

One Flew Over the Cuckoo's Nest (1975). Milos Forman (Dir.). USA: Fantasy Films.

Pulp Fiction (1994). Quentin Tarantino (Dir.). USA: A Band Apart, Jersey Films.

Raiders of the Lost Ark (1981). Steven Spielberg (Dir.). USA: Lucasfilm Ltd.

Rocky (1976). John G. Avildsen (Dir.). USA: Chartoff-Winkler Productions.

Saving Private Ryan (1998). Steven Spielberg (Dir.). USA: Amblin Entertainment, Mutual Film Company.

Schindler's List (1993). Steven Spielberg (Dir.). USA: Universal Pictures, Amblin Entertainment.

Shane (1953). George Stevens (Dir.). USA: Paramount Pictures.

Sleepers (1996). Barry Levinson (Dir.). USA: PolyGram Filmed Entertainment, Propaganda Films.

Slumdog Millionaire (2008). Danny Boyle (Dir.). UK: Celador Films, Film 4.

Some Like It Hot (1959). Billy Wilder (Dir.). USA: Mirisch Company.

Spartacus (1960). Stanley Kubrick (Dir.). USA: Bryna Productions.

Taxi Driver (1976). Martin Scorsese (Dir.). USA: Bill/Phillips Productions, Italo-Judeo Productions.

The Deer Hunter (1978). Michael Cimino (Dir.). USA: EMI.

The Full Monty (1997). Peter Cattaneo (Dir.). UK:

Channel Four Films, Redwave Films.

The Godfather (1972). Francis Ford Coppola (Dir.). USA: Paramount Pictures.

The Green Mile (1999). Frank Darabont (Dir.). USA: Castle Rock Entertainment, Darkwoods Productions.

The Last of the Mohicans (1992). Michael Mann (Dir.). USA: 20th Century Fox.

The Lord of the Rings series (2001–2003). Peter Jackson (Dir.). New Zealand/USA: New Line Cinema, WingNut Films.

The Matrix (1999). Larry (Lana) Wachowski & Andy (Lilly) Wachowski (Dir.). USA: Warner Bros, Village Roadshow Productions.

The Terminator (1984). James Cameron (Dir.). USA: Hemdale, Pacific Western Productions.

The Truman Show (1998). Peter Weir (Dir.). USA: Scott Rudin Productions.

The Untouchables (1987). Brian De Palma (Dir.). USA: Paramount Pictures.

Toy Story (1995). John Lasseter (Dir.). USA: Pixar Animation Studios.

Trading Places (1983). John Landis (Dir.). USA: Paramount Pictures.

Training Day (2001). Antoine Fuqua (Dir.). USA: Village Roadshow Pictures, Outlaw Productions.

Trainspotting (1996). Danny Boyle (Dir.). UK: Channel Four Films.

Unforgiven (1992). Clint Eastwood (Dir.). USA: Malpaso Productions.

Wall Street (1987). Oliver Stone (Dir.). USA: American Entertainment Partners, Amercent Films.

When Harry Met Sally (1989). Rob Reiner (Dir.). USA: Castle Rock Entertainment, Nelson Entertainment.

A special thank you to Charlie, Damien, Jackie, Sarah and Steve.

Printed in Dunstable, United Kingdom

65264527R00198